THE DEFENCE
OF THE
DARDANELLES

For Gilli

THE DEFENCE
OF THE
DARDANELLES

From Bombards to Battleships

Michael Forrest

Pen & Sword
MARITIME

First published in Great Britain in 2012
By Pen and Sword Maritime
an imprint of
Pen and Sword Books Ltd
47 Church Street
Barnsley
South Yorkshire S70 2AS

ISBN 978 1 78159 052 2

Printed and bound in England
by MPG Books Group

Typeset in Times New Roman by
Chic Graphics

Pen & Sword Books Ltd incorporates the imprints of
Pen & Sword Aviation, Pen & Sword Family History, Pen & Sword Maritime,
Pen & Sword Military, Pen & Sword Discovery, Wharncliffe Local History,
Wharncliffe True Crime, Wharncliffe Transport, Pen & Sword Select,
Pen & Sword Military Classics, Leo Cooper, Remember When,
The Praetorian Press, Seaforth Publishing and Frontline Publishing

For a complete list of Pen and Sword titles please contact
Pen and Sword Books Limited
47 Church Street, Barnsley, South Yorkshire, S70 2AS, England
E-mail: enquiries@pen-and-sword.co.uk
Website: www.pen-and-sword.co.uk

Contents

List of Maps

Glossary of Terms

barbette	a gun battery position where the protective parapet is low enough for the gun to fire over it without the need for embrasures
BL	breech-loading
calibre	diameter across the bore of a gun
cm	centimetre
crh	calibre radius head
embrasure	the opening in a parapet through which a gun can be fired
EOC	Elswick Ordnance Company
HMS	His Majesty's Ship
kg	kilogramme
km	kilometre
lb	pound weight
m	metre
mm	millimetre
magazine	a building or structure for the safe storage of gunpowder, shells and charges
pr	pounder (as in the weight of the projectile fired)
QF	quick-firer
RK	Ringkanone (German for ring gun)
RNR(T)	Royal Navy Reserve Trawler Section
RML	Rifled Muzzle Loader
SK	Schiffskanone (German for ship's gun)
SMS	Seiner Majestät Schiff (German for His Majesty's Ship)
SS	steamship
terreplein	a wide, level fighting platform on the rampart behind the parapet
TL	Turkish Lira
TNT	trinitrotoluene
tompion (tampion)	a wooden plug used for fitting into the muzzle of a gun when not in use
traverse	an earth bank positioned across the terreplein of a rampart, dividing it in sections to protect gun crews from shell splinters; the lateral movement of a gun to the right and left
tumblehome	the narrowing of a ship's hull with distance above the water line
VAEMS	Vice Admiral Eastern Mediterranean Squadron

Foreword and Acknowledgements

T*he Defence of the Dardanelles* has been created from many varied sources, some of which have never been published before, with the optimistic objective of shedding new light on the battle between some of the most powerful warships in the world of 1914 against the aged Ottoman fortifications of the Dardanelles. The battleships should have won; everyone expected them to do so, yet they failed at a huge cost in men, material and national prestige.

I was inspired to research this absorbing story when walking the Gallipoli battlefields in 2009 with my stepson, Paul Winnister. Like me, he was fascinated by the stories of hardship and bravery of the troops of all nationalities after the Gallipoli peninsula was invaded on 25 April 1915, but we both wanted to know more of what went before and why the naval assault on the defences was a failure. Paul read the draft manuscript and injected many good ideas and improvements. I would also like to express my thanks to others who read the draft, correcting facts and nomenclature – Duncan Williams, Geoff Hallett and Mike Darling – all members of the Palmerston Forts Society, an educational charity dedicated to the research and preservation of nineteenth-century fortifications. I must also record thanks to Ian Stevenson, archivist of the Palmerston Forts Society, who discovered 1880s' British intelligence documents held at the National Archives that shed light on what was known about the Dardanelles defences decades before they were attacked by British warships.

My thanks are extended to Eric Goossens, proprietor of the lovely Gallipoli Houses hotel on the peninsula, for taking me to the most remote forts and gun batteries that are not accurately located on any maps. I could not have found them without his assistance.

I was lucky to speak by telephone to Tosun Sezen, a Turkish diver who inspected the wrecks of the *Bouvet* and HMS *Irresistible* fifty years after they were sunk and viewed the damage they had suffered. As the centennial of their sinking approaches perhaps there is still a final chance for the decaying wrecks to be investigated by an enterprising dive team before they disappear forever.

The National Museum of the Royal Navy located within Portsmouth's Historic Dockyard has proved invaluable as a source of original information, particularly extracts from the diaries of Harold Tumman of HMS *Harpy* and CPO Young of HMS *Agamemnon*, together with the German Official History of the Naval War 1914-1918. Thanks to the library staff and to Steve Courtney, Curator of Photographs, who sourced the selection of photographs from the Museum's collection that are reproduced in this book. Steve is also a member of the Palmerston Forts Society.

The majority of photographs and all the maps used are my own, but old postcards, photographs and magazine illustrations that occasionally turn up on internet auction sites and at antique fairs have proved to be incredibly useful. One problem has been the choice of photographs to use, as for many of the two dozen forts and gun batteries visited I took twenty or more photographs.

Where appropriate, I have tried to explain technical aspects of the competing guns and the shells that they fired in a hopefully none too technical way. These technical issues can be found as Appendices Seven, Eight and Nine at the end of the book and, when read in conjunction with the main text, go some way to explaining the reasons why the ships' guns could not overcome the shore forts and gun batteries.

I have avoided the use of footnotes, with just a few exceptions, to maintain the flow of the text, but the bibliography does contain a list of my sources. The depth of information contained in the multitude of internet sites – from old newspaper articles to Krupp gun sales figures – has hopefully bolstered my research, so thanks to the dozens of nameless individuals who have placed such information in the public domain, although one such website does deserve a special mention: Piotr Nykiel's excellent www.navyingallipoli.com

Yet a hazard of numerous sources is the possibility of conflicting information – on the few occasions where this occurred I have tried to achieve the most reasonable judgement and therefore accept responsibility for any errors.

Michael Forrest
Emsworth, July 2012

Introduction

There has been much written about the Gallipoli Campaign of 1915 covering the reasons why it occurred, the battles and timeline of events, its aftermath and impact on the Great War: a war that continued for nearly three years after the final Allied evacuations from the peninsula. This book does not intend to cover the same ground. Instead it will focus on the Dardanelles – the stretch of disputed water inextricably linked with the Gallipoli land battles but generally treated only as a prelude to them.

The Dardanelles deserves to have its own story told: the waterway has been a place of conflict from the time of Agamemnon, commander of the Greeks during the Trojan War more than 3,000 years ago, to the powerful pre-dreadnought battleship HMS *Agamemnon* that bombarded the Dardanelles fortifications in 1915.

To cross the Dardanelles by ferry from Eceabat to Canakkale, one travels quickly from the continent of Europe to that of Asia Anatolia, and on a sunny day it is impossible to gaze at the land either side of the Strait and not be moved by its beauty and sense of history. To a twenty-first-century Turk, the journey may conjure up thoughts of heroism and the sacrifice of his country's soldiers and artillerymen who manned the guns defending the narrow strip of water against a fleet of powerful British and French warships, so preventing them from threatening Constantinople. To the descendants of the Allied sailors, marines and later soldiers who fought on the Gallipoli peninsula, it is a reminder of groundless confidence, inadequate intelligence gathering, hapless planning, muddled logistics, poor direction from Whitehall and, ultimately, terrible loss of life.

Admiral of the Fleet Sir John Arbuthnot Fisher, First Sea Lord 1914-1915, wrote the words that have echoed through the last hundred years:

Damn the Dardanelles. They will be our grave.

Sir Edward Carson, First Lord of the Admiralty from December 1916 until July 1917, told the House of Commons:

> The Dardanelles operation hangs like a millstone about our necks, and has brought upon us the most vast disaster that has happened in the course of the war.

Although the eight months of land battles on the Gallipoli peninsula have their rightful place in history, this book will focus on the 500-year history of the shore defences that protected the short channel between two continents. The defences had been tested at different times but, had those defences crumpled in 1915, and had the Allied ships then steamed through the Dardanelles, then it is unlikely that Tommy Atkins and his Anzac and French allies would have ever fought against Johnny Turk on his own soil. On 18 March 1915, a fleet of sixteen capital ships tried to destroy the Dardanelles defences in a massive assault, but failed. The confidence of the Royal Navy was severely dented by this failure, so it reverted to the historically proven strategy of blockade, which it did successfully, bottling up the Dardanelles for the rest of the war.

The strategic idea to force the Dardanelles, destroy the Turkish Navy in the Sea of Marmara, intimidate Constantinople with Allied naval firepower, and so knock Turkey out of the war was a good one; perhaps it could have shortened the war against Germany by two years, as Lloyd George and Winston Churchill both believed. If Turkey had given up in 1914 or in early 1915, there would not have been the campaigns in Gallipoli, Mesopotamia and Palestine; tens of thousands of lives would have been saved; hundreds of thousands of troops and countless amounts of war material would have been directed to fight the Germans on the Western Front in France and Belgium.

Turkey *may* have capitulated if the strategy of forcing the Dardanelles had been successful. The ruling elite, including Enver Pasha, Minister of War, a principal member of the Young Turks triumvirate of the Committee of Union and Progress that ran the Ottoman government, anticipated that Allied warships *would* reach Constantinople. The city was in panic; the Sultan's train was ready for his evacuation; the wealth of the Treasury had been dispersed.

However, history had already proved that the unwelcome passage of warships through the Dardanelles would meet with resistance. Reports prepared by the British Admiralty Foreign Intelligence Committee as early as the 1880s described how the defences should be overcome, and believed that a joint naval and land forces operation was necessary. Yet history was ignored, and in taking the decision to force the Dardanelles with warships alone, the British War Cabinet knew that vessels would be lost in such an expedition: the glittering prize of Constantinople was worth such loss. But no matter how hard the Allied warships tried to destroy the forts and gun batteries with a shattering weight of shellfire, they could not do so, and ultimately were prevented passage by a basic and ugly weapon of modern war – the contact sea mine. If the minefield had been cleared, then, perhaps, the warships could have blasted apart the Krupp coastal gun positions that defended the Strait of Canakkale – the Turkish name for the Dardanelles – and steamed on to Constantinople. It was not to be, and the failure to destroy the defences that protected the minefield forced the Allies to give up the naval campaign and commit to the ghastly war of trench fighting on the Gallipoli peninsula. Incredibly, it was not just the heavyweight fixed guns in the forts that were the decisive ingredient of defence, but also an assortment of field guns, mortars and howitzers, some of them very old and without adequate sights, scattered in the hills and gullies either side of the of the Strait. In 1915, the guns defending the Dardanelles were extremely effective and the gunners were good, often very good, deserving more credit than has generally been given to them.

The duel of warship verses coastal artillery is as old as the history of gunpowder. Although there are historical incidents when warships prevailed over land fortifications, such as the bombardment of the Russian fortress of Sveaborg by the Royal Navy in 1855 during the Crimean War, and then Alexandria in 1882 during the Anglo-Egyptian War, success was rarely assured as there were too many considerations that invariably favoured shore artillery: the elevation above sea level, which helps the defender but inhibits those afloat when firing at clifftop targets; the susceptibility of a warship's deck to plunging fire; the difficulty of gun-laying from a moving ship; and the use of heated shot against wooden ships, to name just a few. With the exception of ketch-rigged bomb vessels, which in the age of sail fired huge mortars at shore targets, or the early twentieth-century big gun monitors fulfilling the same role, warships were primarily intended to combat an equivalent enemy at sea with guns designed for long-range, flat-trajectory fire. Coastal artillery is specifically designed to destroy ships. Coastal guns are fixed to a solid base, and the gun crews are trained to engage moving targets. A ship needs to hold a stable position to be anything like equal to a shore fortification but a static ship is a vulnerable target, so unless it can outrange those guns on land, it needs to be constantly moving to dodge incoming fire. Coastal guns can be dispersed as gun batteries, smaller ones of which may move as soon as they are detected, whereas the ship is a concentrated floating battery. For a coastal gun to be disabled it has to take a direct hit or one so close that its crew are killed, but for a ship to be disabled or sunk, any part of the ship is in danger: its bridge, engines, steering gear, magazines and the integrity of the hull itself.

The destruction of the Russian Pacific Fleet at Port Arthur in 1904 by Japanese land guns demonstrated the weakness of ships versus heavy artillery. Another example of how a warship was lost to a shore fortress is vividly illustrated by the sinking of the new German Admiral Hipper class heavy cruiser *Blucher* on 9 April 1940 by Norwegian shore defences in Oslofjord. The *Blucher* was disabled by just two shells fired from the Oscarsborg Fortress at close range from a 280mm (11-inch) Krupp gun that was forty years old, similar to those protecting the Dardanelles in 1915. The ship was then sunk by shore-launched torpedoes.

An essential factor of the battle between the British and French warships against the Turkish shore fortifications is that these defences were almost entirely dependent on German weapons. This hardware was not rushed in at the first sign of blockade, as Germany did not have the desire, availability or means to do so, but the Ottoman Empire had been purchasing vast quantities of German war materials for forty years. The German arms manufacturer Krupp had become the exclusive supplier of heavy coastal artillery to the Ottomans, and was nearly totally dominant with the supply of field guns. Much-needed ammunition and other essential materials were to only trickle through in the months after the Dardanelles were closed, and it was not until German control of the Balkan railways was achieved did supply ramp up enough to try to meet the demands of the Turkish Army.

The defences of the Dardanelles could have been breached in August 1914 had the British War Cabinet decided to do so; the war with Turkey could have been over before it had begun. Yet seven months later, when the Allies actually tried to force the Dardanelles, the defences were impregnable. The credit for this improvement has historically been given to General Liman von Sanders and his German troops but this actually devalues the efforts of the Turks themselves. Major General Cevat Pasha had recognized the need to strengthen the defences even before British warships appeared on the horizon.

As in any conflict, questions and legends are created that become worthy of investigation to test for validity, and this is certainly true of the Dardanelles battles. Were there any shore-launched torpedo batteries defending the Dardanelles? Just what was the state of the minefield, and did the Turks use drifting mines? Was the French pre-dreadnought *Bouvet* really sunk by a mine or was the sinking caused by a shell from a coastal gun? Did gunner Seyit Ali actually lift a 256kg shell and load it into the breech of a 240mm gun after the crane designed for the task had been disabled? Was the defenders' ammunition so depleted that the forts could not have resisted a second naval assault? Why were the British ships' guns so ineffective against the shore forts? Could the Allies have been successful if they had tried again? Answers to these questions will be found in the following chapters.

Two important nomenclatures need to be identified and explained:

The first is Constantinople, the old Byzantine and then Ottoman name for the city we now know as Istanbul. Historically, Constantinople was an area effectively encompassed by the old city walls. As the period covered by this book – including many of the supporting sources that have provided much of the information – predates the acceptance of the more modern name of Istanbul, so the old name will be used throughout, except for modern references. However, Istanbul itself is an old name but has only been internationally accepted since 1930. It is not just the ancient and cultural capital of Turkey, it is also the principal city of Istanbul Province, which comprises thirty-nine districts and covers both sides of the Bosphorus. Istanbul is the world's only metropolis that is situated on two continents. The other important settlement in the story of the Dardanelles is the town of Canakkale (omitting the modern Turkish alphabet modifications adopted for the phonetic requirements of the language such as the 'Ç' in Çanakkale) and this name is used throughout, except when quoting from British sources, where the name Chanak is used. Current Turkish spelling is used for contemporary place names such as Atatürk Havalimani – Istanbul's principal airport.

The second is the use of the terms 'Ottoman' and 'Turk', which can be confusing. Turkey is recognized today as a parliamentary republican Islamic nation but until the dissolution of the Ottoman Empire after the First World War, 'Ottoman' covered persons of all nationalities and faiths within the cosmopolitan and religiously tolerant empire ruled by its Sultan. 'Ottoman Turks', essentially from the Anatolian heartland of the empire, were deemed to be superior as they dominated the ruling class within the empire. So, regarding pre-

Turkish stamps commemorating the fortieth anniversary of the 18 March 1915 action: the minelayer *Nusret*; Gunner Seyit Ali; the Gallipoli peninsula and the Dardanelles; Mustafa Kemal. (Author's collection)

First World War events, there is general historical acceptance that where Turk is written, one can also read Ottoman, and vice versa; many research sources merrily substitute one title for the other, and this book will do the same when reflecting the spirit of such sources.

The reputations of many British generals, admirals and politicians were blighted in the Dardanelles Strait or in the dirt and mud of Gallipoli – including, temporarily, Winston Churchill's – but the reputation of others began to shine, none more so than Lieutenant Colonel Mustafa Kemal, who would ultimately become Kemal Ataturk, the Father of Modern Turkey. The waste of life and resources that occurred in 1915 still cast a deep shadow over the beautiful Gallipoli landscape and on the historic waters of the Dardanelles, but from these battlegrounds the seeds of the Republic of Turkey were planted. A date celebrated in the calendar of the Canakkale Province – 18 March 1915 – is commemorated each year, and the local university includes the date in its name, Çanakkale Onsekiz Mart University.

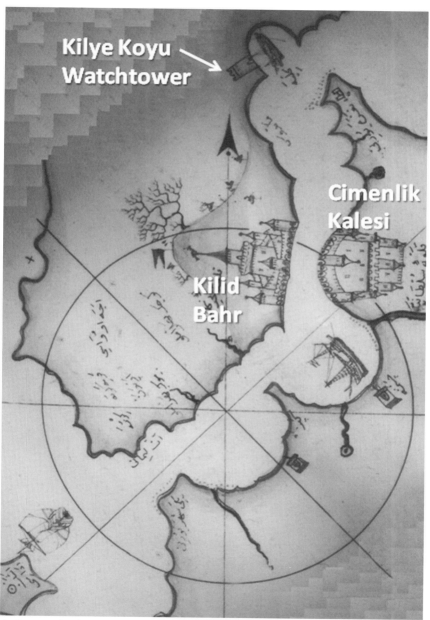

A photograph of a sixteenth-century Ottoman map of the Dardanelles showing the two castles either side of the Narrows – Cimenlik Kalesi and Kilid Bahr – and a watchtower at Kilye Koyu Bay, displayed at Cimenlik Kalesi Museum. The map has been orientated so that north is pointing up. (© Forrest)

CHAPTER 1

A Brief History of the Dardanelles

For 3,000 years the Dardanelles has been significant as a natural barrier between the continents of Europe and Asia Anatolia. It is the southern strait of a busy international waterway linking the Aegean to the Black Sea, via the Sea of Marmara and the Bosphorus, with the ancient city of Istanbul straddling the route between them. The Dardanelles Strait is 38 miles (61km) long measured from the tip of the Gallipoli peninsula to the lighthouse just north of Gelibolu, the town previously known as Gallipoli, where the Sea of Marmara begins. The Strait is a maximum of 4 miles (6.5km) wide and is 330 feet (100m) at its deepest point. It has three squeeze points within the first 16 miles (26km) measured from the entrance: Kepez Point, which is 3,300 yards (3,000m) wide; the Narrows; and Nagara Point. As the name suggests, the Narrows is the crucial tactical feature, 13 miles (21km) from the entrance, barely 1,400 yards (1,300m) wide, of which only about 1,200 yards (1,100m) can safely accept large ships, measured to the 6 fathoms line. A pilot is required for all Turkish ships of 150m or more in length, and this is strongly recommended for other vessels of this size or above in transit. A Traffic Separation Scheme is applied to all vessels. The natural attributes of the Dardanelles, including a sharp turn at Nagara Point where the passage is 2,300 yards (2,100m) wide, coupled with a strong surface current of up to 3 knots that runs out toward the Aegean but with a reverse undercurrent, makes the Strait a difficult waterway to navigate at the best of times but daunting if under fire from defending fortresses.

1

The Dardanelles has been contested on numerous occasions and has been the subject of frequent political manoeuvrings, particularly by Russia, as it is their only access from the Black Sea to the Aegean and then on to the world's oceans. For most of the nineteenth century, the Ottomans made it a condition with the European powers that vessels containing troops or munitions of war were not permitted to pass through the Dardanelles. The London Straits Convention of 1841 closed the Dardanelles and the Bosphorus to all but Turkish warships in peacetime, thereby denying Russia the access they had only recently achieved. The Treaty of Paris (1856) and the Treaty of London (1871) modified but reinforced this requirement. Warships of other nations could transit the Straits on rare occasions such as during the Crimean War or as a part of 'goodwill' visits, but only with the permission of the Sultan. Post-First World War and under the 1920 Treaty of Sevres between the victorious Allies and the defeated Ottoman Empire, the Dardanelles, the Bosphorus and the Sea of Marmara were open to all shipping, both military and commercial, at all times. This treaty was superseded in 1923 with the Treaty of Lausanne, as the now defunct Ottoman Empire was replaced by the Republic of Turkey, but the internationalization of the Straits still continued for another thirteen years. In 1936, this arrangement was updated by the Montreux Convention Regarding the Regime of the Turkish Straits – the Strait of Istanbul or the Bosphorus, the Strait of Canakkale, and the Sea of Marmara – to severely restrict non-Turkish military vessels and prohibit some types of warships such as aircraft carriers, but to provide the free passage of all commercial traffic. It is still applicable today, albeit with some modifications, although the interpretation of the Convention has sometimes been the source of controversy. In April 1982, the Convention was amended to allow Turkey to close the Turkish Straits at its discretion in peacetime as well as during wartime. Since the Montreux Convention was concluded, more than seventy-five years ago, the number of vessels passing through the Turkish Straits annually has increased more than tenfold; according to the Republic of Turkey Ministry of Foreign Affairs website, if measured as tonnage then the figure is more than twenty-five times, giving rise to safety and environmental concerns, particularly due to the amount of tanker and other hazardous cargo traffic.

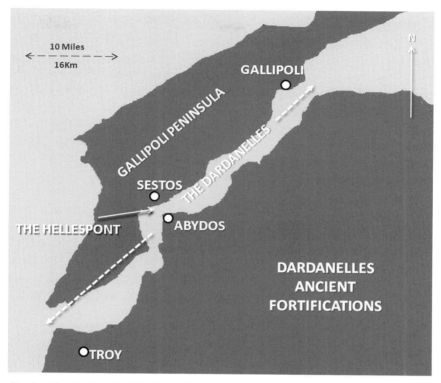

Dardanelles Ancient Fortifications. (© Forrest)

The Dardanelles – early incursions and defence

The name Dardanelles is derived from the ancient Greek city Dardanus in the region Dardania on the Asian side of the Strait, and from Helle, a character from Greek mythology linked to the story of Jason and the Argonauts. According to legend, Helle drowned in the Dardanelles after falling from the back of a winged ram. Helle also gave her name to Cape Helles at the tip of the Gallipoli peninsula and to the Hellespont, which in classical literature was the part of the Strait between Sestos on the European shore and Abydos on the Asiatic shore, close to what is now known as Nagara Point. The original settlers on the Gallipoli peninsula were from Thrace and would have known it at that time as the Thracian Chersonese; they lived in a number of small towns or on farms on either side of the Dardanelles.

The shores of the Dardanelles undoubtedly saw the arrival of hundreds of ships from Sparta, Athens, Ithaca, Thessaly and other such places described by Homer in the *Iliad* during the time of the Trojan War. The first significant military use of the Strait was when Darius I of Persia moved troops across the Hellespont to support the Persian invasion of Europe, circa 500 BC. The ancient Greek historian Herodotus records that Darius's heir, Xerxes I, built two bridges across the 'narrowest part of the Hellespont' to move his army across and so invade Thrace and Greece, circa 480 BC. The bridges were destroyed by a storm before completion, so Xerxes had the flowing water branded with red-hot irons and lashed as a punishment; crueller still, the bridge builders were beheaded. The army successfully crossed at the next attempt by lashing some 300 boats together facing the current to create two floating bridges, suitably anchored to avoid being washed away. Over these boats six large cables were stretched, and on them were fastened strong timbers. Walls were built on either side of the bridges so that the horses and pack animals would not see the water and take fright. In this way more than 200,000 troops crossed from Asia into Europe. In 334 BC, the Greek army of Alexander the Great crossed the Hellespont in the opposite direction to conquer Asia. Two hundred years later, the waterway and its shores came under the administration of Rome.

Christian Emperor Constantine, ruler of the Eastern Roman Empire, or the Byzantine Empire, recognized the strategic importance of the waterway between the Black Sea and the Aegean, and also the commercial significance of the ancient city of Byzantium, which he made his capital city. It was renamed Constantinople after Constantine's death in 337 AD, and for more than a thousand years stood as the gateway that separated Christian Europe from Islam until it fell to the Ottomans in 1453. In the preceding century the Ottomans had advanced from central Anatolia, expanding east toward the Caspian Sea and Arabia, and heading west to cross both the Dardanelles and the Bosphorus into the Balkans. Although the Byzantine Empire was in decline and Constantinople was under economic siege, the city was bypassed and so remained aloof, having a strange sort of neutrality with the invader gobbling up its ancient lands. Life in Constantinople went on in much the same way as before, the population being adequately supplied from the sea by independent trading states such as Venice, Florence and Genoa. Yet beyond the city walls hundreds of Byzantine fortresses were absorbed by the Ottomans, including those at Sestos and Gallipoli. According to eighteenth-century Turkish writer Evliya Celebi in his *Book of Travels*, the hexagonal Greek castle at Gallipoli had a compliment of 300 soldiers but was destroyed by an earthquake in 1356, and the ruin was occupied by Ottoman forces.

The Ottoman Empire had embraced gunpowder early in its rise to power, first using firearms in the late fourteenth century. Bronze cannons soon followed, then, during the final siege of Constantinople, so did massive siege bombards. These cast bronze guns of 5m in length were capable of firing huge stone balls, 80cm in diameter and weighing more than 500kg, for a distance of over 500m. The irony of the Ottoman use of the bombard is that the Hungarian gunfounder, Urban, who was able to produce such a large weapon, first offered it to the Byzantine defenders of Constantinople but they had neither the financial nor material resources to create such a weapon. The Ottomans, under the command of Sultan

The 'Dardanelles Gun' – a Great Bombard displayed at the Royal Armouries Museum, Fort Nelson, Hampshire. Cast by bronze-founder Munir Ali in 1464, it has a bore of 635mm and was capable of firing a 300kg ball to a distance of 1,500m. It is a masterpiece of medieval technology, having been cast in two pieces – powder chamber and barrel – which screw together. In 1866, during his state visit to London, Sultan Abdulaziz gave the Dardanelles Gun to Queen Victoria as a present. (© Forrest)

Mehmed II, were able to accept Urban's services, and the largest super-bombard, measuring more than 8m long, was cast in Adrianople, modern-day Erdine, the capital of the Ottomans in Thrace. Hundreds of men and sixty oxen were required to move the huge weapon 200km to its firing position outside Constantinople. The Ottomans used more than sixty artillery pieces of various sizes to attack Constantinople, but as some guns were cast in the open their quality was poor and may have burst in use. A building was constructed outside Constantinople's city walls in the Galata district specifically for the casting of cannon. This became known as the Tophane (arsenal) and was a centre for Ottoman gun production up to the First World War.

By circa 1400, the Dardanelles were firmly under the control of the Ottomans, but the first use of artillery to attack ships in the Dardanelles was in 1444. Ottoman troops were being transported from the Asian shore to the European shore, and Ottoman guns fired upon Burgundian ships that were trying to prevent the transfer. Although it is not known what type of cannon were used the significance is that the guns were firing at moving targets, whereas the primitive artillery of this time was normally used against static targets.

As the Ottomans absorbed the Byzantine Empire, so they recognized the strategic importance of the Dardanelles. Two castles were built in 1452 to control what we now know as the Narrows – Kilid Bahr (meaning lock of the sea) on the peninsula shore, and Kale-i Sultaniye (castle of the sultan – now known as Cimenlik Kalesi) at Canakkale. Incredibly, a number of the fifteenth-century bombards located at these forts were still in service more than 400 years later. The Dardanelles Gun, now on display at the Royal Armouries Museum of Artillery at Fort Nelson, Hampshire, dates from 1464, and is a magnificent example of medieval technology having been cast in two pieces, powder chamber and barrel, which screw together. This bombard was capable of firing a 300kg ball to a distance of 1,500m.

The powerful Ottoman Navy protected the empire's sea lanes and controlled the waters far into the Mediterranean. The first Ottoman naval dockyard was built at Gallipoli harbour, and became the principal naval base until superseded by the yards built at Constantinople in 1515. During the sixteenth and seventeenth centuries, another important maritime

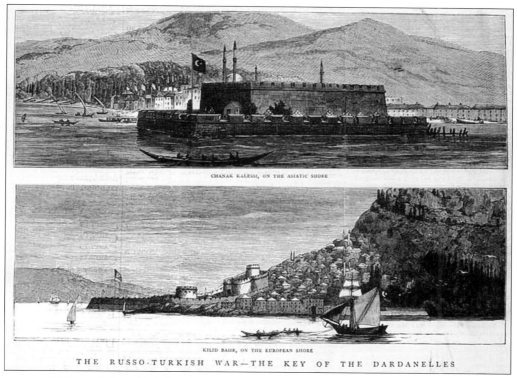

CHANAK KALESSI, ON THE ASIATIC SHORE

KILID BAIR, ON THE EUROPEAN SHORE

THE RUSSO-TURKISH WAR—THE KEY OF THE DARDANELLES

A lithograph from 1877 showing Cimenlik Kalesi and Kilid Bahr. (*The Graphic*, 19 May 1877)

A lithograph from the *Illustrated London News* captioned 'Great gun at Chanak Kalesi, the Castle of the Governor of the Dardanelles', showing a bronze bombard, probably from the fifteenth century, with stone shot stacked behind it. Note the inclined slide to absorb the recoil. (*Illustrated London News*, 12 November 1853)

power – the Venetians – challenged the Ottomans' supremacy and proved to be more than a match for them during a number of gruelling battles in waters of the Aegean and the Dardanelles. The Ottoman Navy experimented with mounting their biggest bombards on a few of their ships, although results were far from satisfactory due to the massive energy of the recoil acting on the wooden hull. It was during the Sixth Ottoman-Venetian War, in the middle of the seventeenth century, that a Venetian fleet blockaded the Dardanelles to prevent Ottoman ships resupplying the armies fighting for islands in the Aegean. After at least four significant naval engagements involving sailing vessels, galleys and galleasses (a larger type of galley with a gun deck) during the years 1654 to 1657, the Ottomans were able to finally clear the threat of blockade. It was at this time that the forts either side of the entrance to the Dardanelles were built – Sedd el Bahr (key of the sea) close to the southern point of the Gallipoli peninsula, and Kum Kale (sand castle) on the Asian shore.

Dardanelles Fortification 1452-1807. (© Forrest)

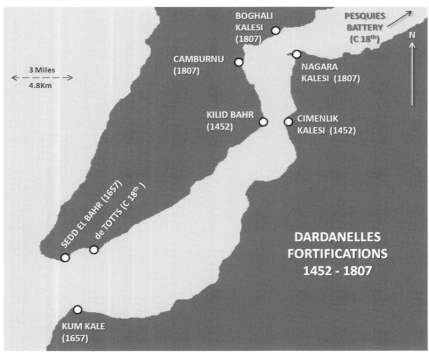

8

The Royal Navy's attempt to force the Dardanelles to threaten Constantinople in 1915 had historical precedence, first in 1807, and then again in 1878.

Admiral Duckworth and the Dardanelles Operation 1807

Turkey closed the Straits to Russian vessels in 1806, encouraged by the French victory over the Russians at the Battle of Austerlitz. Britain, alarmed by this development and fearing that the Russians would be distracted from the war against Napoleon by keeping a large army on the Lower Danube, decided to quickly frighten Turkey by intimidating Constantinople – a similar rationale that was to be applied in 1915. The expectation was that a show of force by the Royal Navy and a few well-aimed rounds into the city would be all that was necessary to scare the Turks into submission, rather than commit to the long and difficult process of transporting and landing an army to take the capital. In November 1806, Admiral Thomas Louis, commanding the eighty-gun *Canopus*, which was accompanied by the frigate *Endymion*, passed through the Dardanelles unhindered, exchanging a traditional friendly salute by cannon with the forts, and anchored off Constantinople to open negotiations with the Turks. Three other British ships had also arrived and anchored off Canakkale, remaining there until Admiral Louis returned. One of the British requirements was that French Colonel Sebastiani, his engineers and artillerymen, engaged in improving the Dardanelles defences, leave Turkey. The stone forts at the entrance to the Dardanelles and at the Narrows had been freshly painted white in 1805 to convey the impression that they were newly fitted. The demand for the removal of the French colonel and troops was ignored by the Turks, frustrating Admiral Louis and British plans. The *Canopus* left Constantinople in late December 1806, but *Endymion* remained until 29 January 1807, when she evacuated the British Ambassador, Charles Arbuthnot, and other British residents.

As diplomacy had failed, so action was required. On 19 February 1807 a fleet of eleven British men-of-war entered the Dardanelles commanded by Admiral Sir John Duckworth: the flagship *Royal George* (100-gun first-rate), *Windsor Castle* (98-gun second-rate), *Canopus* (80-gun third-rate), *Repulse* (74-gun third-rate), *Thunderer* (74-gun third-rate), *Pompée* (74-gun third-rate), *Standard* (64-gun third-rate), and the frigates *Endymion* (40-gun fifth-rate) and *Active* (38-gun fifth-rate). Two bomb vessels – *Lucifer* and *Meteor* – accompanied the rated ships. These were specialized craft with very strong hulls, as each mounted a 10-inch and a 13-inch mortar, the latter capable of firing a 200lb explosive shell to a distance of 2,900 yards. The fleet was fired on by the guns from the entrance fortresses, then from the forts at the Narrows, and again from guns at Abydos and Sestos, but the effects were unimpressive as the forts were inadequately manned. The British ships replied, including the bomb vessels, which also carried 24pr carronades, but the *Meteor's* 13-inch mortar burst, rendering the vessel less than capable of carrying out its role to bombard Constantinople.

A jingoistic newspaper article from *The Penny Illustrated Paper* dated 26 September 1891 describes the action:

> The account which I have condensed from a paper of the period is most amusing showing the audacity of the British tars.... The British ships replied with such precision as to astound the Turkish gunners, who were directed by several French officers. The English vessels, while giving broadsides in response to this terrible crossfire, still kept on their triumphant progress, until above the Castle of Abydos on the Asiatic side, they fell in with the Turkish fleet of thirteen vessels (a 64-gun ship, four frigates, four sloops, two brigs and two gunboats), protected by a big battery on shore of thirty-one guns at the point of Pesquies. [This was an anchorage north of Nagara Point. The guns of this battery were destroyed by Royal Marines landed from the ships.]
>
> Sir John Duckworth scarcely took any notice of the Turkish fleet but sailed majestically on, leaving Admiral Sir Sidney Smith, a splendid seaman, with three men-of-war and two frigates (*Pompée, Thunderer, Standard, Endymion* and *Active*) to deal with the foe. In less than half an hour the Turks were overcome and their ships were boarded by British tars, a few shells dispersing a body of troops assembled in

the rear of the fort.... Of course the fortifications of the
Dardanelles are far stronger than they were in 1807 but the
exploit of the British fleet at that time, we have not the
slightest doubt, could be repeated, if necessary, in 1891.

Although the British ships successfully reached Constantinople, they had
sustained some damage and casualties caused by fire from the shore
batteries and fighting to capture the Turkish ships and the gun battery.
The fleet anchored about 8 miles from Constantinople close to an island
named Prota (now Kinaliada), one of the Princes' Islands in the Sea of
Marmara, where fresh water was available. Admiral Duckworth did not
shell Constantinople, preferring to try to negotiate the surrender of the
city from a position of strength or to draw out the Turkish fleet to fight,
but neither happened. In fact, Sultan Selim III chose to ignore
Duckworth's demands and the Admiral did nothing further to enforce his
presence. Turkish troops briefly occupied Prota and set up a gun battery
to threaten the anchored British ships, but the Royal Marines chased them
off, taking some casualties and capturing two bronze guns, one of which
is now at the Royal Hospital School, Holbrook. After more than a week
of frustration, Admiral Duckworth decided to withdraw to the Aegean,
knowing that this time the Dardanelles fortresses were better prepared
than before. On 3 March 1807 the British ships ran the gauntlet of heavy
guns and ancient bronze bombards once again, with those set up at
Abydos and Sestos, either side of the Hellespont, being particularly
destructive. Most of the vessels were damaged: the mainmast of *Windsor
Castle* was destroyed by a 300kg stone ball from a bombard located at
Abydos; *Royal George* was also hit by a ball from a bombard; and
Canopus had its wheel shot away. All of the ships escaped into the Aegean
but the fleet had suffered forty-two killed, 235 wounded and four missing
during the two-week operation.

There is no record of what damage the British ships inflicted on the
forts and shore batteries but it was probably light, if any at all. The
heaviest guns in the fleet were the 42prs carried by *Royal George*, but
these can be considered puny compared to the balls fired by the bombards.
The exploding shells from the bomb ships could have been effective but
the ships would have to have anchored to be accurate, and clearly this

was not an option for any ship that day. The *Meteor* lost its remaining mortar during this engagement, although not through enemy action but again due to bursting.

Admiral Duckworth's expedition proved to be fruitless as the Turks refused to be terrified by the imposition of British warships in sight of their capital. Retreat was the only option for the Admiral because his ships could not remain unsupported without renewable supplies. With the benefit of hindsight, there was no real value in this incursion into the Turkish waters except in a negative sense: it vividly illustrated that slow-moving warships passing through the narrow Dardanelles without sea room in which to manoeuvre would be at a disadvantage against well-organized shore batteries, and could expect to be damaged, disabled or even sunk. Admiral Duckworth considered the expedition, 'the most arduous and doubtful that was ever undertaken.' In a letter to Russian Admiral Senyavin, Admiral Duckworth prophetically stated that, 'The co-operation of a land force was necessary.'

Duckworth's ships retired from the Aegean. On 6 March 1807 Admiral Senyavin's fleet of ten ships blockaded the entrance to the Dardanelles, closing the Strait to all traffic. After two months, food riots broke out in Constantinople, which led to the Sultan being deposed and his replacement, Mustafa IV, ordering the Turkish Navy to sail and break the blockade. A battle took place off the entrance to the Dardanelles in which the Turkish ships were mauled and retired back into the Strait. The Russian ships followed but withdrew because of the heavy fire from the entrance forts and approaching darkness. Another naval engagement occurred in June 1807 near to the entrance to the Dardanelles – the Battle of Lemnos – in which the Turks lost around one-third of their ships. An armistice between Russia and the Ottoman Empire was signed on 12 August 1807. This was later followed by the Treaty of Kale-i Sultaniye between Britain and the Ottoman Empire, which was finally concluded on 5 January 1809.

After the escape of Admiral Duckworth's ships from the Dardanelles, three new forts were constructed to add additional firepower to the Turkish defences: Nagara Kalesi, close to the battery at Abydos; Boghali Kalesi, on the opposite European shore; and Camburnu, further south on the same side.

Nagara Kalesi built in 1807, after Admiral Duckworth's fruitless expedition through the Dardanelles to threaten Constantinople. Note the low profile of the castle and the cannon embrasures at the water's edge. (© Forrest)

Boghali Kalesi, also built in 1807, after Admiral Duckworth's fruitless expedition. The photograph dates from the 1880s. Note the smooth-bore cannons to the left, the stacked round-shot and the mortar to the right of the tree. (Author's collection)

Relations between the Russians and the Ottomans ebbed and flowed but in 1833, they were allied against Egypt and her supporter, France, in a show of naval force to defuse a threatened incursion through the Dardanelles to seize Constantinople. As a result of this co-operation Turkey agreed under the Treaty of Hünkâr İskelesi that in a crisis the Turkish Straits would be closed to all warships except those of Russia, granting the Russian Navy access to the Aegean via the Bosphorus and the Dardanelles. This was a major prize for Russia but was later rescinded at the London Straits Convention of 1841, concluded between Britain, France, Prussia, Austria, Russia and Turkey. Yet a little more than a decade later, Russia was the enemy once more during the Crimean War of 1853-1856, Turkey then allowing Britain and France to send their warships through the Turkish Straits into the Black Sea. Additional co-operation between the nations during the Crimean War was demonstrated with the building of the Bulair Lines to defend the narrow neck of the Gallipoli peninsula from land attack from the north-east. Much of the planning and construction, including permanent forts, was carried out by British and French engineers.

The Balkans has historically been a flashpoint to wider conflicts, and this was certainly true during the 1870s. A festering crisis in the Balkans encouraged anti-Ottoman revolts from many of the heavily taxed and subjugated peoples of Bulgaria, Serbia and Montenegro. Russia mobilized its army while the principal European powers attempted to mediate. Nevertheless, after two years of fruitless negotiations, Russia declared war on Turkey in 1877. Russia was motivated by the desire to recover its national prestige lost during the Crimean War and to re-establish its Black Sea Fleet and fortified bases. Britain, concerned at Russian expansion toward Constantinople, decided to send warships to the city as a show of force. The Royal Navy was to pass through the Dardanelles uninvited for a second time in seventy-one years.

Admiral Hornby 1878

In January 1878 Admiral Geoffrey Hornby, probably one of the most able naval commanders of his time, was instructed by the Admiralty to go through the Dardanelles and to anchor off Constantinople. After several days of diplomatic manoeuvring while Admiral Hornby's ships were waiting at Besika Bay, a few miles south of the entrance to the Dardanelles, the instruction to proceed was given by the Admiralty. Permission to enter the Strait had been granted by the Turkish military commander and the British ships passed the entrance forts unchallenged, arriving at Canakkale on 25 January 1878. But now the British Government changed its mind, concerned that a Royal Navy incursion may affect the ongoing armistice discussions between Turkey and Russia, so Admiral Hornby was immediately instructed by the Admiralty to return to Besika Bay. However, after further political machinations and numerous telegraphic exchanges between London and Admiral Hornby, he was ordered to proceed to Constantinople, but this time against the wishes of Sultan Abdulhamid II. Not all of the fleet were to proceed, and a number of ships under the command of Rear Admiral Commerell were to act as a guard should the Russians make any attempt on the Dardanelles, Russian troops having already taken some areas of the Gallipoli peninsula.

One of the British vessels under Admiral Hornby's command was HMS *Sultan*, a broadside ironclad launched in 1870, named after Sultan Abdulaziz, who had visited England at the time the ship was laid down. He was the first Ottoman sultan to visit Western Europe and was considered responsible for the modernization of the Ottoman Navy during his reign. By 1876, the year Abdulaziz died, the Ottoman Navy ranked as the third largest in the world after Britain and France.

The British ironclads re-entered the Straits on 13 February 1878 in two lines: Starboard Division (Asiatic side) – *Alexandra* (flagship), *Sultan* and *Temeraire*; and Port Division (European side) – *Agincourt* (divisional flagship), *Achilles* and *Swiftsure*. The weather was appalling, with heavy rain that occasionally obscured the coastline, together with high winds. The ships passed the entrance forts of Sedd el Bahr and Kum Kale at 1015 hrs without challenge, and at about 1100 hrs, snow began to fall, which totally hid the coastline as the Strait opened out to its widest part. The *Alexandra* grounded for a short time but, with the assistance of *Sultan*, was quickly refloated. *The Penny Illustrated Paper* dated 9 March 1878 reported on the passage of the ships, quoting an unnamed naval officer:

Admiral Hornby's ships steam through the Narrows in 1878. The illustration is inaccurate as the ships had formed a single line. (*Illustrated London News*, February 1878)

> At 2.30 pm the ships arrived off the point at which any serious resistance was expected. This was a 40-ton Krupp gun mounted in an earthwork some 3 miles below Chanak.

This location is inaccurate as '3 miles below Chanak' is the Kepez area, where no heavy Krupp guns have ever been located. The '40-ton Krupp gun' refers to the 355mm (14-inch) breech-loading gun set in an earth emplacement located 100m south of Cimenlik Kalesi. Turkey had first ordered heavy Krupp coastal guns from Germany in 1873, and by 1878, Cimenlik Kalesi and other forts mounted many of these guns. A detailed description of the forts and their armaments will be found in Chapter Three.

Admiral Hornby's prepared orders were carried out by each ship as they formed a single line. The ships, making 8 knots against the current, were ready to fight, but would only respond if fired upon first. Riflemen manned the fighting tops; Gatling guns and torpedo defences were readied:

The guns were loaded with heavy charges of powder and shrapnel shell, trained on the beam, and ran out just level with the battery ports. But these messengers of death had a smiling face upon them, for the tompions were in, and everything looked peaceful.... Breathless silence reigned over the ships, broken only by the dull thud, thud of the engines; yet beneath that quietude was the greatest excitement. At the guns stood their crews, one man ready to slip out the tompion, the others to run the gun out, while the captain of the gun stood immoveable, lanyard in one hand, one jerk of which would have sent the enormous shell spinning on its errand. Our hearts were in our mouths as the flagship came abreast of the Chanak gun; the little puff of smoke, the flame, the crash were eagerly watched for, while minutes seemed years. At last relief came; we had passed in peace.

Ironclads were designed to fire from the beam or the side, as in the old-fashioned term the 'broadside', the guns being capable of very limited traverse. The largest gun carried by the ships of Admiral Hornby's squadron was the Armstrong 11-inch RML (Rifled Muzzle Loader) aboard the most modern vessels *Alexandra* (1875) and *Temeraire* (1876). The reference to training the guns 'on the beam' is interesting because none of Admiral Hornby's ships had turrets as we know them today, although *Alexandra* had six 20pr breech-loading guns that were positioned in an upper deck box battery; *Temeraire* was unique (when built) being fitted with disappearing guns in barbettes – open-top emplacements that gave the gun a wide field of fire. The gun was loaded below the deck line and then elevated above the armoured emplacement for firing. The recoil would return the gun below deck for sponging and reloading, safely out of an enemy's line of fire.

In worsening weather conditions, in which visibility reduced so that the ships lost sight of each other, they all successfully traversed the Narrows, guided by good navigation and the leadsman in the chains reporting on the depth of water. There was no firing from the fortifications. At some time after 1530 hrs orders were given to unload the guns. Soon after this the weather and visibility improved, and at 1800 hrs

An 11-inch, 25-ton, Armstrong RML (Rifled Muzzle Loading) gun in an armoured barbette turret aboard HMS *Temeraire* passing through the Dardanelles. On firing, the recoil would bring the gun below deck level for reloading. (*Illustrated London News*, February 1878)

the ships anchored off the town of Gallipoli. The following morning, four of Admiral Duckworth's ships proceeded – *Alexandra, Achilles, Sultan* and *Temeraire* – through the Sea of Marmara to anchor off the Princes' Islands, 10 miles from Constantinople.

Due to international pressures the Russian troops stopped a few miles from Constantinople, and a peace settlement between Russia and Turkey was concluded with the Treaty of San Stefano, almost immediately modified by the Treaty of Berlin. After the cessation of hostilities the British ships withdrew, but Admiral Hornby had a very clear view of the dangers of the Dardanelles and the hazards of resupplying an unwelcome fleet. When still in the Sea of Marmara he wrote to the First Lord of the Admiralty, the politician William Henry Smith[1]:

There seems to be an idea that this fleet can keep the Dardanelles open. Nothing can be more visionary. Not all the fleets in the world can keep them open for unarmoured ships. Small earthworks on the cliffs would always prevent their passage. Guns thus placed, could not fail to stop transports and colliers.

The end of the nineteenth century

Turkey had traditional enemies such as its closest neighbour, Russia, although Britain had never been one of them. Even events such as Admiral Duckworth's expedition in 1807 and the defeat of the Ottoman Navy in 1827 at the Battle of Navarino[2] did not blight the relationship. This was emphasized in the last decade of the nineteenth century, when Turkey, its empire continuing to crumble from within, was still regarded as Britain's friend because of its strategic position. The respected and successful British newspaper *The Graphic* stated in the 17 March 1894 edition:

> Turkey's enemies are England's enemies.... Financially, commercially and politically England is, as she has always been, the best possible friend to Turkey.... Turkey has been crippled and prevented from going ahead by wants of funds. But, in spite of that, she has managed to provide herself with two factors which would be of great value to us in war – viz, a fairly good fleet and a strong system of defence works in the Bosphorus and Dardanelles. In addition to this, she possesses harbours and coaling stations that might be most useful on occasion.
>
> The narrow straits of the Bosphorus, continued further south in those of the Dardanelles, are lined thickly on both shores with forts and batteries. These are heavily armed – several with over forty guns in them. The guns, as a rule, are Krupps. So that with the assistance of their search lights and their minefields it is reasonable to suppose that they should be able to hold back a fleet endeavouring to make its way from the Black Sea southward to the Mediterranean.

Clearly, the emphasis here was that the threat would be from Russia, its fleet sailing south from the Black Sea to gain access to the Aegean, but it would equally apply to a fleet sailing north through the Dardanelles to attack Constantinople. By the end of the nineteenth century, the formidable fortifications of the Dardanelles were well known to military planners of the Great Powers. When combined with the tricky currents and the difficult passage to the Sea of Marmara, it would have been surprising if any aggressive battle fleet could have successfully transited the Straits at this time. Of course, none tried – that was to be a twentieth-century adventure.

Notes

1. The appointment of William Henry Smith as First Lord of the Admiralty, a man with no naval or military experience to govern the Royal Navy, was satirized by Gilbert and Sullivan in the character of Sir Joseph Porter, KCB, in their 1878 comic opera *H.M.S. Pinafore*.
2. The Battle of Navarino was fought on 20 October 1827 during the Greek War of Independence. A combined Ottoman and Egyptian fleet was destroyed by a combined British, French and Russian naval force. It is notable for being the last major naval battle in history to be fought entirely with sailing ships. The northern European ships were better armed than their Egyptian and Ottoman opponents and their crews were better trained, contributing to a complete victory.

CHAPTER 2

Germany and the Ottoman Empire

T he Ottoman Empire was at its zenith in the seventeenth century, when it spanned three continents, controlled much of South-Eastern Europe, Western Asia and North Africa, and ruled over some thirty million people. However, the weak and bureaucratic administration of successive sultans meant that further expansion was impossible, particularly as various alliances ranged against them at different times. Throughout the intervening centuries Ottoman rule clung onto its territories by a harsh regime that steadily became self-defeating, engendering nationalism and then creating revolution from many of the empire's subjugated peoples, notably the Greeks. By the beginning of the twentieth century, the Ottoman Empire had lost many of its North African territories and was under pressure in the Balkans and in Armenia, although it still held much of its territory in Asia, including almost all of the Arab lands.

Early military reform of the Ottoman Empire
The Ottomans had been early advocates of the use of firearms and cannon: it was Europe's first 'gunpowder empire'. Yet by the late eighteenth century, the Ottoman Empire was considered to be in a state of economic decline, caused by numerous military setbacks and internal unrest from its oppressed peoples. However, the Ottomans recognized that some form of military reformation was required, and the services of European military advisors were sought. Foremost in providing technical aid were the French, principally officers such as Claude Alexandre de Bonneval,

who was instrumental in the reform of the Ottoman military system, and Baron François de Tott, who advocated the ideas of mobile artillery units and the use of shore mortars to provide plunging fire onto the decks of enemy ships. A battery known as 'de Tott's' was set up circa 1770 at Eski Hisarlik Point, east of Sedd el Bahr, and still appeared on British planning maps in 1914. The concept of plunging fire from mobile artillery was to be important for the defence of the Dardanelles between the entrance forts and those at the Narrows, combined factors that were to become very significant in 1915, even though howitzers had largely replaced mortars by this time.

During the preceding centuries, the ruling sultans had relied upon the Janissaries, an elite infantry maintained as a standing army, but in 1826 the Janissaries were bloodily disbanded by Sultan Mahmud II because of their cost, misuse of power and resistance to military reform. A new army was created with the use of conscripted troops with defined lengths of service as combatants, auxiliaries and then reservists, and also with the hire of selected professional soldiers such as artillerymen. The Ottoman artillery was divided as *Seyyar* (mobile) and as *Kale* (castle or garrison) forces. Garrison artillery was responsible for the defence of all strongholds and fortified places along the coasts and frontiers of the empire, being loosely attached to the Tophane Müşirliği (Marshal of Ordnance). The Ottomans briefly embraced the machine gun by buying several Gatlings at the end of the 1860s because Russia had done so, but turned down the much better Maxim several years later when the designer, Hiram Maxim, wanted to demonstrate the gun in Constantinople. On his arrival at the War Ministry, Maxim was informed by an English-speaking official, 'Hang your guns; we don't want your guns. Invent a new vice for us and we will receive you with open arms; that is what we want.'

The Ottoman Army at the end of the nineteenth century was far from professional, reliant on only conscript Muslims from certain areas of the empire, and was almost stupefied with inactivity. This was to change prior to the First World War because of the Italian-Turkish War, the catastrophic Balkans Wars and the Young Turks Revolution of 1908. The Young Turks triumvirate of the Committee of Union and Progress was led by Enver Pasha, Minister of War; Djemal Pasha, Minister of the Navy, and Talat Pasha, Minister of Interior. The triumvirate broke up as Turkey joined the war on the side of Germany, but Enver remained as the effective leader of the Ottoman Empire until its defeat in 1918.

The Italian-Turkish War

The Italian-Turkish War of 1911-1912 principally took place in Tripolitania but the navies of the two countries fought a number of actions in the Adriatic, the Aegean, the Mediterranean and the Red Sea. From February 1912, significant efforts were directed to improve the defences of the Dardanelles by laying a minefield and by adding guns, many of which had been withdrawn from the Bosphorus. The passage of merchant ships through the Dardanelles at night was terminated, and pilots were required by all vessels in order to navigate the minefield. By June 1912, an estimated 30,000 Turkish troops were emplaced on the Gallipoli peninsula and on the Asian side of the Strait to resist a possible invasion.

On 19 April 1912, two squadrons of Italian ships, comprising five pre-dreadnoughts mounting 12-inch (305mm) guns as main armament, together with a number of cruisers, bombarded the Dardanelles entrance forts for two hours. The forts returned fire but none of the ships were hit. The Orhaniye Battery, 2km south-west of Kum Kale, was damaged and the barrack block immediately behind the battery was hit. Sedd el Bahr was also damaged, with the Turks sustaining fifteen dead and eighteen wounded. The Italian ships fired 342 shells, to the 150 from the defenders. Turkey promptly closed the Dardanelles to all traffic, which immediately impacted on the Russian grain trade, together with other countries' commercial interests, including Britain. The loss of trade was considerable: an estimated sixty vessels of 4,000 tons or more passing through the Dardanelles each day were prevented from making the transit. Turkey was within its rights defined under the various treaties concluded in previous decades to deny passage to any ships, but after considerable diplomatic pressure the Strait was finally reopened to non-military traffic on 19 May 1912. Sixty mines had been laid in the Dardanelles, which took ten days to remove, and a minelaying vessel – the tug *Semendar* – was blown up during the clearance operation with the loss of twenty-three lives.

On the night of 18/19 July 1912, five Italian torpedo boats entered the Dardanelles to attack Turkish ships at anchor between Canakkale and

Nagara. The torpedo boats had been stripped of all unnecessary weight to increase their speed, and steaming at 15 knots passed the entrance forts almost unnoticed until a searchlight at Cape Helles picked them up. The alarm was then given by signal rockets to alert the defences further into the Strait. The flotilla commander, Captain Millo, in the *Spica*, ordered the boats to increase speed to 23 knots and stay as close to the European shore as possible in an effort to stay below the beams of the searchlights. Under constant fire, but without taking significant damage, the flotilla was stopped by a barricade of hawsers run across the Strait just south of the Narrows. Captain Millo could discern seven Turkish warships, including the destroyer *Peik-i-Shevket,* a few miles to the north but his boats could not continue, so they dashed at full speed back to open sea and all escaped.

The First Balkan War
While the Ottoman Empire was preparing to conclude the war with Italy by signing the First Treaty of Lausanne, Montenegro declared war on the Ottomans on 8 October 1912. In less than two months, the Balkan League of Bulgaria, Greece, Montenegro and Serbia were able to take much of European Turkey through a series of fierce battles. An armistice was signed in early December 1912, but lapsed; the Bulgarian Army threatened Constantinople and Greek warships blockaded the Dardanelles. On 16 December 1912, an Ottoman fleet, including the battleships *Barbaros Hayreddin* and *Turgut Reis*, the cruiser *Mecidiye,* the old ironclad *Mesudiye,* the ironclad frigate *Asar-i Tevfik* and four destroyers, engaged the modern Greek armoured cruiser *Averof*, which was supported by three old battleships and four destroyers. The Battle of Elli was a decisive victory for the Greek Navy and gave them control of the Aegean. All the principal Ottoman ships received damage and sustained casualties, so the fleet scurried back into the Dardanelles covered by the guns at the entrance forts. A few weeks later, the *Asar-i Tevfik* was damaged further by Bulgarian shore guns. The ship was declared a wreck and scuttled by her crew in February 1913, after the removal of her guns, three of which – 150mm SK L/40s – were then located at the Dardanos Battery above the Dardanelles. These guns were to prove highly effective against the Allied vessels in 1915.

To attempt to regain an advantage the Ottoman cruiser *Hamidiye* slipped out of the Dardanelles unnoticed on 14 January 1913 with the purpose to lure the powerful *Averof* to give chase, thereby allowing another Ottoman sortie into the Aegean. The ruse failed, so when the Ottoman ships again emerged from the Dardanelles with the intent of raiding the Greek ships anchored at Mudros on the island of Lemnos, the two fleets met in what became known as the Naval Battle of Lemnos – the title Naval Battle of Lemnos is to distinguish it from the Battle of Lemnos, which took place on 8 October 1912, when Greek marines landed and defeated the island's Turkish garrison to occupy the port of Mudros. As before, it was another victory for the Greeks, and the damaged Ottoman ships again withdrew to the Dardanelles, anchoring close to Nagara Point. On 24 January 1913, the Nagara naval base and the ships at anchor there were attacked by a lone Greek aircraft, a Maurice Farnham floatplane, which dropped four small bombs. This is the first known incident of an aerial attack on ships or a military base in the Dardanelles.

The Gallipoli peninsula was cut off by the Bulgarian Fourth Army during the First Balkan War. The defence of the Dardanelles and the Gallipoli peninsula was reorganized under the Canakkale Strait Forces and Fortification Command, which included the existing heavy coastal artillery regiments, 40,000 troops and more than 100 mobile artillery pieces arranged as defensive groups at Bulair (the narrow 'neck' of the Gallipoli peninsula that separates the Sea of Marmara from the Gulf of Saros), the peninsula beaches from Cape Helles in the south to the north of Suvla Bay, the Asian shore from Canakkale down to roughly opposite the island of Tenedos (now Bozcaada), and a reserve centred on Maidos (now Eceabat). The significance of this disposition of forces is that it was to be essentially the same in 1915 at the time of the Allied landings (Staff Major Mustafa Kemal was deployed in this defence; he was to be back in 1915 to resist the Allied invasion). After the end of the Balkan Wars the defence of the Dardanelles was scaled back down to pre-war levels under the Canakkale Fortified Area Command.

The Ottoman-German Alliance

During the nineteenth century, the Ottoman Navy had been heavily influenced by Britain and continued to be so into the early twentieth century. In 1909, a British Naval Mission under Admiral Douglas Gamble was established in Constantinople to assist with the modernization of the Ottoman Navy. His efforts to reform the decayed navy were daunted by the parlous state of naval affairs that he took over and also by his own ill health, yet against these difficulties he was able to send a small Ottoman squadron into the Aegean on a series of exercises. Gamble was followed firstly by Admiral Hugh Pigot Williams, who clashed with the Ottoman Ministry of Navy, and then in June 1912 by Admiral Arthur Limpus, who had more success in co-operating with the Ministry. Admiral Limpus left only when political tensions and the forming of a German Naval Mission in 1914 made British presence in Constantinople untenable. French influence within Turkey had continued into the twentieth century with the authority within the police force, but this was rescinded with the coming of hostilities.

The Ottoman Army had turned to Germany for help in the 1830s, initially because of the energetic efforts of a 35-year-old Prussian Army officer, Helmut von Moltke, who was requested by Sultan Mahmud II to improve the army. Moltke spent four years advising the Ottomans, travelling across the empire to survey and map large areas, including the defences of the Dardanelles and Bosphorus, and even campaigning against the Egyptians. German arms manufacturer Krupp of Essen began supplying huge amounts of artillery to Turkey from the 1860s, and the Ottoman Army purchased three-quarters of a million German Mauser bolt-action rifles during the latter part of the nineteenth century. Germany and Austro-Hungary went on to become the principal arms supplier to the Ottoman war machine, providing artillery, rifles, light machine guns, mines, shells, cartridges, gas masks, flame throwers and even aircraft during the First World War. There was indigenous arms manufacture in Turkey at arsenals such as the Tophane in Constantinople, generally part-manufacturing and assembling under licence German designs such as the Krupp 75mm field gun. Additionally, German engineering skills had already been utilized to develop the railways in Anatolia, and then a concession was awarded to German companies to extend the existing system to create the Berlin to Baghdad railway.

At the diplomatic level Turkey's choice of Germany to provide fundamental assistance was logical as they needed to align with at least

An illustration of a 400mm Krupp coastal gun, the largest of the type made. (*Popular Science*, 1897)

All that remains of the 400mm gun presented by Krupp to the Sultan Abdulhamid in 1875 is the cut-off breech end, now on display at Cimenlik Kalesi Museum. (© Forrest)

Kaiser Wilhelm II visited Anadolu Hamidiye in 1898 and again 1917, as shown in this photograph. The officer to the Kaiser's right is believed to be Colonel Wehrle. (Author's collection)

one of the European great powers to frustrate Russia, Turkey's traditional antagonist. Britain was excluded because it had taken over administrative responsibilities for the former Ottoman territory of Egypt, and also because Britain was becoming ambivalent and critical of Ottoman actions in Armenia. Sultan Abdulhamid II had a practical reason to favour Germany as it had no border with the crumbling Ottoman Empire and, therefore, no potential expansionist designs. Also, by buying from Germany then, perhaps, their military prowess and prestige would rub off. Germany did all it could to cultivate the relationship by lavishing gifts on the Sultan, including a 'one-off' 400mm (15.7-inch) Krupp gun in 1875 (the breech of this gun is now on display at Cimenlik Kalesi Museum, part of the Canakkale Naval Museum Command), and by providing training for Ottoman Army officers, civilian doctors and engineers in Germany. Germany became the Ottomans' principal export buyer, increasing from about 2,500,000 marks in 1880 to more than

71,000,000 marks in 1905. Kaiser Wilhelm II visited the Ottoman Sublime Porte – the open court of the Sultan at which foreign dignitaries were received – in 1889 and 1898. During the later visit, the Kaiser, sailing in the Imperial Yacht *Hohenzollern*, arrived at Canakkale to the echo of a 101-gun salute from the forts, which were flying German flags. The Kaiser came ashore to inspect the Turkish troops and Krupp coastal guns at Anadolu Hamidiye fort, a short distance south of the town. He was to visit again in October 1917.

The Young Turk Revolution in 1908 overthrew the long-serving Sultan to establish a constitutional form of government, but caused massive upheaval in the process and created a political governing elite. One of the new government's principal objectives was to warn the Great Powers that they were not to intervene in Turkish policies, but after the disastrous Balkan Wars and the loss of Tripolitania to Italy, the new rulers knew that they had to look for outside support. They solicited Britain, France and Russia, but all requests were rejected. The Young Turk leaders confirmed the old Sultan's opinion and turned to Germany.

Two Germans were to have a profound influence on German-Turkish relations – Baron Hans von Wangenheim, German ambassador to Turkey from 1912 to 1915, and Generalleutnant Otto Liman von Sanders, appointed to head the German Military Mission in Constantinople in 1913. Both men carried Kaiser Wilhelm's authorization to develop Turkey as an ally of Germany and to ensure that they take up arms in the forthcoming war. Both were to be successful; von Wangenheim utilizing his considerable diplomatic and persuasive skills; Liman von Sanders relying on his Prussian military efficiency, so much so that he was to go on to command the Ottoman Army defending Gallipoli.

The Ottoman-German Alliance was a secret treaty signed on 2 August 1914 binding the Ottoman Empire to the Central Powers of Germany, Austro-Hungary and Bulgaria, and pledging to follow them to war one day after declaration of war on Russia. The Alliance was concluded by many high-ranking officials, including Enver Pasha and Talat Pasha, but this decision was not wholly supported by Sultan Mehmet V, who had wanted the empire to be a non-belligerent state. Yet by the time the Alliance was concluded, German military assistance to the Ottomans was manifest at all levels.

The *Goeben* and *Breslau*

The clearest example of Germany's overt assistance was the transfer of the battlecruiser SMS *Goeben* and the light cruiser SMS *Breslau* (the Imperial German Navy designated their ships as SMS for *Seiner Majestät Schiff* – His Majesty's Ship), formed as a small squadron under the command of Rear Admiral Wilhelm Souchon, to the Ottoman Navy on 16 August 1914. The *Goeben* had been commissioned only two years earlier and was fast, well-armoured and powerful, mounting ten 280mm SK L/50 (11-inch) guns in five twin turrets plus twelve 150mm (5.9-inch) and twelve 88mm (3.5-inch) guns. The poorly executed pursuit of the *Goeben* and *Breslau* across the Mediterranean by the Royal Navy is outside the remit of this book, but the impact on Turkish-German relations is relevant. Unknown to the British pursuers, who had expected the ships to head for the friendly Austrian port of Pola in the Adriatic (now Pula, Croatia) or to try to exit the Mediterranean by running through the Strait of Gibraltar, Ambassador von Wangenheim had used his considerable influence to persuade Berlin to direct the ships to Constantinople. The Ambassador had the advantage of direct communications with Berlin via the powerful radio in the German-built, 8,000-ton Hamburg America Line passenger ship *Corcovado*, moored as an accommodation vessel offshore of the German Embassy in Constantinople.

Although the passage of a belligerent country's warships through the Turkish Straits was still banned under the treaties of the previous century, von Wangenheim arranged with Enver Pasha for the safe passage of the *Goeben* and *Breslau* through the Dardanelles and their transfer to the Ottomans. In reality, it was the Ottoman Navy that was transferred to the Germans as Admiral Souchon was to take command of it. This was a considerable coup for von Wangenheim and for Germany, and had a very considerable influence on future events.

The ships had anchored off Constantinople several weeks earlier as a part of a publicized 'flag-waving' visit to impress the Sultan and the ruling Turks. Their unexpected return was at first seen as an apparent embarrassment for the reluctant hosts as the ships were from a country that was now at war, but it proved to be momentous as the transfer of the vessels to Turkey was a part of a larger sequence of political manoeuvres. Also, Turkey took consolation as Britain had only recently denied them two new capital ships, the *Sultan Osman I* and the *Reshadieh,* seizing both for service in the Royal Navy (respectively HMS *Agincourt* and HMS *Erin)* shortly before they were to be handed over to the Ottoman Navy. The ships were part paid for, the money having been raised by public subscription across the Ottoman Empire, and the crews were in England waiting to accept them. The Turks still owed two years' worth of quarterly payments totalling £846,400, but Britain offered to pay £1,000 per day as a fee to use the ships and guaranteed that they would be delivered when the war was over, providing that Turkey remained neutral throughout the period of conflict. Although the seizure of the ships to bolster the Royal Navy was both legal (the payments were subsequently returned) and understandable in the circumstances, in hindsight this was a fateful decision taken by Winston Churchill as First Lord of the Admiralty. The damage to British credibility was too much for the Turks, convincing them to align with Germany rather than with Britain.

The escape of the *Goeben* and *Breslau* across the Mediterranean had been significantly assisted by the 8,000-ton passenger liner and cargo ship SS *General* of the German East Africa Line under the command of Captain Fielder. The ship had been commandeered by Admiral Souchon in Messina at the announcement of the mobilization of German forces, and was to prove vital to the warships' escape to Constantinople by providing coal and radio communications. The ship was disguised by repainting her multicoloured funnel to all black, so as to appear as a Dutch mail steamer of the Rotterdam Lloyd Line. Admiral Souchon could not communicate directly with Constantinople because of having to use Athens as a relay station, which was administered by the French, so as the ships steamed closer to the Dardanelles, the *General* became the wireless relay as she pursued a different course to Smyrna (now Izmir). According to the German Official History, it was while at this port that an important message for Admiral Souchon was received by the *General* from the German Admiralty via Constantinople:

> Come in; demand the capitulation of the fortress. Take a Dardanelles barrage pilot.

The signal was duly transmitted on to Admiral Souchon, and the *Goeben* and *Breslau* arrived off Cape Helles at 1600 hrs on 10 August 1914, holding position as the *Goeben* hoisted the flag signal to request a pilot. Not knowing what reception to expect, the ships were ordered to action stations with guns loaded and ready to fire on Sedd el Bahr and Ertugrul at the southernmost tip of the Gallipoli peninsula, and on Kum Kale and Orhaniye on the Asian side. There was a short wait and then a Turkish torpedo boat appeared from the Strait flying a 'Follow me' signal flag. The two German warships entered the Dardanelles at 1717 hrs, steaming slowly in line astern around the two lines of mines that had been recently laid. At 2135 hrs, the ships anchored off Canakkale, where they were out of reach of their pursuers, unless the British ships were prepared to fight their way into the Dardanelles. This action was not on the British agenda at this early stage of the First World War, the belligerent countries having been at war for less than a week, and Britain was not even at war with Turkey at this time.

German General Hans Kannengiesser, who was to later command the southern defence of the Gallipoli peninsula after the landings on 25 April 1915, then later the XVI Army Corps at Anafarta to the north, was with Enver Pasha at this crucial time. Enver carefully considered the situation and then issued the instruction that British warships were to be fired on if they attempted to follow the German ships. Kannengiesser described the moment as, 'We heard the clanking of the portcullis descending before the Dardanelles.'

At the time the German ships were anchoring off Canakkale, so the *General* was preparing a clandestine departure from Smyrna; the German Official History explains:

> As darkness had fallen, the Turkish guard boats were no longer at their stations, so the passage through the minefield had to be made without a pilot. During the night the *General* kept close under the dark slopes of Mitylene [a region and a town on the island of Lesbos] and reached next morning the entrance to the Dardanelles unmolested.

Soon after the *General* entered the Dardanelles on 11 August, the British light cruiser *Weymouth*, armed with 6-inch guns and commanded by Captain William Church, attempted to enter the Strait by trying to

The *Yavuz Sultan Selim*, ex-*Goeben*, under steam at Constantinople and passing the Maiden's Tower lighthouse, which can just be seen above the ship's bow. (Courtesy of the National Museum of the Royal Navy)

negotiate a safe passage. Two Turkish torpedo boats requested that the *Weymouth* 'heave to' 3 miles from the entrance to the Strait, and circled around her to ascertain the ship's name but ignored her signals. After the torpedo boats returned to the Strait, Captain Church allowed the cruiser to gently drift toward the coast but two blank warning shots from one of the shore forts corrected this mild challenge. *Weymouth* maintained a watch on the entrance to the Dardanelles and, on the morning of 12 August, another Turkish torpedo boat came out. A Turkish Army lieutenant came aboard to inform Captain Church that the entry of his ship into the Dardanelles was prohibited and, anyway, the two German ships had been purchased by the Turkish government. Although the official transfer did not take place for a few more days, a public announcement had been made in Constantinople on the day that the ships had passed through the Dardanelles, and the Turkish press reported it in the newspapers. The *Goeben* was renamed *Yavuz Sultan Selim*; the *Breslau* as *Midilli*.

On 16 August the *Yavuz Sultan Selim* and the *Midilli* were anchored off Constantinople as a part of a naval review held in the presence of the Sultan. The ships raised the Turkish ensign and the crews donned the traditional Turkish fez to welcome aboard Djemal Pasha, the Turkish Minister of Marine, and to celebrate the ships' transfer to Turkey. On 27 October, the *Yavuz Sultan Selim* and the *Midilli* shelled Russian Black Sea ports, prompting Russia to declare war on Turkey, with Britain and France following suit on 5 November.

Krupp guns and the Ottoman Empire

Alfred Krupp inherited his late father's bankrupt cast steel factory in 1826 and visited Britain to learn the art of steelmaking; he was to go on to create one of Europe's premier steel companies. Fried Krupp of Essen, an abbreviation of Friedrich Krupp, who launched the family's metal-based activities in 1810 by building a pioneering steel foundry in Essen, was to last as an arms manufacturer until Germany's defeat in 1945. Initially, the company was involved with the manufacture of high quality steel railroad products, such as the patented seamless railway tyre. So significant was this product that Krupp utilized three interlocking tyres as the company's trademark, but later as an arms manufacturer this was mistakenly assumed to be the muzzles of three interlocking gun

The Krupp name and trademark on a 240mm L/22 at the Kucukanafarta Battery, Gallipoli. The trademark represents three interlocking steel railway tyres, not gun muzzles, as is often assumed. (© Forrest)

barrels. Krupp began forging steel gun barrels from 1843, although there was no interest from the Prussian military until much later. After exhibiting a 6pr muzzle-loader at the Great Exhibition held at London's Crystal Palace in 1851, then a 12pr muzzle-loader at the Paris World Fair in 1855, the Krupp armaments business began with an order from Egypt for a total of thirty-six guns. Soon after this, Russia ordered guns for coastal defence. However, production of heavyweight artillery pieces did not begin in quantity until after the Austro-Prussian War of 1866, which

A Krupp C73 L/24 displayed at the Royal Armouries Museum, Fort Nelson, Hampshire, showing the unique cylindro-prismatic wedge breech mechanism. (© Forrest)

was to lead to unification of all the northern German states, as long strips of coastline had been absorbed and needed to be defended using large calibre naval guns on coastal mountings. By the time of the Franco-Prussian War of 1870-1871, the Imperial German Army had adopted Krupp steel guns as field pieces, whereas the French were still using bronze. The step change for Krupp was the introduction of the unique cylindro-prismatic wedge breech mechanism, and such guns were designated 'C73', being of two distinct bore sizes – 88mm for field artillery and 78.5mm for horse artillery. Krupp began to offer these impressive guns to overseas buyers, although export models were slightly different calibres as the 88mm became 87mm and the 78.5mm became 75mm. The C73 was stronger, more powerful and quicker firing than the

A lithograph of a Krupp C73 defending Alexandria Harbour in 1882. (*Illustrated London News*, July 1882)

old smooth-bore muzzle-loading guns, firing a 7.4kg (16.4lb) shell to a range of 6,500m (7,100 yards).

The first contact the Ottomans had with the German gun manufacturer Krupp was with an enquiry in 1860, and forty-eight muzzle-loading guns were delivered for trials in 1861. Following the success of the trials, sixty-four field pieces were ordered in 1863, and 127 in 1868, all of these guns being muzzle-loaders as per the original delivery. This association between customer and supplier would last until the end of the First World War as Krupp steadily ousted all other gun suppliers, including Britain's Sir William G. Armstrong & Company, for both the Ottoman Army and Navy. By the end of the 1860s, 284 Krupp guns had been delivered or were on order, although most, if not all, of the Ottoman artillery were still smooth-bores. Turkish-manufactured bronze guns were still being used during the Russo-Turkish War of 1877, but were steadily being replaced by steel. Whilst bronze guns of the same bore, length and charge weight would have a similar range to those of steel, the rate of wear was three times faster. Krupp was soon shipping both fully finished guns to Constantinople and those requiring additional work, such as boring, which would be carried out at the Tophane.

In 1869, Krupp opened a representative agency in Constantinople led by Otto Dingler, who would successively run it for twenty years. By 1873, Krupp had already sold 1,384 guns to Turkey, the number increasing to more than 2,800 of all types in the early 1880s. During the 1870s, the Turkish Army alone purchased 1,816 Krupp guns.

Turkey's confidence in German military and administrational abilities increased, and in 1883, a German Military Mission was established in Constantinople. The chief of the mission was Baron Kolmar von der Goltze, a 40-year-old general with extensive military service, including being on the staff of the distinguished Prince Frederick Charles of Prussia during the Franco-Prussian War. Alfred Krupp regarded German diplomats abroad as his salesmen so, in addition to his duties as Mission Chief, General von der Goltze was instructed to encourage the Turks 'to buy their guns from the firm of Krupp.'

In 1875, the Turks placed an order worth 900,000 Turkish Lire with Krupp for 500 steel guns, the majority of which were field guns. Apparently, the Grand Vizier (essentially the Ottomans' most powerful man after the Sultan) expressed concern about the amount being spent because there were suggestions of corruption in awarding the arms contracts. This was undoubtedly true as in a letter sent in April 1878 by Otto Dingler, Krupp's agent in Constantinople, he requested 'additional funds for "Baksheesh" to pay an anonymous friend.'

The system of bribes was still true some thirty years later. In 1910,

The Fried Krupp display at the 1876 Centennial International Exhibition held in Philadelphia, USA, showing 355mm and 280mm Coastal Guns and C73 Field Guns. (*Harper's Weekly*, 1876)

General Herbert Kitchener passed through Constantinople en route from India to England to receive his field marshal's baton from King Edward VII. His stay in the city had been short but he was alarmed at the influence the Germans had and the amount of money they spent in bribes at all levels of the Ottoman administration. This type of arrangement was unacceptable to British Foreign Secretary Edward Grey. Kitchener wrote of his concern privately to Lady Salisbury:

> We are out of it altogether, as the present [British] ambassador does nothing and the German does as he likes.

The Krupp Company of Essen was successfully selling guns to the home market and to countries all over the world. In 1876, the company displayed both 280mm (11-inch) and 355mm (14-inch) coastal defence guns at the Centennial Exhibition held in Philadelphia, Germany having taken a large area within the Machinery Hall. To further promote their armament business Krupp held artillery demonstrations for international buyers at a huge proving ground owned by the company at Meppen, in northern Germany. Krupp sold to governments in South America, East Asia, Scandinavia, Iberia, Western Europe and the Balkans, yet of all overseas buyers, Turkey was the largest, taking about 14 per cent of all international purchases and 60 per cent in the Balkan region alone. By 1912, Turkey had purchased 3,943 Krupp guns of all sizes. Krupp sales to other Balkan states over the same period were: Romania 1,450; Bulgaria 517; Greece 356; Austria-Hungary 298; Montenegro twenty-five; Serbia six. The majority of guns purchased by Turkey during its long association with Krupp were generally outdated models from the Krupp portfolio because of the need to control purchase costs. The Turks were notoriously bad payers, an issue that was to continuously plague the sale of British-built, Armstrong-armed, ironclads to the Turkish Navy.

Coastal guns
Turkey purchased a total of 134 Krupp coastal defence guns in two distinct batches defined by barrel length – 101 of the L/22 type (the barrel length being twenty-two times the calibre) in the mid-1870s, and 33 of the L/35 type (the barrel length being thirty-five times the calibre) in the mid-1880s (see Appendix One, Krupp Coastal Defence Guns purchased by Ottoman Turkey) – but thereafter focused on buying field guns and quick-firers. The reasons for this change of policy are clear as there were only so many ports or straits to defend, and by the size and nature of the empire, a large army dependent on mobile artillery was essential. The Dardanelles forts were equipped with seventy-eight coastal defence guns, twenty-two of which were the long-barrel L/35 type, reflecting the significance of the Strait (see Appendix Two, Krupp Coastal Gun locations on the Dardanelles); others were located at Smyrna, in Tripolitania, and on the Bosphorus. According to *Der Krieg in Den Turkischen Gewassern* by Hermann Loren, written in 1926, the guns defending the Bosphorus in 1914 were two 355mm L/35, two 280mm L/24 (the L/24 suffix may be an error and, perhaps, should be L/22),

A German postcard, circa 1880, of the Krupp Works at Essen, showing the assembly of coastal guns. (Author's collection)

twelve 240mm L/35, ten 240mm L/22 and nine 210mm L/22. The guns identified in Appendix One and Appendix Two are of the RK type – *Ringkanone* or Ring Gun – in that the gun carriage is traversed by means of a pivot at the front and two sets of wheels that run on rails. In 1873, Turkey also purchased other RK Krupp guns but of smaller calibres, such as 120mm L/24 (120 purchased), 150mm L/14 (fifty purchased) and 150mm L/26 (230 purchased). Some of these guns were located at Dardanelles fortifications such as Kum Kale and Cimenlik Kalesi, and others in batteries to augment the defence of the Narrows. Later, and with the threat of an Allied battle fleet attack, many of the batteries were relocated to the hills and gullies on both shores of the Dardanelles south of the Narrows, and this will be explained in more detail in later chapters.

CHAPTER 3

The Fortification and other Defences

The shape of the shore on the Gallipoli peninsula from Eski Hisarlik Burnu, where the huge Turkish Martyrs' Memorial now stands, to Kilid Bahr at the Narrows is almost a straight line, with steep hills that plateau at the south of the peninsula and gullies that plunge down to the shore. The nature of the Asian shore is generally flat at the south-western end but becomes hilly as the coast is followed toward Canakkale. As the shores draw closer, so they create a funnelling of the Strait, which squeezes the sea room available to large vessels. Coupled with commanding views, the hills and shores of the Dardanelles have proved to be well-suited for coastal artillery. During the five centuries since the earliest fortifications were built they have expanded, improved, fought and then decayed. Some areas of land are still restricted by Turkish military requirements today, but there are no active fortifications on the shores of the Dardanelles, although evidence of many forts and batteries still exist, some with now forgotten nineteenth-century armaments. Together with sea mines and the threat of shore-launched torpedoes, the defences of the Dardanelles proved to be decisive during the First World War. As recently as October 2009, a First World War sea mine was discovered submerged at a depth of only 5 metres, but was successfully destroyed by bomb disposal engineers: a stark reflection of the waterway's turbulent past.

In the Turkish calendar one day above all others is regarded as the Dardanelles fortifications day of glory – 18 March 1915 – when a combined battle fleet of British and French warships failed to open the passage to the Sea of Marmara because they were unable to destroy the guns that were preventing mine clearance operations. The sinking of two powerful ships that day – *Irresistible* and *Ocean* – were caused by mines. However, the guns from the forts and batteries seriously damaged *Suffren*, *Gaulois*, *Agamemnon* and *Inflexible* (which also hit a mine) and scored numerous hits on other ships too. The *Bouvet* was also lost but there is debate over whether she hit a mine or was struck by a shell that penetrated a magazine. This question will be considered in a later chapter. An estimate of the number of Turkish guns defending the Dardanelles in March 1915 is 238; this includes 177 howitzers, field guns, ships' guns, quick-firers and mortars, all of various calibres, and sixty-one coastal defence Krupp guns of 210mm to 355mm (see Appendix Two, Krupp Coastal Defence Guns Location at the Dardanelles; Appendix Three, Dardanelles Gun Batteries – 18 March 1915). Originally there had been seventy-eight coastal guns but seventeen were destroyed during the initial actions that were focused on the entrance forts in November 1914 and February 1915.

No large Allied warship penetrated more than around 7 miles (11km) into the Strait because of the extensive minefield, excluding vessels such as the minesweepers, picket boats and Allied submarines, so the challenge of the Narrows with its fixed torpedo tubes and 355mm (14-inch) guns firing at a range of just 700 yards (650m) was never faced. The question that has been asked repeatedly since 1915 is this: could Allied surface ships have successfully passed through the Dardanelles had they tried again after the disastrous action of 18 March? As with the loss of the *Bouvet*, the answer to this question can be found in a later chapter.

The fortifications are arranged on both the European side of the Dardanelles (the Gallipoli peninsula) and on the Asian side. The construction of forts was generally complimentary, building a fortress on each side of the Strait at the same time to provide a gauntlet of artillery against an attacker. There can be confusion with the names of the forts because of various spellings for one location, some due to changes from the original Ottoman Turkish to modern Turkish, others because of the interpretation in German or the simplification to English, i.e. Anadolu Hamidye can be spelt Anatoli Hamidiye in German but was also known as Hamidieh I to British planners. To further confuse, these planners

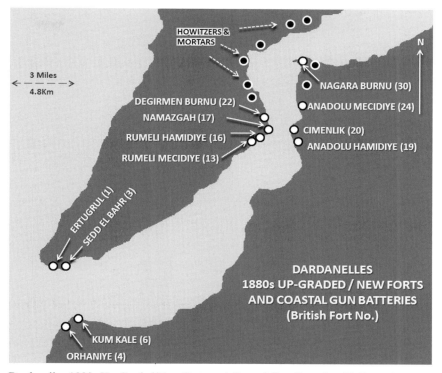

Dardanelles 1880s Up-Graded/New Forts and Coastal Gun Batteries. (© Forrest)

identified all the fortifications and some semi-permanent mobile artillery positions by Fort Number, for example, Hamidieh I was known as Fort No. 19. For the sake of expedience within this account the full title including the Turkish word *'Tabyasi'* or 'Fort' will be avoided, the example above having been simplified from Anadolu Hamidiye Tabyasi to Anadolu Hamidiye.

The distinction between the titles 'Castle' and 'Fort' in the Dardanelles can blur and is worth clarifying. The European castle was invariably made of stone, perhaps transported a considerable distance. As the product of a feudal system a castle can be considered as a private stronghold for a king, ruler or nobleman, and also a place of refuge for those vassals dependant of such an auspicious person. A fort is positioned for militaristic purposes to defend a specific geographical location or to hold a garrison of occupation. It is made of local materials, whenever possible, is totally functional and is unlikely to be considered as comfortable or grand as a castle. The Ottomans were prolific fortress builders across the empire, and although castles (*Kalesi* in Turkish) were built on the shores of the Dardanelles, such as Nagara Kalesi located at Abydos Point, Boghali Kalesi on the opposite shore, and Kale-i Sultaniye (later known as Cimenlik Kalesi) at the Narrows, only Cimenlik comes close to the concept of a castle because of its keep. Kilid Bahr on the opposite shore also has a central keep, but these castles were not the homes of regal persons. Their defined purpose was to control the Strait and keep open the Ottoman lines of communications; therefore, they should be considered as offensive structures designed to deny the passage of enemy ships. The early castles of the Dardanelles could have resisted attack by assaulting ground troops at the time they were built because they were self-contained behind walls, but the later forts were flat, open structures and generally undefended at the rear, although some had loophole walls for riflemen.

From the perspective of an attack coming from the Aegean, the principal fortifications were arranged in two clusters, each as a specific defence group: those at the entrance to prevent access into the Dardanelles, and those at the Narrows to engage any ships that did gain entry but to prevent their progress through to the Sea of Marmara. Of course, should an attack come from the north, that is from the Black Sea, and assuming these vessels had not been stopped by the Bosphorus fortifications, then the Dardanelles forts groups had a reverse function. Either way, they were there to deny an enemy passage.

When Admiral Hornby's ironclads passed through the Dardanelles in February 1878, ready to exchange fire with the fortresses but not having to do so, there were a number of Krupp guns that, had they been fired, could have seriously damaged the ships. The renowned British war correspondent for the *Daily News*, Archibald Forbes, who was covering the Russo-Turkish War in 1877, wrote about the fortifications of the Dardanelles:

> The forts at the entrance to the Dardanelles are not of much account, being somewhat ancient type, and though constructed of masonry, would soon be knocked to pieces by

the fire of modern artillery. These batteries contain no heavy guns, most of the pieces being smooth-bores of an old pattern; and though of late a few Krupps guns have been added there is nothing which would do much damage to an iron-clad passing at a distance. From the entrance to the Narrows there is nothing in the way of defences; but there are two well placed and constructed forts, the one called the Namazieh Battery, at Kilid Bahr, and the other, Medjidieh, a little to the north-west of the town of Chanak, can deliver a crossfire that would make it very warm for a few minutes for any vessels attempting to pass against the will of the Turks. In Fort Medjidieh there are two 12½-ton Armstrong guns, besides some ten 15-centimetre Krupp guns. The Namazieh Battery's armament, too, is very heavy, consisting as it does some eight 22-centimetre Krupps. These are the strongest forts about the Dardanelles, and the only ones likely to inflict much damage upon a hostile fleet, although there are three others which would still have to be passed. One of them, like Namazieh, is of modern construction, and mounts a few Krupps of small calibre, but the others are like those at the entrance, and not much to be feared.

He went on to write about other fortifications using Krupp guns:

Where the channel of the Bosphorus begins to narrow, is a very formidable array of batteries, well arranged for crossfire. Two of them are of recent construction, and mount fourteen very heavy Krupp guns each, quite capable of piercing the armour-plating of most ironclads.

The entrance forts
The entrance to the Dardanelles is just over 2 miles (3.5km) wide, and controlled by Sedd el Bahr at the southernmost tip of the Gallipoli peninsula on the European side and Kum Kale on the Asian side. Both forts were built during the reign of Sultan Mehmet IV from 1657 to 1660, by order of Grand Vizier Koprulu Mehmet Pasha to architect Mustafa

Aga. The range of cannon at that time was barely sufficient to completely cover the gap between the two forts, but it significantly reduced the amount of free passage available to an unwelcome ship and would have deterred all but the most audacious.

Sedd el Bahr was constructed of roughly-dressed stone veneer with rubble stone infill, rectangular at 150m by 125m, with walls 3m thick and 9m high, topped with crenellations. Four large diameter corner towers dominated, and smaller intermediate towers were on the north-west wall either side of a gated entrance. When first built, heavy guns such as bombards were at shore level, both at the base of the seaward-facing south tower and in gun ports of the south-eastern wall. Sedd el Bahr was reinforced with additional batteries in the late eighteenth to early nineteenth century, and again in the 1860s. Three of the corner towers were then used as ammunition stores. In 1883, Krupp coastal guns were installed and reported by British intelligence as six 280mm L/22s arranged with two facing south-west, one due south and three to the south-

Plan of Krupp Coastal Gun positions at Sedd el Bahr, circa 1906. (© Forrest)

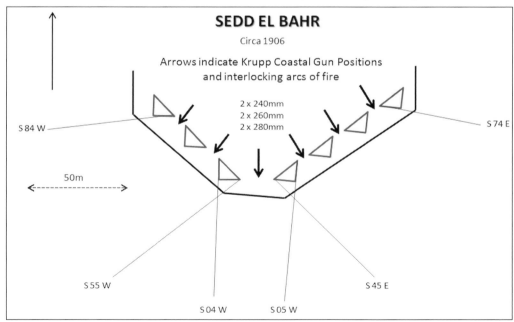

Sedd el Bahr before the First World War with Krupp L/22 guns installed. The tower to the left was to be destroyed by naval gunfire on 3 November 1914. (Author's collection)

east, all with a large arc of fire. The actual complement of these guns was discovered to be slightly different after the Allied occupation of the fort: two 240mm L/22, two 260mm L/22 and two 280mm L/22. In addition, four 87mm field guns were in the immediate vicinity of the fort. All these guns were at an elevation of 20m above sea level, and the entire south-eastern wall of the fort was removed during the armaments upgrade. Traverses were located between the guns, each with a sunken magazine for sixty rounds of ready-use ammunition. Another magazine was located under a raised terreplein. Barracks, officers' quarters and store buildings were constructed within the perimeter, and two searchlights were located in or near to the fort. Sedd el Bahr was known as Fort No. 3 to British planners. A fortified barrack had been constructed on a low hill to the rear of the fort during the 1850s, but this was not considered to be a significant defence in 1914.

A battery was constructed 600m to the west of Sedd el Bahr for two Krupp 240mm L/35 guns during the late 1880s' improvement of the Dardanelles coastal defences. The Ertugrul Battery, identified as Fort No. 1 by British planners, was built with masonry revetments and three earth-covered magazines located in the traverses. Its position is elevated 25m above what came to be known as V Beach for the landings on 25 April 1915. A white stone barracks was constructed 100m behind the battery,

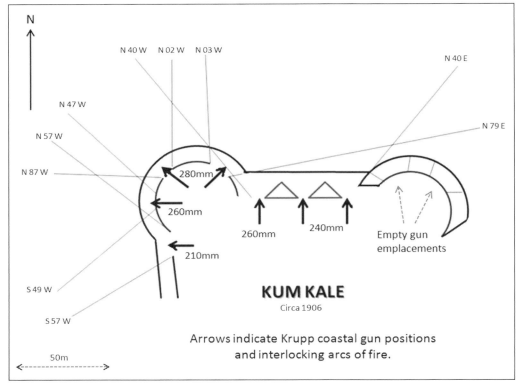

Plan of Krupp Coastal Gun positions at Kum Kale, circa 1906. (© Forrest)

which was visible over the guns, and so was an easier ranging target than the guns themselves.

Kum Kale (Fort No. 6) was a rectangular masonry castle, slightly larger but similar to Sedd el Bahr and built at the same time, directly south of it across the entrance to the Strait. The walls and towers of the original castle still stood in 1914, but had been superseded by an earth and masonry fortification along the shore with a similar history of armament upgrading as its northern neighbour, culminating in a complicated mixture of Krupp guns: one 210mm L/22, two 240mm L/22, two 260mm L/22 and two 280mm L/22, plus a 150mm L/22 and a 150mm L/26. It was a clever arrangement as ships approaching from the south-west would see nothing of the fortification until they came under fire from it. Most of the large calibre guns date from the 1870s, but, according to Archibald

Forbes' account, few, if any, were installed when Admiral Hornby sailed through the entrance in 1878. In addition, a number of field guns were in position, so the logistics of supporting such a variety of ammunition requirements must have been difficult, but this characteristic seems to have been apparent at many of the forts. Two searchlights were located in or near the fort.

The Orhaniye Battery (to the British it was Orkanie or Fort No. 4) is located 2km to the south-west of Kum Kale, being built at the same time and of similar design to Ertugrul and also equipped with two Krupp 240mm L/35 guns for long-range defence. Elevated 40m above sea level, the location has a commanding position. A British plan held by The National Archives (reference: WO301/476) from 1906 shows that the coastal guns were supported by two batteries of 87mm field guns, one battery at either side. As with the Ertugrul Battery, barracks and stores were sited dangerously close to the rear of the guns, and they were first

A photograph from the 1890s of two Krupp L/22s, possibly at Kum Kale. Note the side arm equipment to load the gun. (Author's collection)

damaged by Italian shelling in 1912 and then destroyed during a naval bombardment on 3 November 1914.

As formidable as all these guns at the entrance forts may have seemed the majority were of the short-range L/22 type purchased in the 1870s, whilst only the long-range L/35s at Ertugrul and Orhaniye dated from the late 1880s. These defences did not prove effective during the Italian-Turkish War of 1911-1912, and although they may have deterred Greek warships from entering the Dardanelles in the First Balkan War, they were out-ranged by the Allied naval bombardment in 1914. The armament of all four forts would be subsequently destroyed by naval gunfire and landing parties.

The Narrows forts

The two forts that command the Narrows are Kilid Bahr and Cimenlik Kalesi. They are the oldest of all the forts on the Dardanelles, having been built in 1452, during the reign of Sultan Mehmet II, the Conqueror. As this is the narrowest part of the Dardanelles, at barely 1,400 yards (1,300m) wide, the range of the up to thirty bombards and smaller guns per fort would have been sufficient to sweep the water clear of enemy ships.

Kilid Bahr was built in 1452 on the European shore at the Narrows. The curtain wall was built during the sixteenth century. (© Forrest)

Kilid Bahr on the European side is a beautiful construction with the three curved bastions, each 40m in diameter, arranged in a clover leaf shape that sweeps upwards to reflect the slope on which the castle is built. A triangular central keep connects to the high outer walls, and this is also curved and free of any projections, being designed to deflect away enemy shot. Ancient cannons were located at the crenellations in the outer walls, but the heavy bombards would have been at ground level. Much of the inner castle was constructed using stones taken from the site of the ancient city and castle of Sestos. In the sixteenth century, Sultan Suleiman, the Magnificent, strengthened and extended the outer curtain walls, adding a gate tower. In the 1840s, a new battery was built a short distance to the south of Kilid Bahr and is known as Namazgah (Fort No. 17), which was

A photograph showing two Krupp 210mm L/22 guns at Namazgah, close to the southern tower of Kilid Bahr. (Author's collection)

updated in 1893 with Krupp guns. Most of this fort's guns were located in two lines of embrasures to create a 'V' shape with 250m flanks, one facing south and the other facing north-east, with ready-use magazines set in the traverses and the main magazine located under the raised terreplein. Two more guns were positioned close to Kilid Bahr and other guns at the point facing across the Strait toward Cimenlik Kalesi. The

51

guns were at an elevation of 10m above the water and of two different barrel lengths: seven 210mm L/22, five 240mm L/22, two 240mm L/35, and two 260mm L/22. The mixed barrel lengths (and therefore range) were used in many of the Turkish fortifications of the Dardanelles, reflecting the different dates of armament installation. The rear of Namazgah was protected by a 4m high loopholed wall and defendable gated entrance.

Just to the south of Namazgah is Rumeli Hamidiye (Hamidieh II or Fort No. 16) built in 1896 and equipped with two Krupp 355mm L/35 guns set in masonry revetments with earth-covered magazines in the traverses, being similar in layout to the Ertugrul and Orhaniye batteries. One kilometre further south again is Rumeli Mecidiye (Fort No. 13), built with seven gun emplacements but equipped with six Krupp guns: four 240mm L/35 and two 280mm L/22, all facing south. The design is similar to the other forts close by, with earth-covered magazines in the traverses between the guns.

When the war was declared in 1914, these forts and batteries were organized under a single command with the 2nd Heavy Artillery Battalion Headquarters located at Namazgah. Captain Mehmet Hilmi Bey,

A photograph taken at Namazgah in the late 1890s showing two Krupp L/22, 210mm or 240mm, *Ringkanones* on their carriages. Note the magazines to each side, and also Cimenlik Kalesi just 1,500 yards away on the other side of the Narrows. (Author's collection)

A Krupp 240mm L/35 now located at Rumeli Mecidiye in a restored gun emplacement. Note the figure of the artillery officer. (© Forrest)

commanding the L/35 guns, wrote in his memoires *Canakkale was not Passed*:

> The batteries on the European side – the Rumeli Mecidiyesi with four 24 cm guns, the Rumeli Hamidiyesi with two 35 cm guns, Namazgah with two 24 cm guns were reorganized as one battery under my command. We were given a projector for night spotting & observation and we also received light four-wheeled guns. We entrenched the 24s at 32 metres and the 35s at 40 metres distance from each other and the guns were placed on wooden platforms of a metre high and a 3 to 4 metre wall in front for shelter at the front.

53

The keep of Cimenlik Kalesi. (© Forrest)

The fifteenth-century stone-built Kale-i Sultaniye (Cimenlik Kalesi) at Canakkale is directly opposite Kilid Bahr across the Narrows. Its outline is rectangular, 150m by 100m, with the long sides running east-west; the walls are 5.8m thick and strengthened by corner and intermediary towers on three sides. Inside the walls is a stone-built rectangular keep with base dimensions of 29m by 44m, 22m high with 7m thick walls. In 1876, a Krupp 355mm L/22 was located in an earth emplacement 100m south of Cimenlik facing south-west but with a very narrow arc of fire. To the north of this gun, close to Cimenlik's south-west tower, were two 280mm L/22 guns with wider arcs of fire. It was this small battery that concerned Admiral Hornby during his passage through the Narrows in 1878.

THE FORTIFICATION AND OTHER DEFENCES

The arrangement of coastal guns at Cimenlik was changed in the late 1880s. The east wall facing the Strait and a part of the south wall were demolished, and two guns faced across the Strait and two down toward the entrance of the Dardanelles. The expense magazines were located as traverses between the guns. As with other forts, the guns were of different bore and barrel length combinations: one 355mm L/35, one 355mm L/22, one 240mm L/22, and one 210mm L/22. A British plan (The National Archives reference: WO301/481) from 1906 shows that a mixture of 120mm and 87mm field guns, and 150mm howitzers were located both north and south of the fort, although these were redistributed at the beginning of hostilities in 1914. To the British planners Cimenlik was known as Hamidieh III or Fort No. 20.

Anadolu Hamidiye (Hamidieh I or Fort No. 19) is located just over 1km to the south of Cimenlik, and was equipped in the early 1890s with nine Krupp guns located just a few metres above shore level – seven

The south-western corner of Cimenlik Kalesi in 2010, showing the ramps up to the Krupp coastal gun emplacements and a selection of First World War field guns and howitzers. (© Forrest)

Anadulo Hamidye today taken from the Dardanelles. The arrows indicate the former Krupp gun positions in the low profile of the fort. (© Forrest)

240mm L/35 and two 355mm L/35 – arranged in a line facing south-west with a view straight down to the entrance of Dardanelles. These big guns would be the first from the Narrows to engage any ships that had cleared the entrance as they came into range. Construction was similar to the forts on the opposite shore, earth emplacements with masonry revetments and ready-use magazines in the traverses.

Three forts were located north of Canakkale. On the peninsula side of the Strait is Degirmen Burnu (Fort No. 22), one kilometre north of Kilid Bahr, which because of its position had no opportunity to engage a target unless there had been a breakthrough of enemy vessels from the south. Degirmen Burnu was an old fort that was remodelled and extended in the early 1880s, being equipped with seven Krupp guns facing due east at an elevation of 10m above the water: six 240mm L/22 and one 210mm L/22. The guns were arranged in a line 30m apart with ready-use ammunition magazines between them, each containing fifty rounds. The main magazine was close by, as was the gunners' barrack block. Directly opposite on the Asian side of the Strait is Anadulo Mecidiye (Fort No. 24) built in the late 1870s and heavily armed with a mixture of Krupp guns: three 280mm L/22, three 260mm L/22, three 240mm L/22, one 210mm L/22, and three 150mm L/22. The gun emplacements were arranged in a rough 'L' shape, one side longer than the other so most of

Anadulo Mecidiye today taken from the quay at Canakkale. The arrows indicate the former Krupp gun positions. (© Forrest)

the guns faced south-west down the Strait, the others facing north-east covering the water across to the town Maidos (now Eceabat). The rear of the fort was protected in the same way as Namazgah, with loopholed wall and defendable gated entrance.

Further north on the Asian side, approximately 5km from Canakkale, is Nagara Kalesi, located at Nagara Point, near to where the ancient city of Abydos once stood. Construction of the castle was started in 1807 as a result of Admiral Duckworth's passage through the Dardanelles in the same year. The old fortifications at Nagara Kalesi consisted of a 10m high tower, 25m in diameter, and a 3m high wall pierced with gun positions just above sea level. The castle, which still stands today, was equipped with up to thirty-five smooth-bore muzzle-loading guns when it was built. The updating of these defences commenced in 1852, but was to take more than twenty-five years to complete. When finished it comprised an earthen redoubt and stone revetments in front of the gun emplacements that housed Krupp guns of the following types: one 260mm L/22, six 240mm L/22 and five 150mm L/26. To British planners Nagara Burnu was known as Fort No. 30.

At the beginning of the First World War the Narrows area was defended by sixty-one old but heavy Krupp guns (210mm or greater), thirty-one on the European side of the Narrows and thirty on the Asian side.

In the 1870s, the construction of additional gun batteries on both shores between Canakkale and Nagara Kalesi had taken place. These were small redoubts, where both 150mm howitzers and 200mm mortars were located in open barbette positions, where the gun fired over the crest of a defensive parapet. These were later removed and consolidated at selected fortifications, such as Yildiz.

A Krupp 150mm L/26 howitzer at an unknown location. (Author's collection)

A pair of Krupp howitzers, probably 87mm, dating from the early 1870s, although the photograph is from the 1890s. This location may be above the Dardanelles or the Bosphorus. Note the shell in the centre foreground. (Author's collection)

A pair of Krupp howitzers, probably 87mm, guarding another location. Note the side arm equipment to service the guns. (Author's collection)

The condition of the Dardanelles defences in 1914

Admiral Wilhelm Souchon had successfully brought the battlecruiser *Goeben* and the light cruiser *Breslau* to the safety of the Dardanelles, and then steamed on triumphantly to Constantinople as Turkey covertly aligned itself with Germany but still pleaded armed neutrality to the world. During the passage through the Strait, Admiral Souchon had taken time to observe the decrepit condition of the fortifications and later discussed the subject with German General Otto Liman von Sanders and Lieutenant Commander Hans Humann, German Naval Attaché in Constantinople. In 1913, General Liman von Sanders was appointed Director of the German Military Mission in Constantinople and tasked with the modernization of the Turkish Army. As Inspector General he has been credited with improving the army's efficiency through 1914, and then as the commander of the Turkish defence of the Gallipoli peninsular against the Allied invasion in 1915.

The Germans were very aware of the need to improve the defences, and proposed the addition of German troops to bolster the Turks. The Dardanelles forts had been in action in 1912 against the Italian Navy, and the area had been heavily defended during the First Balkan War, but the Turkish authorities in Constantinople still had a general sense of lethargy. The defences had commanded the Strait for centuries and had been upgraded at great expense with powerful coastal artillery in the 1880s, so complacency pervaded some higher levels of the army. However, the gunners were far from professional, being poorly trained and lacking discipline in even basic soldierly skills such as guard duty. Together with the complex mix of ammunition to serve the old guns, the lack of range-finding equipment, insufficient searchlights, and need for improved communications between the forts and batteries, the Germans considered the defences neglected and inadequate. The German Official History records the following comments:

> The condition of the material and the training of personnel at Chanak fortress in the Dardanelles, and at the Bosphorus fortress of Kawak, was so poor that the enemy would have no difficulty in penetrating into the Straits.... Vessels for duty afloat, mines, torpedo batteries and searchlights, guns, ammunition, rangefinders, observation posts, apparatus for transmitting orders, telephones – all were lacking. Neither the Turkish officers nor those of the German Military Mission stationed in them were coast-artillerymen.

However, orders to reactivate the fortifications had been given before the arrival of Admiral Souchon, probably because of the constant threat of the Greek armoured cruiser *Averof* that had battered the Ottoman warships in 1912 with its British-made EOC (Elswick Ordnance Company) 9.2-inch guns. The Canakkale Fortified Area Command was under the command of Brigadier General Fahri Pasha during and after the Balkan Wars, but in 1914, Major General Cevat Pasha replaced him. He immediately requested an up-to-date defence plan for the Dardanelles from Turkish Army General Headquarters, but when this was not forthcoming he prepared his own assessment of the condition of the defences, including an appraisal of the likely actions of an attacking fleet and how the defences should respond. His opinion was that as the outer forts were out-ranged by modern battleships they would fall, shifting the responsibility for main defence to the fortifications at the Narrows. His judgement was to prove correct. On 31 July 1914, fortress commanders were alerted to prepare for war and to expect reinforcements.

Berlin's response to the request for German troops was rapid, and by the end of August, some fifteen officers and more than 300 naval gunners and mine technicians had arrived. They were commanded by Admiral Guido von Usedom, who was appointed as Inspector General of Coastal Artillery and Mining, with Vice Admiral Johannes Merten liaising with Major General Cevat Pasha and his staff in Canakkale.

Germany was connected to Constantinople by railway through Austro-Hungary, Serbia or Romania and Bulgaria, but the route via Serbia could not be used for war supplies as she had been attacked by Austro-Hungary in July 1914, defending her territory for nearly a year until then attacked by Bulgaria. Later, Britain and France allied with Serbia in what would become the Salonika Campaign. The Central Powers were also forbidden from moving military equipment through Romania, so the transportation of German troops along either route was disguised as they wore civilian clothes. The Romanian route was more heavily used but after discovering military stores hidden in double-bottomed railway wagons or concealed in barrels of beer, this route was supposedly closed. However, the bribery of Romanian officials ensured that this rail link was actually kept open. One way of transporting heavy material was by barge along the river Danube to Rustchuk (now Ruse) in Bulgaria, then transhipment by railway. Bulgaria joined the Central Powers in September 1915, thereby allying with Turkey, which had given up an area of land along the Maritza River in return. Bulgaria attacked Serbia and later Romania, ultimately securing rail links between Germany and Constantinople, which then allowed greater amounts of munitions to feed the Ottoman war machine. The amount of war supplies sent to Turkey in the period between August 1914 and the latter half of 1915 may not have been great, but German propaganda suggested an inexhaustible supply to discourage Allied planners and demoralize commanders on the ground during the Gallipoli Campaign. Much later, submarines were to bring in some high-value technical equipment and supplies. Sir Louis Mallet, British Ambassador to Constantinople from October 1913 until hostilities were declared, reported to London that 540 cases of Mauser rifles, 6,000 cases of ammunition, together with thirteen rail trucks of other war materials had arrived from Germany.

With the arrival of the *Goeben* and *Breslau* and their combined crews of over 1,400, a total of more than 1,700 German sailors were in Turkey by September 1914; by the end of the year the total number of German Navy and Army personnel was around 3,800. A number of German sailors were distributed to selected Turkish ships such as the battleships *Turgut Reis* and *Barbaros Hayreddin*, the torpedo cruiser *Peik-i Shevket* and a number of torpedo boats.

For the short time the *Goeben* and *Breslau* were anchored off Canakkale they significantly enhanced the defensive firepower available should British ships have steamed in after them. Whilst the *Weymouth* was the first British ship to arrive off the entrance to the Dardanelles, she was soon joined by others, including three more Town class light cruisers – *Chatham*, *Dublin* and *Gloucester* – from Admiral Troubridge's First Cruiser Squadron. Three 12-inch gun battlecruisers also arrived – *Indefatigable*, *Indomitable* and *Inflexible* – the latter as the flagship of the British Mediterranean Fleet commanded by Admiral Sir Berkeley Milne, plus smaller and lighter armed vessels such as destroyers. Had these warships entered the Dardanelles in clear breach of Turkey's neutrality, they would have certainly had to fight to pass the forts but may have caught one or both of the German ships at anchor (the *Goeben* departed Canakkale ahead of the *Breslau*) or in the Sea of Marmara. And by doing so, they would have arrived off Constantinople as an imperial show of force, as Admirals Duckworth and Hornby once did, perhaps with better results than those nineteenth-century expeditions. At this time the defences of the Dardanelles were at their weakest than at any time in the next four years, including the sparse minefield, so a successful passage *may* have been achievable in August 1914. It needed two fundamental ingredients for success: the British Government's audacity and boldness from Admiral Milne. Yet it was not contemplated and so remains a great 'what if?' scenario.

The core of the Canakkale Fortified Area Command lay with its fixed coastal guns organized as the 2nd Artillery Brigade with three regiments: 3rd Heavy Artillery Regiment on the Asian shore of the Narrows (Cimenlik, Anadolu Hamidiye, Anadulo Mecidiye and Nagara Burnu); 4th Heavy Artillery Regiment on the peninsula shore of the Narrows (Namazgah, Rumeli Hamidiye, Rumeli Mecidiye and Degirmen Burnu); 5th Heavy Artillery Regiment at either side of the entrance to the Strait, with the 1st Battalion at Sedd el Bahr and Ertugrul; the 2nd Battalion at Kum Kale and Orhaniye. The regiments were well stocked with heavy coastal gun shells (210mm and above): the 3rd Regiment with 2,429; the 4th Regiment with 3,486; the 5th Regiment with 1,679, together with large quantities of smaller calibre shells for the field gun batteries attached to each regiment. Depot magazines recorded an additional 5,616 shells available.

Other Turkish troops were involved to provide specialist support to the defences, arranged as detachments and companies: Fortified Area Ammunition Depot, Searchlight Detachment, Fortress Engineer Company, Engineer Construction Company, and a Communications Company. In 1912, there were two detachments for underwater warfare, one for mines and the other for torpedoes, but in 1915 they were merged to form the Mine Detachment.

Fortifications between the entrance and the Narrows

Although German involvement with the defences was ramping up by the end of August 1914, the Turks had already begun to activate improvements, motivated by the British ships that patrolled off the entrance of the Dardanelles. There was little that could be done to improve the coastal guns situation other than to consolidate the ammunition, ensure enough competent gunners and provide an adequate communications infrastructure, but Cevat Pasha was able to request two infantry divisions and several mobile artillery batteries. Turkish military resources had been seriously depleted due to the Italian-Turkish War and the recent Balkan wars, where hundreds of guns and thousands of men of had been lost, but

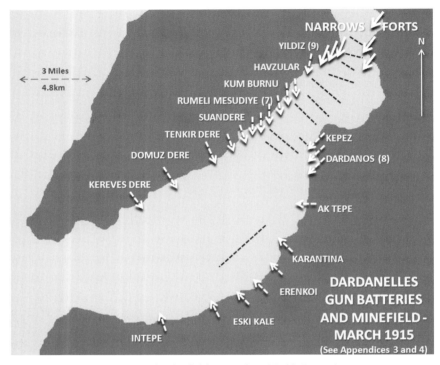

Dardanelles Gun Batteries and Minefield – March 1915. (© Forrest)

some additional guns were found and despatched to the Canakkale Fortified Area Command. The Howitzer Zone, which would form along both sides of the Strait below Kepez to prevent sweeping of the minefield, was now organized as the 8th Heavy Artillery Regiment and commanded by German Lieutenant Colonel Heinrich Wehrle. More than twenty gun batteries were dug-in on the heights either side of the Dardanelles, including eight 150mm howitzer batteries, and others consisting of a mixture of calibres and types, including: 75mm and 87mm field guns, 120mm howitzers, 150mm mortars and Nordenfeldt machine guns. In early 1915, three 6-inch/45 ship's guns were located at Rumeli Mesudiye Battery (Fort No.7), these having been recovered from the wreck of the *Mesudiye*, which had been sunk by British submarine *B11*. Two important batteries were already established – the Yildiz Battery (Fort No. 9) south-west of Kilid Bahr, set approximately 80m above sea level, and the

Dardanos Battery (Fort No. 8) overlooking Kepez Bay on the Asian side at an elevation of about 100m. Yildiz was a permanent fortification with six Krupp 150mm L/26 guns supplied from four earth-covered magazines set in the traverses, plus four 87mm L/24 mortars with their own deep magazine. A stone store and accommodation block was located more than 100m to the rear. Dardanos was originally equipped with two naval Krupp 150mm SK L/40 (SK – German designation *Schiffskanone*) quick-firers but was supplemented in August 1914 with three more from the *Asar-i Tevfik*, a Turkish ironclad built by the Thames Ironworks of London in 1870. The ship's original guns were replaced with the L/40s during a 1903 refit, but the *Asar-i Tevfik* ran aground and was scuttled in 1913. The 150mm SK L/40 was an obsolete naval gun that had been successfully

Two Krupp 150mm L/26 howitzers of the type emplaced at the Yildiz and Ak Tepe batteries, now at the Cimenlik Kalesi Museum. (© Forrest)

adapted for land use on a field carriage, although at Dardanos each gun was mounted in a traversing armoured turret. The battery was in an exposed position on the top of a hill, so it was accessed via a winding trench at the rear.

As significant as the heavyweight coastal artillery may have been, it was the numerous smaller calibre guns and mobile field pieces (see Appendix Three, Dardanelles Gun Batteries – 18 March 1915) that were to constantly disrupt British and French minesweeping operations: the failure to clear these mines was to be disastrous for the Allies on 18 March 1915. On 26 February, the day that minesweeping began, the 8th Heavy Artillery Regiment had 7,627 high explosive shells for its 150mm field guns and 602 armour-piercing shells for its 210mm mortars.

The minefield

Submerged electro-contact mines using black powder explosive were first used in the Dardanelles at the time of the Russo-Turkish War of 1877-1878, being hurriedly laid off Suandere Bay, Sarisiglar Bay, in the shallows off Namazgah fort, and in two echelons across the Narrows. An English officer, known as Woods Pasha, supervised the operation but according to a British intelligence report now held in The National Archives (reference: ADM231/8 No. 93, March 1886) it was considered to have been carried out 'in a very rough and ready manner'.

These mines were removed when hostilities ended but sixty similar mines were again laid in 1880 during a period of international tension, and possibly yet again in 1885. A remote detonation technique using electrically-fired mines activated from a shore command position was considered, as was the laying of dummy buoyant mines on long moorings, so as to hamper the movement of ships even if they avoided striking them (no record of any such methods have been discovered).

The minefield at the time the *Goeben* and the *Breslau* entered the Dardanelles in early August 1914 would have had limited success against an invading battle fleet, as it was only two lines totalling forty-eight mines laid on 4 and 6 August at a depth of 4m to 4.5m. A third line of forty mines was laid on 15 August. The minefield was a hazard but not a deterrent to commercial traffic, which still carefully ploughed up and down the Dardanelles in designated paths, although these were to be mined at the end of September 1914, so completely closing the Strait. The expansion of the minefield became a high priority with the laying of what would become, by 18 March 1915, a total of 403 mines of various types moored at a depth of 2.5m to 4.5m and at various spacing up to 100m apart (see Appendix Four A, Dardanelles Minefield up to 18 March 1915). During the minelaying operation twelve exploded, which slightly reduced the effective number of mines to 391, unless they were replaced.

As events progressed and British planners evaluated what they knew of the minefield there was the additional concern about drifting mines, given the strong current flowing out of the Dardanelles. The deliberate sowing of drifting mines was banned under the Hague Convention and a mine was supposed to deactivate itself if inadvertently released from its sinker, but this continued to be an unpredictable threat to the Allies. Generally, the Turkish mines were old and unreliable, but others were of French, Russian or Bulgarian manufacture. After Russia declared war on Turkey on 2 November 1914, Russian destroyers were constantly sowing contact mines at the Black Sea entrance to the Bosphorus in the hope of sinking Turkish warships, merchantmen and colliers. Later the Russians employed the world's first minelaying submarine for this purpose, the *Krab.* Turkish minesweepers would recover as many Russian-laid mines as possible, to sow them in their own minefields in the Bosphorus and the Dardanelles.

In this phase of the war, the northernmost line of mines in the Dardanelles was from Canakkale lighthouse across the Narrows to a position close to the Degirmen Burnu fort; nine more lines crossed the Strait further south to a line between the Suandere Bay and Dardanos. The last line of mines that was laid prior 18 March 1915, and conclusively the most effective, used the German E-Mine with a 330lb (150kg) charge of gun cotton, activated by the crushing of the Hertz horn, which released an electrolyte to trigger the firing mechanism. This mine was also known as a 'carbonite' type as the released electrolyte makes an electric circuit between a carbon and a zinc plate to form a simple battery capable of generating enough current to ignite the mine's electrical detonator.

The inspired laying of the eleventh line of twenty-six mines on the night of 7/8 March 1915 by the *Nusret,* commanded by Lieutenant Commander Tophaneli Hakki Bey, was orientated differently to the other

The seagoing replica of the *Nusret* minelayer moored alongside the Canakkale Naval Museum. (© Forrest)

The *Nusret's* deadly cargo, albeit replica mines on their sinkers. (© Forrest)

lines, as instead of crossing the Strait as a barrier it was parallel with the Asian coast in Erenkoi Bay. It had been observed that this was an area where the Allied battleships regularly steamed to exit the Dardanelles after shelling the Narrows forts, and this line of mines was to be responsible for the sinking of the *Ocean, Irresistible* and possibly the *Bouvet*, and seriously damaging the *Inflexible*. Incredibly, the British were unaware of this critical hazard, and after the event concluded that the ships had been sunk by Leon torpedo mines. The Leon torpedo mine was designed to oscillate up and down in the water as it drifted with the current, and so pass under the nets that could screen a capital ship. It was only after the end of the First World War that the Allies were aware of the true reason for the loss of the ships.

German Vice-Admiral Merten took command of minelaying operations from 4 February 1915. By this time, nine lines had already been laid by the Turks, using four vessels, although German technicians

Dardanelles Minefield – 18 March 1915. (© Forrest)

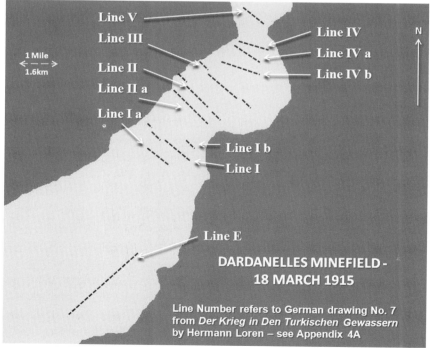

69

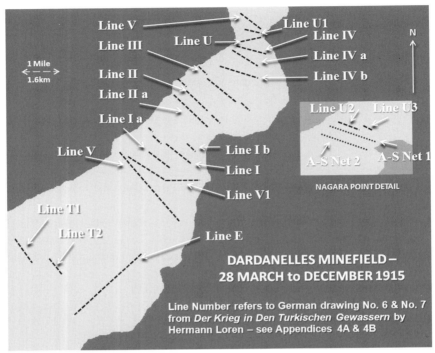

Dardanelles Minefield – 28 March 1915 to December 1915. (© Forrest)

had been providing practical assistance. Most of Turkey's minelayers and minesweepers were vessels converted from another purpose, the *Selanik* and *Initbah* being converted tugs. Another ship that laid mines in the Dardanelles, the *Samsun*, may also have been a converted tug, although there was a destroyer of this name. However, the 360-ton *Nusret* was a modern German purpose-built minelayer commissioned in the Turkish Navy in 1913, and could carry forty mines. Two more short lines of mines were laid after the failure to force the Dardanelles on 18 March 1914, nine on 28 March and another ten on 31 March. These were much further to the south of the main minefield, staggered off the Gallipoli shore as a precaution against another Allied mass attack, although there is no record of these actually being struck by any British or French warships. Of course, there was not to be another big ship assault but destroyers became very active in the later absence of battleships. From May until December

1915, 154 more mines were laid to extend the original minefield and to restrict the passage off Nagara Point, together with two anti-submarine nets (see Appendix Four B, Dardanelles Minefield and Anti-Submarine Nets from 28 March to December 1915). Powerful 60cm searchlights were positioned at various locations along both shores, both fixed and mobile, from the entrance to positions at Nagara Point.

As the transportation links from Germany to Constantinople improved with the opening of the railway after Bulgaria entered the war, even more mines were sown in the Dardanelles: 207 in 1916 and 223 in 1917. Additional anti-submarine nets were strung across the Dardanelles both above and below the Narrows, reaching to a depth of 67m (220 feet).

The Turkish Navy

The formation of a German Naval Mission in Constantinople in 1914, replacing the British Naval Mission, welcomed the two new additions of the *Yavuz Sultan Selim* and *Midilli* (ex *Goeben* and *Breslau*) to the Turkish Navy, together with the responsibility for the Navy under Admiral Souchon. The German Official History records the state of the Turkish Navy at this time:

> For decades the service has been confined to accommodation, victualling, clothing and theoretical instruction.... Since 1877 no Turkish man-of-war has gone out of the Bosphorus into the Black Sea. Consequently, the personnel had not got their sea legs.... Target practice had practically never taken place, neither had signal exercises or torpedo practice.... Practical navigation had broken down. Technical work, for which the Turk has in any case no aptitude, was in a very bad way. The engineers of all grades were not equal to the requirements of their posts and seniority. Accordingly hulls, armament and engines were not in a condition to comply with German naval officers' requirements. All sorts of things were missing; for instance, the heavy guns of the battleship *Messudieh* had not been in her for years; on board other ships individual guns were missing.

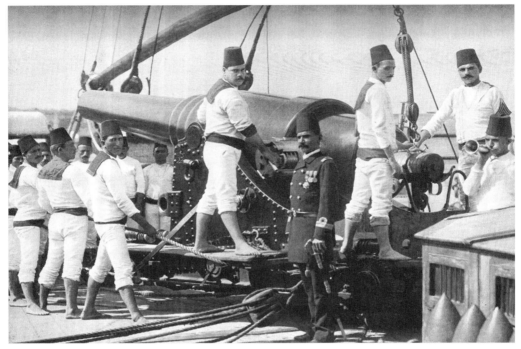

Gun drill aboard the Ottoman ironclad *Osmaniye* after her 1894 refit. Note that the shell is about to be loaded into the open breech of the 240mm Krupp gun. (Author's collection)

Although antiquated and neglected the Turkish Navy did have two warships with guns powerful enough to have challenged the British ships (excluding the recently acquired *Yavuz Sultan Selim* and *Midilli*) – the *Turgut Reis* and the *Hayreddin Barbarossa*. These were ex-German Brandenburg class battleships of 10,000 tons displacement, each armed with four 280mm L/40 Krupp guns, and at various times they were anchored off Maidos between the Narrows and Nagara Point under the command of Commodore Arif Bey, second in command of the Turkish Navy after Admiral Souchen. When the warships were at anchor they had steamers tied up against their vulnerable sides to counter the threat of a torpedo attack by submarine. On 6 March 1915, the *Queen Elizabeth* shelled the forts at the Narrows with indirect fire from her position off Gaba Tepe, the Aegean side of the Gallipoli peninsula. The *Hayreddin Barbarossa* returned fire over the peninsula but without serious effect due to inadequate fire control. A Turkish artillery spotting team had been positioned on a hill but without any telephone communications back to their control at Maidos, the peninsula town close to the anchored Turkish warship. Pre-arranged star shell signals were used instead but these attracted the attention of the British ships' guns, so the spotters had to keep moving around. Yet this was also true for the *Queen Elizabeth* that was under fire from field guns as well as those of the *Hayreddin Barbarossa*, and she moved off, being unable to stabilize a position to provide accurate fire. Chief Petty Officer Young aboard HMS *Agamemnon* observed what happened:

> Our guns destroyed a farm used as an observation station. The 'QE's' job was to fire clean over the Gallipoli peninsular into the forts of the Narrows.... The Turks' object seemed to be to keep her on the move as she requires to be stationary for this job: nothing much was therefore accomplished, as she had to shift berth two or three times.

On 25 April, the *Turgut Reis* gave indirect fire over the Gallipoli peninsula, this time at the Allied landings at Ari Burnu. By now an improved spotting system using telephones and beacon points with pre-defined bearings had been established by the Turks to improve fire accuracy. After a few rounds the battleship quickly steamed off into the Sea of Marmara because of a report that a submarine had been seen north of the Narrows; this was the Australian *AE2*. The *Hayreddin Barbarossa* was in action again on 3 May, and this time her indirect fire hit the *Swiftsure* and sunk a transport.

The *Turgut Reis* returned to Constantinople in June 1915, after a shell exploded on deck. She was laid up until 1918, although some of her 105mm guns were removed and sent to add weight to the Dardanelles defences. The *Hayreddin Barbarossa* was torpedoed off Bulair and sunk by submarine *E11* on 8 August 1915. The *Mesudiye* was the only Turkish ship actually used as a floating battery in the defence of the Dardanelles, but she was torpedoed by the *B11* in Sarisiglar Bay while providing protection to the minefield. Had she not been sunk on 13 December 1914, the 40-year-old *Mesudiye* would have been ineffective against the Allied ships, even against the pre-dreadnoughts. The *Mesudiye* was a central battery ironclad built in Britain by the Thames Ironworks in 1874 and, when commissioned, was considered as one of the most powerful ships in the world with her heavy armour and 10-inch RML (Rifled Muzzle Loading) guns. The ship was refitted in 1903 in Genoa, but the intended 9.2-inch Vickers breech-loading replacement guns were not fitted to the turrets as they had not arrived, so wooden dummies were installed instead! By 1914, the ship still had these useless imitations and, although the guns were now available from store in Constantinople, she was considered to be in such a poor condition that a refit was untenable. The *Mesudiye* was fitted with 6-inch/45 Armstrong's as secondary armament, and these were later recovered from the wreck to be used at a number of batteries either side of the Dardanelles.

The Ottoman Navy had purchased two submarines in 1886-1887 from Barrow Shipbuilders, which were sent to Constantinople disassembled for reassembly at the Taskizak Naval Shipyard. The first of the pair was the *Abdul Hamid*, which has the distinction of being the first submarine to fire a live torpedo underwater; the second was the *Abdul Mecid*. Each were armed with 14-inch (350mm) Whitehead torpedoes, but the boats were coal-fired and proved to be unpractical and limited in range and speed. Early twentieth-century technical author Frederick A. Talbot described the testing of these Turkish submarines in the Bosphorus:

> They displayed an unconquerable desire to make acquaintance with the seabed.... The Turkish government never succeeded in coaxing or forcing a crew to man them.

Turkey's pre-First World War torpedo boats were sourced from Britain, Germany and Italy, forty-seven being purchased in various classes from 1888, the most modern seventeen being from 1910 to 1913; torpedo armament increasing from three 15.7-inch (400 mm) to four 17.7-inch (450mm) torpedoes. One of these, the German-built *Muavenet-i Milliye,* sank the old pre-dreadnought *Goliath* in Morto Bay on 13 May 1915. As with most other munitions used by Turkey at this later time, the torpedoes were probably of German manufacture of the C/07 Coastal Defence Type. This was unguided torpedo, 450mm diameter, 5.5m long, which carried a 110kg TNT warhead to a range of 1,500m; propulsion was by Brotherhood compressed air system. The number of torpedo boats operating in the Dardanelles and the Sea of Marmara on anti-submarine and escort roles was increased after the Gallipoli invasion.

Shore-launched torpedoes
A further threat to any unwelcome warship penetrating the Dardanelles was the use of shore-launched, or locomotive, torpedoes. These were first considered by British intelligence circa 1880, but, together with tethered mines (at this time referred to as fixed torpedoes), were dismissed as ineffective in a memorandum dated 11 August 1880 by Admiral Sir Geoffrey Hornby, who had led a British squadron through the Dardanelles in 1878.

> I do not apprehend that torpedoes, either fixed or locomotive, can, with the varying force of the current and the numerous eddies, prevent ships passing. Those laid in 1877 by Captain Woods of the Turkish Navy, were, in his opinion, ineffective, and the Turks had great difficulty in finding them when their war ended.

However, by the twentieth century, shore-launched torpedoes were back on the agenda, and a British plan (reference: The National Archives WO301/477) from 1908 of the fort at Sedd el Bahr identifies such a position outside the fort facing south-east, and that the ammunition towers also contained torpedo stores. In subsequent operational planning two British destroyers were specifically detailed to deal with this threat. A British map (reference: Imperial War Museum ref: Chart No. 2429) dated August 1914 shows six torpedo tube positions in the Dardanelles; two on either shore at the entrance; two on either shore near Kepez Point; and two on either shore at the Narrows. German maps of the Dardanelles (reference: *Der Krieg in Den Turkischen Gewassern* by Hermann Loren) do not show torpedo positions at Sedd el Bahr, and there are no official records of torpedoes being discovered by the landing parties that followed the bombardment in February 1915 or by the occupying Allies after the invasion on 25 April. According to the diary Herbert Reely of HMS

Inflexible, a landing party that went ashore at Sedd el Bahr on 26 February 1915 discovered 'a 36-inch searchlight with dynamo complete and two torpedo tubes mounted on a raft'. German maps do show torpedo batteries on both sides of the Strait at the Narrows, at or close to Kilid Bahr and Cimenlik Kalesi, so it is reasonable to believe that these were the only shore-launched torpedo locations in the Strait. According to the British journalist and naval historian H.W. Wilson, at Kilid Bahr there were three 18-inch torpedo tubes, for which there were only five torpedoes. In a newspaper report by an American journalist following the action of 15 March 1915, he stated:

> That they [the Turks] had secret land torpedo-tubes ... one in
> plain view and out of service on March 18.

No accurate details of shore-launched torpedoes in the Dardanelles have yet come to light. An explanation for this may be that they were not located in bomb-proof casemates at the water's edge with cages that could

A 14-inch torpedo launcher, which was designed to be rolled into the water for firing, now on display at the Canakkale Naval Museum. (© Forrest)

be lowered into the water, such as at the Oscarsborg Fortress in Oslo Fjord, (see Introduction and the sinking of the German heavy cruiser *Blucher*) but in mobile launchers, which could be run into the water from the shore to discharge the torpedo. Such an example constructed around a 14-inch torpedo tube using a compressed gas system as propellant, possibly removed from one of the unsuccessful submarines of the 1880s, does exist in the Canakkale Naval Museum Command. Assuming that this device used a German-supplied torpedo, it could have been a C35/91 350mm with a warhead of 40kg TNT, but this would have been largely ineffective because of its short range of around 400m. Another idea was that the Turks had mounted 18-inch torpedoes on two barges that could have been moored either side of the channel. A further suggestion is that the torpedo tubes were suspended below a pier built out from the shore at Kilid Bahr, a simple and realistic arrangement, and one such pier is believed to have existed close to Kilid Bahr at this time. These credible proposals could have worked, although the pier and anchored barges would have been very vulnerable to enemy fire, particularly as any ships that had succeeded in passing through the minefield would be advancing with all available guns blazing.

Turkey had taken an interest in the use of coastal defence torpedoes as early as the 1870s, when Egypt, which was then an Ottoman province, proposed to protect Aboukir Bay with the wire-guided Lay torpedo. Invented by American John Lay, the 26-foot long torpedo carried 90lb of dynamite or gun cotton, and was powered by compressed carbon dioxide gas driving a small engine linked to a propeller. It was steered by electrical commands from a shore-based helmsman to the rudder via a cable that ran out as the torpedo moved forward, but the range of 1 to 2 miles was limited by the amount of cable carried and the helmsman's vision with binoculars. The torpedo ran at a sedate 9 knots close to the surface of the water and carried two flags, one fore and one aft, to indicate its position – very helpful to the gunners on the ship being attacked – but this visual marker technique was used by other contemporary torpedoes at the time. Supposedly, the flags could be lowered as the helmsman steered the torpedo closer to the hostile vessel; at night two rear-facing lamps were the aid to guidance. The Lay torpedo was demonstrated to Hasan Pasha, Ottoman Minister of Marine, in the Bosphorus in November 1882, and was successfully guided to its target – a 60- to 90-foot gap between two moored cutters – during both day and night trials. An 'Improved Lay' version with a heavier explosive and a reputed speed of 12 to 16 knots was sold to the Russian government for them to manufacture; ten were made but proved unsatisfactory.

A Royal Navy officer, Lieutenant Sleeman RN, wrote a paper entitled 'The Lay and other Locomotive Torpedoes considered for the purpose of Coast Defence, and also as the armament of Ships, Torpedo and Submarine Boats' in 1883 for The Royal United Services Institution, in which he extolled the virtues of the Lay torpedo and illustrated just how effective it would be in the defence of the Dardanelles. He determined that there were five locations at the entrance to the Strait that would provide total coverage against attacking ships, plus further positions both sides of the Strait at Kepez and at the Narrows. This potential arrangement could have influenced British planners in later years, hence the previously mentioned British map from 1914. Lieutenant Sleeman also suggested that a larger Lay torpedo had a range of 2,650 yards (2,400m), so torpedoes could also be launched wherever the Dardanelles narrowed north of Canakkale; at Nagara Point, Cape Peskieri (Pesquies Point) and near to the town of Gallipoli.

Also in the 1880s, another type of torpedo defence was offered to the Ottomans by American engineer and inventor Hiram Berdan, a former US Civil War general famous for the Berdan rifle, which became standard issue for the Russian Army for more than twenty years. Berdan's interests included many aspects of munitions, and when living in Constantinople he began to devise a weapon for underwater warfare. His idea was for a projectile to run along the surface of the water steered by an operator pulling tiller lines, using a sighting mast to follow its course and position after launching, not unlike Lay's design. General Berdan quoted the Ottoman government for the building of two bomb-proof torpedo stations, one either side of the entrance to the Dardanelles, each equipped with fifty torpedoes. A small factory to manufacture Berdan torpedoes was to be established in the dockyard in Constantinople. In addition, he suggested an additional 200 torpedoes were required plus twelve small steamers, presumably as torpedo boats, to protect the Ottoman Empire's other harbours. The quote for the 300 torpedoes alone was £150,000; no further reports on Berdan's Ottoman venture have been traced.

CHAPTER 4

Ships versus Forts

Before any thought of provocative action was taken by the British warships patrolling off the Dardanelles to prevent the escape of the *Goeben* and the *Breslau*, a constant stream of telegraph traffic passed between the Admiralty in London and Admiral Milne, soon to be replaced by Admiral Sackville Carden. As events in Constantinople quickly unfolded it was realized that the German warships, now transferred to the Ottoman Navy, were unlikely to exit the Dardanelles after all, but the British ships remained. The anticipated closing of the Strait by the Turks was precipitated on the night of 26-27 September 1914, when a Turkish torpedo boat was intercepted by the Royal Navy and turned back as it tried to enter the Aegean. The Dardanelles were closed the following day by order of German General Eric Weber, a defence specialist reporting to Admiral von Usedom. The immediate effect of closing the Strait was to halt Russian grain exports and material imports, so as to begin a slow strangling of the Russian economy, which eventually contributed to her political and military collapse. Over the next few weeks hundreds of cargo ships passed through the Bosphorus heading south, but being unable to proceed further soon bottled up at anchor off Constantinople. The closure of the Dardanelles also badly hurt the Turkish economy because of the loss of passage revenues and customs duties. According to Henry Morgenthau, the American Ambassador to Constantinople, this dramatic decision had been a part of Germany's plan regardless of what the Turkish Cabinet wanted, and that they had only been looking for an excuse to do so. There is no doubt that the German ambassador, Baron Hans von Wangenheim, had an inordinate amount of influence over the principal Turkish personalities such as Enver Pasha, encouraging him to undertake actions that were, ultimately, good only for Germany.

As Britain and Turkey diplomatically tiptoed around each other to avoid war, German pressure on their in-country hosts to close the British Naval Mission in Constantinople and replace it with a German Naval Mission strained Anglo-Turkish relationships further. At the end of October, German Admiral Souchon, now a Turkish Vice Admiral, was instructed by Enver Pasha to take the *Yavuz Sultan Selim,* the *Midilli (Goeben* and *Breslau*) and several Turkish warships into the Black Sea to attack Russian bases in Sevastopol, Feodosia, Yalta, Odessa and Novorossiysk. This surprise action began on 26 October 1914, and forced Russia to declare war on Turkey; as a Triple Entente ally, Britain had to support Russia. The first shots in the war against Turkey were fired by British ships on 3 November 1914, two days before France and Britain's formal declaration of war.

Prominent in the decision to force the Dardanelles in 1915 was Admiral John Arbuthnot 'Jacky' Fisher, a man perhaps best known for his energy and enthusiasm to reform and modernize the Royal Navy for service in the twentieth century. By the beginning of the First World War, Lord Fisher had already retired after sixty years of service but, aged seventy-four, he was recalled as First Sea Lord to replace the incumbent Prince Louis of Battenberg, who was forced to retire because of his German antecedents. Fisher was never completely convinced that a wholly naval action in the Dardanelles would be successful, often changing his support for the operation, much to the irritation of those that shared the responsibility, including Winston Churchill. Fisher had been the captain of the innovative Victorian ironclad *Inflexible* during the bombardment of Alexandria in 1882, and was critical of the effectiveness of ships in action against shore forts:

> One point which has to be borne in mind when ships engage forts is that the ship has to hit the gun or crew; the fort has only to hit the ship.

Admiral Fisher was acquainted with the Dardanelles, having sailed through them in 1900 aboard a Royal Navy fleet scout, HMS *Surprise.*

This vessel, although armed, had been built in 1885 with a high standard of accommodation, specifically for the transportation of diplomats and high-ranking officials. At the time of his visit, Admiral Fisher was in command of the powerful and prestigious Mediterranean Fleet but he chose to sail to Constantinople in a vessel similar to a yacht. At Canakkale he was met by Turkish Vice Admiral Husni Pasha who accompanied him to the capital.

British intelligence and the Dardanelles

It is certain that British intelligence officers inspected the defences of the Dardanelles, possibly covertly on land, years before the First World War, and the opportunity to view the fortifications from the deck of a British ship enabled a progressive account of their development to be maintained. An 1886 report by the Admiralty Foreign Intelligence Committee (reference: The National Archives: ADM231/8 No. 93, March 1886) described in detail the natural features of the Dardanelles, the condition of the fortifications and communications between them, and other relevant facts such as the numbers of artillerymen and their efficiency. The same document refers to an 1883 report in which is described just how these defences should be overcome, and believed that a joint naval and land forces operation was necessary (see Appendix Five, Extracts from the Foreign Committee Paper (No. 93), 1886).

An officer named Charles Woods, who was involved with mining the Narrows in 1877 (see Chapter Three), is credited with carrying out a reconnaissance of the defences in 1906, and filing a report with the General Staff and Naval Intelligence, although this may not have been circulated to all interested departments at that time. Based upon the detailed drawings from 1908 of forts such as Sedd el Bahr, and also from the Admiralty's own intelligence documents now held in The National Archives, some of this information must have been examined. Where the information was duly considered, the conclusions were uncomplimentary about the state of the defences and the disposition of the guns, suggesting that fast-moving ships could have a chance of success of breaking through. Woods apparently posted copies to the General Staff and to Naval Intelligence again early in 1915, before the decision to destroy the fortifications and so control the Dardanelles were taken. However, in

1906, the British Committee of Imperial Defence – an advisory planning council established to provide guidance to the Prime Minister on military strategy, which included the First Sea Lord and the Chief of the Imperial General Staff – had also considered the passage through the Dardanelles under fire, and had reached a different conclusion in a memorandum prepared on the subject. They believed that a combined army and navy operation was essential but that the prospect of success was not worth the risks involved:

> A mere naval raid into the Sea of Marmara being a dangerous and ineffective operation, the work will have to be undertaken by a joint naval and military expedition having for its objective the capture of the Gallipoli peninsular and the destruction of the forts which at present deny entrance and exit from these waters.

The principal author of the memorandum presented to the Committee of Imperial Defence was Major General Sir C.E. Calwell, who had actually visited the Dardanelles before 1906 and had taken careful note of the topography and the defences. In August 1914, he searched for the memorandum but found only a note in the file concerned to say that by order of Sir H. Campbell-Bannerman, Prime Minister at the time the memorandum was written, it had been withdrawn. At a later date, General Calwell discovered that Prime Minister Campbell-Bannerman had perceived that it was a matter of quite exceptional secrecy, and dreaded the disastrous results if the Turks were to learn that British naval and military authorities believed that an attack upon the Dardanelles was virtually impracticable. General Calwell recorded in his memoires:

> Tell the Turk that, and our trump card was gone.

Another important report that was available to British military operations in London early enough to have influenced their planning was that provided by Colonel Cunliffe-Owen, the Military Attaché in Constantinople in 1914. He had conscientiously surveyed the Gallipoli peninsula defences, reporting on the German activities in the area, the forts and gun batteries, mines, torpedo tubes, searchlights, and even the dummy guns that puffed smoke that were later to confound the ships' fire control officers. This highly significant information, which concluded that a joint naval and military attack was necessary to secure the passage through the Dardanelles, was available at the War Office by September 1914, but it was not given due consideration then or when the Mediterranean Expeditionary Force was formed under General Sir Ian Hamilton.

Early in 1915, and after the slow process of the reduction of the shore fortifications by naval firepower had began, the former head of the British Naval Mission in Constantinople, Admiral Limpus, wrote a comprehensive appreciation of the Dardanelles situation to Rear Admiral Richard Phillimore, commander of the 2nd Battlecruiser Squadron, but who would become the Principal Beach Master controlling the Cape Helles landings in April 1915. In this study he concluded that a landing action was necessary to secure the forts and batteries, particularly as he considered that it was the Germans rather than the Turks who were conducting the defence. Even Admiral Fisher had reached the same conclusion:

> The bombardment of the Dardanelles, even if all the forts are destroyed, can be nothing but a local success, which without an army to carry it on can have no further effect.

Regardless of what advice may have been available, Winston Churchill's zeal to force the Dardanelles by naval assault alone carried the project but ignored the perils. An important factor in the decision process was the recent success of big guns on heavy fortifications: the German artillery bombardment of the Belgian forts at Antwerp and those along the river Meuse at Liege and Namur. One of the most significant of these attacks was the shattering of Fort Loncin by a 420mm howitzer shell that penetrated the main magazine to blow the fort apart, killing hundreds of soldiers in the explosion. The Belgian forts dated from the late 1880s and had been designed to resist the guns of that time, but as the calibre of the shells had become larger so the defences had become relatively weaker. The upgraded Turkish defences surrounding the Dardanelles were of a similar age to the Belgium forts but were of a different, technically inferior, design. The Belgium forts were of unreinforced concrete with guns in armoured cupolas, therefore far better protected than the vulnerable open gun emplacements of the Dardanelles. However, it appears that British defence planners ignored the fact that the plunging fire of howitzer shells was much more effective on fixed fortifications than the flat trajectory of projectiles fired from ships' guns. One reason for this obvious oversight was the spectacular success of destroying an ammunition magazine at Sedd el Bahr during the opening bombardment by Allied ships. However, the decision to shell the entrance forts on 3 November 1914 was not as a prelude to an attack on the Dardanelles or to soften them prior to an invasion of the Gallipoli peninsula – it was a demonstration of Allied naval strength and superiority – and took place two days before war with Turkey had been formally declared.

3 November 1914

The French pre-dreadnoughts *Suffren* and *Verite* and the British battlecruisers *Indefatigable* and *Indomitable* opened fire on all four of the forts at the entrance to the Dardanelles at 0650 hrs. The British ships fired from a range of 15,000 yards (13,370m), out-ranging the four Turkish 240mm L/35 guns located at Ertugrul and Orhaniye, although these guns did reply ineffectively, perhaps just one round each. The damage inflicted on Ertugrul, Orhaniye and Kum Kale during the seventeen-minute bombardment was minimal, little more than throwing earth around, which was soon cleared after the ships had withdrawn. It was a different story at Sedd el Bahr as the fifteenth-century west stone tower took a direct hit, blowing up the powder and shells stored in the tower and those placed outside it, and displacing a number of guns. However, the shells stored outside the magazine were unlikely to have been filled with explosive, unless being transported to the guns for firing. Most probably they were empty cores awaiting filling with black powder, which has to be done under controlled conditions. Total casualties across the four forts were 150 men, forty of whom were German, many having been killed when a barracks was hit.

The most significant aspect of this attack was that it galvanized the defenders to increase their efforts to improve the fortifications and

Sedd el Bahr in 2010. The right-hand tower was destroyed by a direct hit on 3 November 1914. (© Forrest)

The remains of the destroyed tower at Sedd el Bahr. On the far side of V Beach, left of the Helles Memorial, is the Ertugrul Battery (indicated by an arrow). (© Forrest)

communications between them. Although locally the soldiers and technicians were already working hard to achieve this goal, the bombardment opened the eyes of the lethargic Turkish military command. Had the 3 November attack been immediately followed up by the fleet entering the Dardanelles, pressing on to attack the forts at the Narrows and then steaming on to the Sea of Marmara, *perhaps* the goal of reaching Constantinople to intimidate Turkey may have been successful. However, the minefield had been strengthened by this time, now comprising five lines, totalling 171 mines.

The big gun competition: Armstrong, Vickers and Krupp
The battle between the British warships and the Turkish fortifications can be loosely considered as an extension to a long-running competition between two commercial arms manufacturers – the Sir William G. Armstrong & Company of Elswick and the Fried Krupp Company of Essen – both companies having courted Turkey from the 1860s, and both having been successful with their sales. Krupp guns fed the Ottoman Army as it slowly tried to modernize. Armstrong guns were generally specified for the Ottoman Navy as it strove to equip with new ironclads, many of which were built in Britain, and these vessels were to form the core of the Ottoman Navy toward the end of the nineteenth century. However, this 'core' turned out to be rotten as these ships were often ineptly used, if used at all, many of them simply corroding at anchor until they were useless.

The Armstrong business was to later become the Sir William G. Armstrong Whitworth Company, although the armaments production was known as the Elswick Ordnance Company (EOC). The Elswick Ordnance Company was originally created in 1859 to separate William Armstrong's armaments business from his other interests, as Armstrong was then Chief Engineer of Rifled Ordnance for the War Office, and the company's main customer was the British Government. Armstrong held no financial interest in EOC until 1864, when he left government service.

In 1914, the British ships that were to engage the Dardanelles forts were fitted with Armstrong/EOC guns and also those made by Vickers Limited, a relative newcomer to British arms manufacturing that started in this business in 1887. The main armaments of the British capital ships

HMS *Cornwallis* firing her 6-inch guns at shore targets. Note the anti-torpedo net booms standing out from the side of the ship. (Courtesy of the National Museum of the Royal Navy)

were of three calibres: 10-inch (254mm) on the *Swiftsure* and *Triumph*; 15-inch (381mm) on the *Queen Elizabeth;* 12-inch (305mm) guns being fitted to the remainder of the warships. The main armament of the French pre-dreadnoughts *Bouvet*, *Verite*, *Gaulois*, *Charlemagne* and *Suffren* were also 12-inch (305mm) (see Appendix Six, British and French Battleships used in the Dardanelles campaign up to the 18 March 1915).

Against this formidable Allied arsenal were the Turkish Krupp guns. Based on the calibres 240mm to 355mm (9.5-inch to 14-inch) the Krupp *'Ringkanones'* appear almost as equals, but as the naval guns were of significantly longer barrel length, so they should have out-ranged the shore guns. Although this was true against the short barrel Krupp L/22s, the long barrel L/35s could out-range many of the ships' main armament (see Appendix Seven, The Power of the Guns, Table of Comparison: British, French and Turkish Main Armaments).

HMS *Queen Elizabeth's* 'A' and 'B' 15-inch gun turrets. (Courtesy of the National Museum of the Royal Navy)

The new super-dreadnought *Queen Elizabeth* carried high hopes of success, as the range of her 15-inch guns and the weight of fire she could deliver made her the most powerful warship off the Turkish coast. However, the ship was considered so valuable that she was not to be exposed to close fire from Turkish guns within the Dardanelles, and she had to be constantly protected from possible torpedo attack. From early March 1915, she fired blind over the Gallipoli peninsula at the Narrows forts but the fall of the shells was rarely determined accurately. Yet, strangely, German General Hans Kannengiesser and other staff officers erroneously believed the British ships had accurate plans of the peninsula and that they were able to easily pinpoint targets for destruction.

Colonel Maurice Hankey of the Royal Marine Artillery, who became a coastal defence analyst to the War Division of the Naval Intelligence Department, Secretary to the Committee of Imperial Defence in 1912 and then Secretary to the War Council in November 1914, visited Gallipoli during its later occupation to inspect the damage at Sedd el Bahr and Ertugrul. He was not impressed, later writing to Prime Minister Herbert Asquith:

> One gun which had received a direct hit was knocked to pieces. Otherwise ... the guns were not damaged by shellfire.... I am pretty well confirmed, therefore, in my original conviction that forts cannot be knocked out permanently by ships. The naval guns, when directed against shore targets, are spectacular but unconvincing.

However, as a result of the fortunate but misleading success against Sedd el Bahr, British planners were over-optimistic of the ships' guns effectiveness. They had calculated that five to ten 15-inch shells from *Queen Elizabeth* would be sufficient to reduce each of the entrance forts to a point where the 12-inch guns of the older ships could close in to finish them off at short range; the quantity of ammunition required would therefore be small. The same process could then be applied to destroying the forts around the Narrows at no great expense in shells. This was considered prudent because as war began there was a shortage of all munitions for both the British Army and the Royal Navy. Ultimately, the shortage of shells that became known as the 'Shell Scandal' was to bring down Asquith's Liberal government in May 1915, which was then re-formed as a coalition with the Conservatives.

The First Sea Lord, Admiral Fisher, concerned with ensuring that the warships in Home Waters should be the priority for ammunition because the threat of German action was more likely to be there, instructed that the ships engaged in the Dardanelles should have only sufficient enough to achieve their purpose. Firing was to be economical, no salvos, one gun at a time with reduced charges whenever possible, and the use of secondary armament when circumstances allowed. Winston Churchill did not agree and was to later write that the ships at the Dardanelles were:

Two examples of 12-inch shells of the types fired by the British ships attacking the Dardanelles fortresses in 1914 and 1915, on display at the Royal Armouries Museum, Fort Nelson, Hampshire, right to left: pointed; capped for improved armour-piercing. (© Forrest)

> Needlessly inhibited by the need to conserve shells.

The ships bombarding the fortifications of the Dardanelles had the advantage that their targets were not moving, so the only compensation necessary would be for the movement of the gun platform – the ship itself – and that sophisticated range finding would not be necessary when shooting at a fixed target (see Appendix Eight, The Director Fire Control System). But if a moving warship firing at a static target has an advantage, particularly if outside the range of the defending guns, why then was the bombardment of 3 November 1914 less than satisfactory, apart from the destructive hit on Sedd el Bahr? This question can also be asked in relation to the rest of the ships versus forts actions during the campaign: the answer is that the naval shells fired were not of the correct type to inflict the necessary damage, as the combination of shell, explosive filling and type of fusing were designed to attack ships, not shore targets (see Appendix Nine,

Shells, Fillings, Fuses and Charges). The spectacular explosions had little damaging effect, and the smoke and clouds of debris thrown in the air made it additionally difficult for a ship's fire control officer to pinpoint the targets set in low earth emplacements, particularly if spotting from up to 15,000 yards away. Also, if more than one ship is firing at the same target, which shell from which ship is falling where? Of course, the Navy recognized this potential point of confusion and tried to avoid it, but in the heat of action this did happen.

Aircraft were used for gunnery spotting but these had limitations caused by bad weather, pilot inexperience, poor target recognition, poor aircraft reliability and low flying ceilings due to the minimal power of their engines, which then made them vulnerable from ground fire. Although the aircraft did carry an early form of wireless telegraphy, which turned out to be hopelessly unreliable, on most occasions there was an inevitable time delay of the aircraft returning to their bases so that the corrections could be telegraphed to the warships. The Royal Navy's first aircraft carrier, *Ark Royal*, a merchant ship converted to a seaplane tender with workshops and able to carry aircraft in a large hold, arrived off Gallipoli in February 1915. Although the ship was equipped with five seaplanes (100hp Sopwith Type 807), two land-based aircraft (80hp Sopwith Tabloid) were delivered by being catapulted over the bow to land at a prepared airstrip. The seaplanes could also take off over the bow of the ship, and then return by landing close to the tender, where they were lifted to the deck by the use of one of two steam-powered 3-ton cranes, then into the hold via a sliding hatch.

More aircraft arrived as the campaign developed through 1915, and were based at the islands offshore, initially Tenedos and then Imbros, and for a few months at an advanced aerodrome at Cape Helles. Observation balloons attached to merchant ships such as the *Hector* with a direct telephone line to speed the communications were also used, but balloons were disadvantaged by not having an over-the-target view and that they invariably attracted the attention of the Turkish gunners.

A key objective of the 25 April 1915 Gallipoli landings was to take the 700-foot (331m) high point of Alci Tepe (Achi Baba to the British), which has views to both the Aegean and the Dardanelles, to facilitate accurate spotting of naval gunnery and field artillery. This objective was never achieved.

CHAPTER 5

The Reduction of the Fortifications – The Beginning

Vice Admiral Sackville Carden, the British naval officer in command of all Allied ships off the Dardanelles, including those of the French under Admiral Guepratte, is credited with the February 1915 seven-phase plan to destroy the fortifications of the Dardanelles and control the waters beyond:

Reduction of the entrance forts
Reduction of the defences up to the Narrows
Reduction of the Narrows forts
Clearance of the minefield
Reduction of the forts above the Narrows
Control of the Dardanelles to allow safe access to the Sea of Marmara
Operations in the Sea of Marmara and off Constantinople.

Contrary to earlier ideas this was not to be a rush through the Dardanelles but a slow, methodical reduction of the opposition, which would take a considerable amount of time, consume a large quantity of ammunition and, unfortunately, occur during a seasonal period of bad weather. Admiral Carden's plan was approved by the War Council but was apparently met with serious reservations by the French, who were not even consulted, and had only the wavering support of significant naval men such as Admiral Fisher. With hindsight, the expectation that a purely naval action would be successful was simplistic and naive, particularly

A stylised panoramic view of the Dardanelles from the *Illustrated War News* dated 10 March 1915. Note how the illustrator has made Kum Kale a grand castle, the hills into mountains, and has drawn in the erroneous line of mines at the entrance to the Strait. (*The Illustrated War News*, 10 March 1915)

when the British intelligence sources had always indicated that a combined navy and army operation was required to secure the Dardanelles.

At the time of the declaration of war against Germany in August 1914, the British Committee of Imperial Defence became the War Council, and an early agenda item was strategy in the event of war with Turkey. However, as the events in France and Belgium unfolded so the pressure to send troops to the Western Front dominated all minds, including Winston Churchill's and that of the Secretary of State for War, Field Marshall Herbert Kitchener. The demands being made on Britain's small but professional army meant that no troops could be made available for other areas of operation, so any campaign against Turkey would need to be a naval enterprise. The prospect of co-opting Greek assistance to use their army as an invasion force was considered in August 1914, but dismissed. The Dardanelles Commission, which was set up in 1916 to investigate the Dardanelles naval campaign and the subsequent Gallipoli expedition, concluded, amongst many things, that the entire undertaking was ill-conceived, poorly planned, lacked the element of surprise, and that the scale of the difficulties were not understood (reference: The National Archives CAB 19/1). The decision to initiate the operation without an adequate examination of the risks involved, resources required and levels of co-operation necessary between sea and land forces was, at best, cavalier. The date chosen for the opening action to destroy the entrance forts was 19 February 1915, coincidentally exactly 108 years to the day since Admiral Duckworth had forced the Dardanelles.

19 February 1915

As with the bombardment method applied on 3 November 1914, the entrance forts would first be shelled at long range to soften them and, hopefully, to destroy most of the guns and magazines. Unlike the previous action, the ships would then close in through medium ranges, finally and decisively firing at a range of just a few thousand yards. The first shots were fired at 0951 hrs by *Cornwallis* aiming at Orhaniye (Fort No. 4) at a range of 9,500 yards, soon followed by the *Triumph* at a range 7,700 yards indirectly firing from the Aegean at Ertugrul (Fort No. 1) over the tip of the Gallipoli peninsula. At 1032 hrs the *Suffren* began firing at Kum

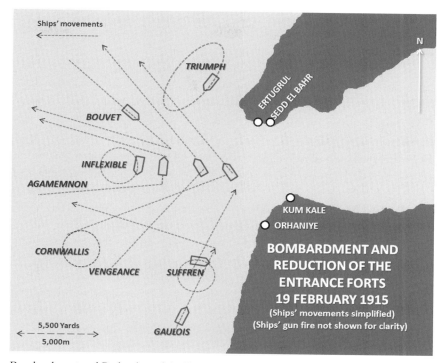

Bombardment and Reduction of the Entrance Forts – 19 February 1915. (© Forrest)

Kale (Fort No. 6) at a range of 11,800 yards, the ship having anchored 2 miles off the Asian coast to provide a steady firing platform, with the *Bouvet*, which was due west of Cape Helles, observing the fall of shot. Admiral Carden in *Inflexible* ordered the other ships to anchor but *Cornwallis* was unable to do so in deep water due to a problem with a capstan, so she was replaced by *Vengeance*, which had been observing north of Rabbit Island. The *Cornwallis* then took up a spotting role. The *Inflexible* anchored at 1150 hrs west of Cape Helles and fired on Ertugrul from a range of 15,400 yards, but the two 12-inch rounds fell short, so she moved 2,500 yards closer to continue the action, firing eighteen more rounds at anchor. The range of *Inflexible's* 12-inch guns firing a 2crh (calibre radius head) shell was 16,450 yards, just enough to have engaged a target at 15,400 yards, but as she had to move closer to do so, it suggests that the guns of this veteran of the Battle of the Falkland Islands were badly worn or that the charge strengths were inadequate. None of the forts replied, but a spotter aircraft reported that all of the guns were still in position.

At 1400 hrs, the ships began to close the distance to their targets but they were ordered not to anchor, instead steaming directly at the forts then turning away, firing as each gun found a target, then to run in again to ever shorter ranges. At 1500 hrs, *Inflexible* moved to a position 11,000 yards from Sedd el Bahr to fire five more rounds into the ruined fort, with the *Bouvet* and *Cornwallis* steaming even closer. The *Triumph* stayed to the north of the peninsula, now shelling a field gun battery at Tekke Burnu (identified as Fort No. 1b). *Vengeance* and *Suffren* took on Kum Kale at 7,000 yards, then, as Kum Kale was silenced, *Suffren* directed rapid fire with her secondary guns at Orhaniye from only 5,000 yards.

The attack continued until 1640 hrs, when Admiral Carden ordered a ceasefire for the opportunity to examine the forts from the ships and by aircraft, as there were two seaplanes reported airborne at this time. Through the clouds of smoke and settling dust the observers concluded that the forts had been overwhelmed, as they were in ruins and were deserted. *Vengeance* closed to within 4,000 yards of the entrance to the Strait, and as a calm settled across the water so both the Ertugrul and Orhaniye batteries opened fire with their 240mm L/35 guns, thoroughly surprising the ship's crew and Admiral John de Robeck, who was aboard. Field gun batteries from both shores then joined in, so the *Gaulois*, *Suffren* and *Cornwallis* closed to add supporting fire. The *Bouvet* also steamed in, firing salvos over the *Vengeance* and *Cornwallis* as they moved away from the shore guns. *Inflexible* fired nineteen rounds at Orhaniye but soon after this Admiral Carden ordered a recall as the light was behind the ships, so silhouetting them to the west, although none of the Allied ships had been hit. At 1730 hrs, the ceasefire was signalled and the ships retired. *Agamemnon* had arrived to join the fray only ten minutes earlier and also became a target, being straddled by several shells. Those aboard *Agamemnon* believe they had scored three direct hits on Orhaniye from a dozen shells fired, principally from the 9.2-inch secondary guns and at least one from a 12-inch, but the battery still stubbornly fired at the retreating ships. Spotter aircraft had been aloft to assist with gunnery control but wireless equipment failure had meant that they were close to being useless. However, the pilots were able to report the emergence of unexpected howitzer and mortar batteries and, perhaps for the first time, appreciated that the maps that the Allies were using were badly inaccurate.

The bombardment had lasted more than seven hours, with a large quantity of shells consumed, and although observers from the ships and aircraft had concluded that the four forts had appeared to have been devastated by explosions, the smoke and earth thrown in the air actually masked what was soon realized as ineffective shelling. It was to be a portent of what was to follow during the next month. In reply, the Ertugrul Battery had fired only six rounds and Orhaniye perhaps twenty-one rounds, but after the massive Allied barrage, the Turkish and German casualties were only ten killed, including German Navy Lieutenant Woerman, as the artillerymen had sheltered from the beginning of the action until running to the guns late in the afternoon.

Ertugrul Fort after its capture and being used as a wagon park. Note that the closest of the two Krupp 240mm guns is still emplaced, although the sliding breech has been removed. Steaming past in the background is the French pre-dreadnought *Henri IV*. (Courtesy of the National Museum of the Royal Navy)

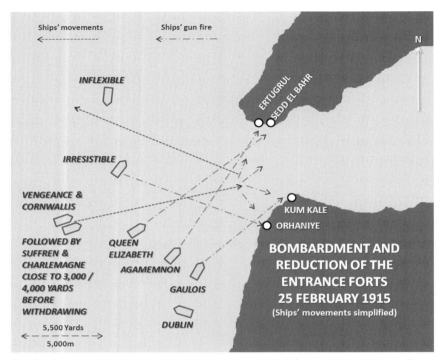

Bombardment and Reduction of the Entrance Forts – 25 February 1915. (© Forrest)

25 February 1915

Admiral Carden reported:

> The result of the day's action of 19 February showed apparently that the effect of long-range bombardment by direct fire on modern earthwork forts is slight.

He changed his plan for the next attack which was not until the 25 February, having been delayed due to bad weather conditions. This day was clear and bright, well suited to observing the fall of shells. The attack was to be at long range to start with, then at long and short range simultaneously, so as to dominate the forts while the more accurate fire from the closing ships reduced them. Four ships were anchored in a long arc off the entrance to the Dardanelles, each with a specific target: *Queen*

Elizabeth 11,600 yards south-west of Cape Helles; *Agamemnon* between her and the Asian coast, 10,000 yards from Ertugrul; *Irresistible* 11,500 yards west of Orhaniye; and *Gaulois* 7,500 yards from Kum Kale but close-in to the Asian shore so that her fire was almost indirect. Four other ships were to work as pairs – *Vengeance* with *Cornwallis*, *Charlemagne* with *Suffren* – to close within 3,000 yards of the forts. Admiral Carden in *Inflexible*, west of Cape Helles, issued an operation order that instructed *Agamemnon* to use three-quarter charges for her 9.2-inch and 12-inch guns; likewise *Queen Elizabeth* for her 15-inch guns; and *Irresistible* to use full charges for her 12-inch guns. The light cruiser *Dublin* steamed slowly off the Asian coast, tasked to spot for the *Queen Elizabeth*. Firing began just after 1000 hrs but, unlike 19 February, the forts began to reply almost immediately with accurate fire. The two 240mm L/35 guns at Ertugrul quickly found *Agamemnon* and she was hit amidships, then six more times in just a few minutes as she up-anchored to steam out of range. The total casualties were surprisingly light, just three killed and seven

Fragments of Turkish cast iron shells. The reverse of this postcard is inscribed: HMS *Agamemnon*. Pieces of Turkish shell fragments picked up onboard after an engagement. CPO T. Frost. (Author's collection)

seriously wounded. The damage to the ship was not serious as some of the shells hit the superstructure and others broke up on impact, while the armour-piercing shells punched holes through the ship's plates but without causing severe explosions. These had plunged from a high angle due to the extreme elevation of the Turkish guns, and should have caused more damage but were the 'Old' type non-capped shells. Had they been the 'New' type armour-piercing or high explosive shells, streamlined and with a greater amount of explosive filling, then they would have certainly wreaked far more havoc (see Appendix Nine, Shells, Fillings, Fuses and Charges). As *Agamemnon* retired, so the Ertugrul shifted its attention to *Dublin*, which was also being targeted by a field gun ashore. *Dublin* was ordered out of the range of fire, so Ertugrul switched target again, swiftly straddling the *Gaulois*, which had been firing on Kum Kale. The *Gaulois* responded by directing her fire at Ertugrul, and *Inflexible* took on the observation role for the *Queen Elizabeth*, which was also firing on this two-gun battery. The *Queen Elizabeth's* guns took time to find the range and it was not until her sixteenth and seventeenth rounds that she scored direct hits, one of which dismounted one of the Krupp guns. *Agamemnon* returned to the fray, again firing on Ertugrul, so that the plucky battery was finally put out of action and the barracks to the rear was destroyed. The *Agamemnon* fired a total of 123 rounds during the action from her 9.2-inch guns, only twelve of which used Lyddite as a bursting charge, the others being powder-filled (see Appendix Nine, Shells, Fillings, Fuses and Charges). The forts and field guns replied with fifty-six shells against her.

At 1215 hrs, Admiral Carden ordered the first fast run-in against the now silent forts, with *Vengeance* leading *Cornwallis* by five cables (approximately 1,000 yards), heading directly for the entrance of the Strait and firing as they did so. The *Vengeance* turned sharply to port at 4,000 yards from the forts, the *Cornwallis* following in a wider arc three minutes later, firing as the guns bore on Orhaniye and Ertugrul, neither of which replied. The run was successfully completed by 1322 hrs, so Admiral Carden signalled that the *Suffren* and *Charlemagne* were to make the second run, which began at 1410 hrs. The French ships came in at 12 knots, firing from 9,000 yards until the range was down to 3,000 yards, when they each turned to port and steamed out of the firing zone. There had been only one ineffective return shot fired from Kum Kale. The action had been entirely successful as the Ertugrul guns had been disabled beyond repair, almost all of those at Sedd el Bahr and Kum Kale were out of action, and one gun at Orhaniye was smashed and the other disabled.

At just after 1500 hrs, minesweeping trawlers approached the entrance to the Dardanelles and went almost unmolested, apart from sporadic and inaccurate fire, being covered by *Albion* on the Asian shore and *Triumph* on the Helles shore. The minesweepers worked through the night, from the entrance to 4 miles up the Strait, but no mines were discovered. In fact, this was because there was not a minefield at the entrance of the Dardanelles at all; a British map (reference: Map M-78-000266 – Imperial war Museum / Western Front Association) dated February 1914 incorrectly shows a line of sixty-one mines across the entrance between

The barrel of a Krupp 240mm L/35 and the remains of its mounting at the Ertugrul Battery facing directly across the entrance to the Dardanelles. (© Forrest)

La Guerre 1914-1915
Visé Paris 317

AUX DARDANELLES
La flotte alliée – Vue des hauteurs du fort détruit de SÉDUL-BAHR

A French postcard of Sedd el Bahr during the Allied occupation, showing a destroyed Krupp L/22 gun. Offshore are two destroyers, a transport, a Canopus class pre-dreadnought (two funnels with smoke) and either *Lord Nelson* or *Agamemnon* directly in line with the gun. (Author's collection)

Sedd el Bahr and Kum Kale, which may explain why minesweepers were employed here.

26 February 1915

The minesweepers returned during the morning of 26 February accompanied by four destroyers and three pre-dreadnoughts – *Albion*, *Majestic* and *Triumph*. The battleships steamed through the entrance of the Strait, firing at the forts with their secondary armaments but without reply, with *Albion* targeting an observation post at the old de Tott's Battery and a supposed shore-launched torpedo position. At the limit of the swept area the ships began to fire with their main armament at Dardanos (Fort No. 8) some 12,500 yards away. The distance was within range of the aged ships' guns but close to the maximum, so the elevation was at high-angle and the shots inaccurate; the battery was undamaged, contrary to British reports. The Dardanos Battery was equipped with five Krupp 150mm SK

L/40 quick-firers in traversing armoured turrets with a range of 13,800m (15,000 yards) at maximum elevation of 20 degrees. The range quoted was when the guns were new but as these ex-ships' guns dated from the 1890s, the range of them was probably less than ideal, although still just enough to have replied to the incoming fire. Dardanos did not fire at all that day but unseen howitzers and field guns did reply to the shelling; constantly making the ships change position. The minesweepers worked in pairs close to the Asian shore, concentrating in the area of Karanlik Bay, yet sweeping an area that was actually devoid of mines. The Turkish gunners did not trouble the minesweepers on this occasion, probably amused at the fruitless work and sensibly wishing to conserve their ammunition. Two destroyers ventured farther into the Strait toward Kepez Point as if to invite a response, possibly unaware that they were fast approaching the southernmost line of mines. The destroyers were in range of Narrows forts but did not present a sufficiently valuable target for the big guns emplaced there, but were fired on by closer shore batteries, so turned away without taking damage. All ships were recalled late in the afternoon but *Majestic* had received a small-calibre hit below the waterline, although it was not serious and did not put the ship out of action. The Dardanelles had been patterned with buoys that acted as range markers for the shore guns, and these were promptly sunk wherever they were found.

A Naval Signal from VAEMS (Vice Admiral Eastern Mediterranean Squadron) to 'Courbet' (presumably a code name as French Courbet class vessels were serving with the 1st Armée Navale in the Mediterranean at this time, although Admiral Lapeyrere's flagship *Jean Bart* had been torpedoed in December 1914 and was in Malta for repairs) dated 27 February summed up the events of the day, although it incorrectly mentions *Vengeance* not *Triumph*:

> Sweeping carried out inside Straits up to 4 miles from entrance. No mines found. *Albion* and *Majestic* supported by *Vengeance* entered to limit of swept area shelling fort No. 8 and new battery on Asiatic shore. Firing ineffective from Fort 8, which was hit several times by *Albion*. Two batteries apparently 6-inch and some field guns on hill SW of Arin Kioi caused considerable annoyance and small material damage but no casulties. Aerial reconnaissance having

failed to locate these batteries in the morning these will be destroyed tomorrow.

March 1915

On 1 March, the same pattern of attack as 26 February was employed, achieving the same frustrating results. This time *Albion* and *Triumph* fired on Dardanos while *Majestic* and *Ocean* engaged the mobile guns with secondary armament, often close enough to the shore to use the ship's 12pr QF quick-firers. Another penetration into the Strait was made on the afternoon of 2 March with three different pre-dreadnoughts – *Canopus*, *Cornwallis* and *Swiftsure* – using a new attack route close the Asian coast, so providing less clear targets for the howitzers. Dardanos came under intense fire for more than two hours and did not reply until 1615 hrs, accurately targeting *Canopus*, which took three hits, including one that wrecked the wardroom. All three ships had sustained only light damage and slight causalities, but decided to withdraw.

A 210mm mortar of the type used by the Turks to defend the Dardanelles, although this photograph from 1911 shows a German gun crew. (Author's collection)

A relief sculpture at the base of the Turkish Martyrs' Memorial at Eski Hisarlik Burnu showing Turkish gunners in action. (© Forrest)

Similar operations continued on other days but any Allied ship incursion into the Dardanelles brought a hail of return fire from various calibre field guns, howitzers and 210mm mortars. The latter had considerable punch with a shell weighing 120kg, but there were only a small number of them and they had limited range. However, the range of the Rumeli Mesudiye Battery (Fort No. 7) on the Gallipoli shore, comprising three 6-inch/45 ship's guns from the sunken *Mesudiye*, covered the entire width of the Strait. The majority of the guns set up in the shore batteries were firing shells weighing from 7kg to 45kg, and although the shell type and burster charges were insufficient to mortally damage the armour-plated warships, they were serious enough to kill sailors and damage open gun positions. While their effectiveness was harassment for the capital ships by discouraging them from anchoring to stabilize their own fire, it was to prove deadly against the minesweepers that were tasked to clear a passage for the big ships.

On 5 March, the *Queen Elizabeth* began the indirect shelling of the Narrows forts by anchoring out to sea, west of the Gaba Tepe headland, firing her 15-inch guns at a range of approximately 18,500 yards. Three ships were selected to enter the Strait to spot and communicate the fall of the shells – *Cornwallis*, *Irresistible* and *Canopus* – but because of the harassing fire from the shore batteries they could not anchor, so would run up the Strait in succession at twelve-minute intervals, turning 5 miles south of Kepez to run back down. Two observation aircraft were to supplement each ship's report but one crashed due to engine failure, while the pilot of the second aircraft was wounded by ground fire and returned to base. At noon, the *Queen Elizabeth* began to fire on Rumeli Mecidiye (Fort No. 13), and after eighteen rounds began to accurately drop shells into the fort. After ten more rounds she redirected her fire at Namazgah (Fort No. 17), but after only five rounds hit Rumeli Hamidiye (Fort No. 16) instead, midway between the two other forts, as a large explosion was seen at this location.

Indirect shelling was resumed on 6 March, targeting Cimenlik Kalesi (Fort No. 20) but this time with only *Albion* spotting from a stationary position in what was determined as 'dead water', free from enemy fire as it was close to the Gallipoli shore. The *Queen Elizabeth* and *Albion* were protected by other capital ships, both in the Strait and off Gaba Tepe, but the results of the shelling were disappointing. A Naval Signal from VAEMS dated 7 March describes the action of the day before:

> Operations 6 March *Queen Elizabeth* supported by *Agamemnon* and *Ocean* continued indirect bombardment of Fort No. 20 but owing to interference from howitzers who found her range at once and made accurate shooting she was obliged to shift berth twice, finally to position 2,100 yards from front attack. In consequence she only fired eight rounds. Howitzers could not be located and seaplanes owing to engine trouble were unable to reach sufficient height for observation. Ships inside Straits – *Vengeance*, *Albion*, *Majestic*, *Prince George*, who fired on batteries 7 and 8 and were fired on... one was hit by 12-inch shell. *Queen Elizabeth* and majority of ships inside were hit but suffered no serious damage and no casualties.

On 7 March, five battleships entered the Strait, each with selected targets, *Charlemagne, Suffren* and *Gaulois* on the Gallipoli side targeting Dardanos and howitzer batteries at Erenkoi village, and *Agamemnon* and *Lord Nelson* firing at Rumeli Mecidiye and Anadolu Hamidiye. The two British ships followed the French, passing them as they slowed to engage the shore batteries, steaming directly toward the Narrows and commenced firing at 1230 hrs, with their forward guns at a distance of 14,000 yards. At 12,000 yards, they each turned starboard across the Strait to fire broadsides. Chief Petty Officer Young of the *Agamemnon* recorded in his diary (referring to his ship and the *Lord Nelson*):

> *'Aggie'* and *'Nelson'* had been ordered to bombard forts No. 13 & 19 in the Narrows. We expended more ammunition in the two hours that we have all the time up here: seventy-six rounds 12-inch & 145 rounds 9.2-inch. Total weight of metal being about 53 tons. Not a bad afternoon's work for a day of rest. It doesn't seem quite the English style to choose a Sunday to try and murder each other. Perhaps they thought the Turk followed the line of some of us, in bed Sunday afternoon and so catch him napping.

Yet the Turkish and German gunners were not napping. Their return fire was accurate and concentrated, straddling the ships and deluging the decks from huge columns of water thrown up by the salvos of shells. Captain Herbert Fyler of the *Agamemnon* described the return firing from Rumeli Mecidiye (Fort No. 13) and Anadolu Hamidiye (Fort No. 19) in his report dated the 8 March:

> At 12.40 pm Fort No. 13 opened fire with four heavy guns and five minutes later hit the ship. At 12.50 pm. Fort No. 19 opened fire with five heavy guns. The firing was then heavy, accurate and well directed and projectiles from both Forts were ranging up to 14,500 yards. Much annoyance was also caused by 6-inch howitzers and numerous Field Gun Batteries. The time of flight of the heavy guns was thirty-five seconds and the angle of descent about 30 degrees. The shells

burst well and into very minute fragments, highly dangerous
in exposed positions, but failing to penetrate any thickness
of metal. At 1.33 pm the ship was again struck by a 9.4-inch
or heavier projectile and ten minutes later a shell (probably
a 14-inch) struck and went through the Quarterdeck, making
a hole 16 feet round, into the Wardroom, wrecking it and the
Gun Room below.

Although *Agamemnon* was struck by at least eight shells, amazingly, no
serious damage or casualties were sustained. The *Lord Nelson* was also
struck several times, including being hit in a bunker above and below the
waterline, and had to steam to Mudros for repairs.

Minesweeping

Although the sea mine had been introduced decades earlier, minesweeping
was in its infancy at the beginning of the First World War and the earliest
Royal Navy minesweepers were not specifically designed for the task, being
converted North Sea trawlers. Manned by civilians from the Royal Navy
Reserve Trawler Section, the RNR(T), the crews were experienced to the
hard work as trawler men and therefore believed in their own capacity to
trawl for mines. Hundreds of such vessels were successfully employed in
keeping the waters around the British Isles free of mines, although there
were losses due to the hazards of the job. The minefield of the Dardanelles
had to be cleared, so this task required the trawler minesweepers. As tough
as the trawler men were, not surprisingly, they baulked at the job when they
came under fire from the shore guns. Royal Navy volunteers were to later
take over the mission, some from the large resource of crews of those ships
lost on 18 March 1915, but as the minesweepers were progressively
damaged, destroyed or just became unserviceable, so the minefield
remained almost completely intact. The RNR(T) in the Dardanelles were
formed as three groups – two from Lowestoft and one from Grimsby –
twenty-one vessels in all, supported by up to twenty-four French
minesweeping trawlers, but not all arrived, and by 18 March 1915, only
about half of those that had were still operational.

The trawlers were relatively small vessels at 200 to 220 tons gross and
110 to 120 feet long, but with a wide beam of 20 to 24 feet to contain the

The minesweeping trawler *Star of Empire* (No. 318) full troops and en-route to X Beach on 25 April 1915. In the background is HMS *Implacable*, which arrived off the Dardanelles on 23 March 1915. (Courtesy of the National Museum of the Royal Navy)

catch when fulfilling their intended purpose. The trawlers were modified with armour plating protection but this added considerable weight to them, so that a vessel's plodding three-cylinder steam engine, which had not been upgraded, was strained even before they tackled the Dardanelles' strong out-flowing current. Therefore, the minesweeping trawlers moved very slowly and offered good targets to the shore gunners. The minesweeping actions were always supported with destroyer and heavier escorts, but early activities of sweeping at the entrance to the Dardanelles were entirely fruitless as it had been carried out where there were no mines located. The trawlers worked in pairs 500 yards apart, dragging 2.5-inch diameter steel cable between them supported by water kites to maintain the cable depth. Once a mine was caught, the trawlers had to try dragging it out of the field into shallow water or breaking the securing cable so the mine would surface to be destroyed by rifle fire. Ideally steaming as overlapping pairs to form a staggered sweep, this was rarely possible because of the constant artillery harassment, and the process was generally ragged, if it progressed at all. The draft of the trawlers meant that they could be as vulnerable as any other vessel operating in the minefield.

From 1 March, minesweeping switched to a night-time operation, and on that night seven trawlers (three pairs and a leader) with five escorts, one of which was the light cruiser *Amethyst*, were employed. The trawlers were picked up by searchlights and then came under fire from the shore batteries, causing panic amongst the crews and a rapid retreat. The searchlights were to be the curse of the night operations, but were to become targets themselves from the protecting destroyers. Searchlights on mobile mountings could shift position, switching on, switching off, and then popping up at a different location a short time later to repeat the process. On the night of 3 March, another attempt at sweeping was made, but the efforts were wasted as no mines were collected. Yet as the almost nightly sweeping operations persisted, some successes were achieved, such as on the night of 11 March, when three mines were destroyed. It took a considerable time to reach and sweep the mines against the strong current, so a new technique of entering the lower extent of the minefield, turning the vessels, attaching the sweeper gear and then sweeping with the current was attempted. This method was equally fraught as on 11 March, the *Manx Hero* (No. 339) was destroyed by a mine it had just collected as it swept down on her stern. As the number of trawler minesweepers reduced, so smaller and slightly faster Royal Navy picket boats were employed towing explosive charges to try to cut the mine cables. These 50-foot long steam-powered boats were multi-purpose launches, equally known as a Pinnace, which were little workhorses for the larger ships as they acted as ferries and communication vessels.

The French also attempted sweeping operations using their own converted vessels fitted with cable cutters, but these also proved entirely unsuitable for the task and were quickly withdrawn. In the early hours of 14 March, *Amethyst* was hit and sustained more than fifty casualties, half of whom were killed. Daylight sweeping resumed after two weeks of poor night-time results.

Another problem that hampered the minesweeping efforts was establishing the actual location of those mines that had been cleared, as darkness, incoming fire, disorientation and the strong current, all served to often baffle the crews and confuse the planners trying to gauge where the gaps had been created. It is possible that some of the mines in the line laid by the *Nusret* on 7/8 March in Erenkoi Bay were swept up but none of the minesweeper crews could identify this location. If they had, then this decisive obstacle may have been eliminated before the massed battleship assault, and possibly may have changed the entire course of events. In fact, in the three weeks prior to the Allied attack on 18 March 1915, only twelve mines were destroyed by sweeping, representing a wholly inadequate return for all the efforts and losses sustained. The task was made virtually impossible by the inadequacies of the equipment employed and the tenacity of the Turkish gunners manning the howitzer and field gun batteries. Often, the guns that were in action against the sweepers at night had been moved to a new position by the following day. It was hard enough to identify their positions during the night engagements, so when Allied ships came back to shell them during the day the guns could be miles away, frequently firing from the far side of a hill so that they could not be spotted in daylight at all. The Turks further confounded the fire controllers on the ships by using dummy guns, steel tubes that would puff smoke during daylight actions.

Beagle class destroyers had arrived off the Dardanelles early in the campaign but half of them were despatched back to Britain in November 1914, some going for refitting and others as channel escorts for a few months. However, the needs for better minesweeping determined that all sixteen of this class of vessel were fitted with sweeping gear, being despatched to Malta in pairs for the work to be done and arriving back off the Dardanelles between early to mid-April 1915. The Beagle class destroyers were the last of the type built with coal-fired engines driving steam turbines and capable of 27 knots. Their speed reduced when dragging the sweep but the vessels still had the power to act as competent minesweepers. Displacing between 860 to 940 tons, with dimensions of 275 feet by 28 feet beam, and armed with three 12pr quick-firers and a 4-inch Mk VIII/40 gun, they were small but energetic fighting vessels to take on the shore batteries. As with the trawlers, the destroyers worked in pairs for sweeping, each ship dragging a water kite, the kites linked by the sweep wire.

During the landings of 25 April 1915, and under cover of *Albion* and *Cornwallis*, which had entered the Dardanelles to shell shore batteries further up the Strait, ten destroyers began sweeping under the charge of Captain Prentiss in *Wolverine*. On the following day the *Agamemnon* went to the limit of the minefield to shell ships at anchor at Canakkale, and suddenly the accompanying destroyers swept up three mines that bobbed to the surface 300 to 400 yards ahead of the battleship. Midshipman Henry Denham aboard the *Agamemnon* described them as 'pretty new mines, copper, fairly bright and very big', and that everyone blazed away at them, exploding one but sinking the other two. He noted that the shore batteries had not fired on the *Agamemnon*, as if to lure her into the minefield. On the following day destroyers went further up the Strait but caught only one mine, which exploded in the sweep near to *Grampus*. During a similar sweeping operation on 28 April, *Wolverine's* bridge was a hit by a shrapnel shell, wrecking the bridge and killing the captain. Sweeping with the destroyers continued for the next week but they accounted for only a few more mines.

In addition to the minesweeping destroyers, requisitioned commercial cross-channel ferries were also used as Fleet Sweepers, becoming known as HM Minesweepers *Newmarket*, *Hythe*, *Reindeer* and *Clacton*. Armed with two 12pr quick-firers for defence, these vessels were not used exclusively in this role but also as general cargo and troop carriers. Although all the minesweepers and destroyers exercised as a flotilla, practising to clear the Dardanelles minefield in a concerted effort that would be integral to another attempt to force the Dardanelles, they were never actually to attempt to do so. Harold Tumman of HMS *Harpy* wrote in his journal:

> Sunday 9 May 8.00 am. Coaled from collier; 130 tons after which we joined up with *Amethyst* (Capt. D) and remainder of flotilla, on south side of Imbros Island, and exercised general minesweeping, in preparation for our impending rush through the 'Narrows' (which, by the way, shows no immediate prospect of materialising).

Once the idea of the fleet forcing its way through to the Sea of Marmara was abandoned the destroyer's role as a minesweeper was essentially over in the Dardanelles. The Royal Navy's first purpose-built minesweeping sloops – the Flower class – began operations in mid-1915, but none were deployed to the Dardanelles.

Landing parties

After the naval bombardment on 25 February, and when weather permitted, Allied landing parties of marines and sailors went ashore both at Cape Helles and at Kum Kale, clearing the forts of any defenders and to destroy what guns, ammunition and equipment remained. At first they were able to move with comparative ease but for irregular shots from the few remaining Turkish troops who had pulled some distance back, but resistance progressively stiffened. On 26 February, a combined force of marines and sailors from the *Vengeance* were landed at the pier close to the ruin of Kum Kale, and was soon in action

A heroic image of a Royal Marine landing party in action. (*The War Illustrated*, April 1915)

against Turkish soldiers, apparently backed up by Germans. It was on this occasion that the only Victoria Cross for attacking the Dardanelles forts was awarded. Lieutenant Commander Eric Gascoigne Robinson led a demolition party toward the Orhaniye Battery, tasked to ensure the destruction of the 240mm L/35 guns and also two new artillery pieces that had been located from the air. The sailors' white uniforms made them easy targets for the Turkish defenders who, although some distance off, were still able to provide accurate rifle fire. The light cruiser *Dublin* shelled windmills close to the village of Yeni Shehr, directly ahead of Robinson's party, to reduce some of the resistance, but flanking fire from inland still persisted. Robinson pushed his men on using all available cover to reach the artillery battery, which was unmanned, the gunners having fled, although that was not immediately known to him. To avoid taking casualties from snipers Robinson went on alone to lay the charges, returning for more and making the approach a second time. He was said to be 'Strolling around ... under heavy rifle fire. Like a sparrow enjoying a bath from a garden hose.'

With the guns destroyed the party pushed on, discovering that Orhaniye was deserted, but one of the two Krupp coastal guns could still operate, so the mounting of this gun was blown up. Robinson's bravery for this action, and for further acts of valour including the later attack in a picket boat on the grounded and captured British submarine *E15,* was recognized with the award of a Victoria Cross. *The London Gazette,* dated 13 August 1915, recorded the following entry:

> Lieutenant Commander Robinson on 26 February advanced alone, under heavy fire, into an enemy's gun position, which might well have been occupied, and destroying a 4-inch gun returned to his party for another charge with which the second gun was destroyed. Lieutenant Commander Robinson would not allow members of his demolition party to accompany him as their white uniforms rendered them very conspicuous. Lieutenant Commander Robinson took part in four attacks on the mine fields - always under heavy fire.

A Naval Signal from VAEMS to 'Courbet' dated 27 February stated:

> Demolishing parties were landed at 2.30 pm from *Vengeance* and *Irresistible* at Kum Kale and Sedd el Bahr respectively as the enemy had been seen retiring from these localities. After having been shelled from inside Straits, forts No. 3 and 4 were demolished, No. 6 partially. Two new 4-inch guns concealed near tomb of Achilles[1] were destroyed. These had been firing on our ships and minesweepers and could not be located. Four Nordenfield [sic] guns covering entrance were destroyed. Enemy encountered in Kum Kale village were driven out over Mendere Bridge which was partially destroyed. Our casualties here one killed, three wounded.

In another incident on the same day, men from *Irresistible* and *Vengeance* were injured by flying debris when a charge laid at the Ertugrul Battery was fired before they had retired to safety. Surprisingly, after the severe bombardment, four of the coastal guns at Sedd el Bahr were found intact before being blown up with explosive charges. A battery of six field guns located in the east-facing arches of the old fort were discovered and destroyed. In the book *History of the Great War: Naval Operations Volume II* by Sir Julian S. Corbett the guns are described as '15-pounder field guns'; they were probably Krupp 75mm L/30s, which fired a 14.5lb shell (nominal).

Turkish soldiers were never very far from the positions they had vacated and constantly sniped at the landing parties, and as time passed so their confidence increased and they became bolder. After days of poor weather, the 4 March dawned a beautiful day, with no wind and a cloudless sky, so another major landing action was put in progress, but it was one that the Turks expected and were determined to repel. Navy boats were mustered – picket boats pulling cutters – and set off for the two shorelines, a company of marines and a navy demolition party for each. Attendant warships shelled the ruins of the forts yet again, hopefully driving out the defenders who percolated back after the previous incursion. A demolition party from the *Lord Nelson* led by Lieutenant Commander Dodgson was instructed to destroy the immobile but serviceable Krupp 240mm at Orhaniye, which although now jammed and unable to traverse because of the damage to its mounting, could still fire. The landing party made slow progress, being powerless to climb the hill to the battery due to enemy fire until the area had been cleared, and it took several hours to achieve this objective. The village of Yeni Shehr, just south of Orhaniye, which had been set ablaze on previous occasions, was targeted yet again by the ships as mobile howitzers were emplaced and the whole area was alive with Turkish troops. The assault toward Orhaniye moved slowly on but the resistance increased, much of the rifle fire coming from the fortification itself. It was clear that the objective could not be reached, so a retreat was ordered by Colonel Mathews commanding the marines, with reserves covering the withdrawal. The evacuation was under continuous fire and recovery of wounded men from Kum Kale carried on until after dark. The operation had entirely failed, costing seventeen men killed, twenty-four wounded and three missing.

Things were no better at Sedd el Bahr. After landing at the camber close to the fort, the marines had spread out but met fierce opposition in the village and ruins of the castle. Turkish soldier Sergeant 'Mehmet' (a generic name applied to the Turkish soldier, similar to the British 'Tommy Atkins') was to say after the action:

> I was on duty with my squad. The enemy ships started to land after they had bombarded the coast intensely. Meanwhile we got off the place where we had been concealed, lay down and started to fire at the enemy. The enemy was also lying down and firing at us. We were very close to each other. For a while the mechanism of my gun did not work. Because of the anger, I threw the gun. Seeing this, an enemy soldier stood up and started to fire at me. Immediately, I drew my fortification shovel and attacked him. I didn't remember how many people I hit. When I opened my eyes, I was in a tent of sanitary.

Chief Petty Officer Young of *Agamemnon* reported a similar incident in his diary:

> A Sergeant of Marines got detached and was wounded. Others went to his assistance but before they could reach him a polite Turk came out of a house and bashed his head in with the butt end of his rifle. It will be pleasant to fall into the hands of the Turks apparently.

The marines and sailors withdrew under cover of a bombardment from the ships. Two Nordenfeldt machine guns were destroyed, but the raid cost the lives of three men.

Notes

1. The tomb of Achilles is a tumulus, a short distance behind Orhaniye, known as Kum Tepe. Heinrich Schliemann, the archaeological excavator of the ruins of Troy in the 1870s, identified this as the tomb of Achilles but there is also a larger tumulus known as Kesik Tepe, located 2.5km south of the Orhaniye Battery, where it is believed that Alexander the Great sacrificed to Achilles on his way to Troy.

CHAPTER 6

The Reduction of the Fortifications – The Hammer and the Anvil

German and Turkish gun crews

As soon as the Germans had arrived in the Dardanelles they had taken on many of the gunnery responsibilities, both assisting the Turks to improve their skills and providing the control and discipline required for effective gun crews. However, not all forts and gun batteries were manned by Germans, Turkish gunners being by far the greater majority, but there was a large German contingent at Anadolu Hamidiye under the command of Captain Wossidlo. An American journalist, whose name is unfortunately not recorded, wrote an article about his experiences in Canakkale in 1915 that was reproduced in 1938 as 'Yesterday's Wrong Turning':

> For a month I had wasted my time…. My only profit was to polish up on my German with the German officers and gunners in the forts. These Germans were restless, too. They had volunteered 'for hazardous service, place unspecified' and had made the unexpected trip to far away Constantinople. But all they had experienced of hazard had been at the card table. They were a breezy lot. They manned the five long-range guns in the Dardanelles defences, 14-inch cannon which fired behind earthwork, and fourteen 9-inch, equally older guns with shorter range. The Turks had, in all,

ten forts but only three with any pretensions, and only nineteen guns were worth the concerns of a modern fleet. All nineteen were in charge by these pleasant, impatient Germans.

While the gunners were sure their biggest guns could sink a battleship at 14,000 yards, they did not believe they could hold the Narrows against a determined attack. On that score there was no pussy-footing. The job, as they saw it, was to make the attack as costly as they could.

It was no secret that the forts were short of ammunition. The fact wasn't advertised, but we newspaper men knew it. We knew that the shells had been ordered, but in good Turkish fashion were slow in coming. We knew that the supply on hand was hardly enough for one day's good fighting.

But all of us, Germans and Turks and neutrals, had began to doubt that the Allies were coming. Their activities were not being pushed.... But the Germans were elated because it wasn't aggressive work. They had come to think that they had frightened the British naval leadership.

The Dardanelles defences were visited by Henry Morgenthau, American Ambassador to Constantinople, on 16 March 1915 at the suggestion of Enver Pasha. Morgenthau was escorted by Colonel Djevad Pasha to Anadolu Hamidiye, describing the fort's location as 'ideal' because of its clear view to the entrance to the Dardanelles. He was not impressed with the earth construction of the fort or with the elderly guns with their 'rusted exteriors', and believed that the stock of ammunition was low. At the Dardanos Battery he was puzzled by the fact that the Allied fleet, despite its large expenditures of ammunition, had not been able to hit it, although, 'The land for nearly half-a-mile around it had been completely churned up.'

The Ambassador assumed that this was because of poor gunnery, but a German officer who was a part of the tour believed that it was actually due to the hilltop location of the battery, as a skyline target is hard to hit due to the mirage effect. Morgenthau later recorded that about 4,000 shells

A photograph of activity at Anadolu Hamidiye. Note the officers in fezzes to the left and what appear to be neat stacks of rifles to the right. In the centre distance is Cimenlik Kalesi. (Author's collection)

were fired at the battery, up to and including 18 March 1915, and that the gun turrets received only superficial damage. However, eight gunners were killed, including the battery commander, Lieutenant Hasan, and his deputy, Second Lieutenant Mevsuf. The battery's name was later changed to Hasan Mevsuf in commemoration of the men.

Travelling further south on the Asian side of the Strait, the Ambassador visited another battery located on the unseen reverse of a hill near Erenkoi village, one of a number of batteries in this area where Krupp howitzers were located. He described that there were more concrete gun positions than guns themselves, as the guns were regularly moved from one emplacement to another as soon as the fleet obtained any accuracy, and that he saw a team of sixteen buffalo moving a howitzer. He was also shown one of the dummy guns that frequently fooled the naval fire control officers: an elongated section of sewer pipe. The gunner in charge of this 'contraption' was linked by telephone to a real howitzer team:

> When the command came to fire, the gunner in charge of the howitzer would discharge his shell, while the man in charge of the sewer pipe would burn several pounds of black powder and send forth a conspicuous cloud of inky smoke.

Later the same day Henry Morgenthau crossed from Canakkale to Kilid Bahr to visit the Namazgah fort, Rumeli Hamidiye and possibly Rumeli Mecidiye:

> The batteries showed signs of heavy bombardment. None had been destroyed, but shell holes surrounded the fortifications.

He described a show drill put on by the Turkish artillerymen, and to the command of a bugle call, they all rushed to their positions:

> Some were bringing shells, others were opening the breeches, others were taking the ranges, others were straining at the pulleys, and others were putting the charges into place. Everything was eagerness and activity.... Above the shouts of all I could hear the singsong chant of the leader, intoning the prayer with which the Moslem has rushed to battle for thirteen centuries.

Ambassador Morgenthau began the return journey to Istanbul that evening, 16 March. Two days later, the Allied ships attacked in force.

18 March 1915

The British commanders had recognized the conundrum with which they were faced: the minefield had to be cleared to allow the Allied ships to break through the Dardanelles and into the Sea of Marmara, but the fortress guns and mobile defences either side of the Strait had to be destroyed before the minesweepers could operate successfully. Admiral Carden was under pressure from Winston Churchill to carry the fight forward regardless of the difficulties so far encountered, but Carden was ill with worry and the strain of command. On 15 March 1915, he stood down and was succeeded by Admiral John de Robeck, who was fully conversant with the situation, having been off the Dardanelles since the beginning of February. The attack was scheduled for 18 March.

Intelligence reports indicated that the Turkish guns of all sizes were so very short of ammunition that they could not maintain an effective defence for very much longer; just one big assault – a hammer blow – on the defences would be sufficient to finally destroy any resistance. The ships were to be organized in divisions or lines, co-ordinated waves of heavy fire on the defences, so furious that they would quickly give up. To ensure the destruction of the Narrows forts, some of the battleships had to hold their positions against the current to ensure accuracy of fire, while others steamed to the very edge of the minefield before turning away to allow another wave of ships to attack. Secondary guns were to engage the howitzers and field guns on the flanks of the assault, thereby allowing the minesweepers to proceed. It was a spectacular plan involving sixteen capital ships entering the Dardanelles: nearly a quarter of a million tons of battleships and seventy ships' guns of 10-inch (254mm) or more, plus all the smaller calibre secondary armament. It was hoped that after two hours of bombardment the Turkish guns would have been sufficiently neutralized to allow minesweeping to commence, clearing a passage 900 yards (820m) wide on the Asian side.

The day before the attack the minefield was inspected from the air and a 'general' signal was sent from VAEMS dated 17 March 1915 at 1750 hrs:

> Seaplane over Narrows at 11:45 reports only seven of the mines reported yesterday SE from Suandere River now in place and in shoreward appear to have dragged further towards entrance. They show a wash on surface and do not appear to be very deep, nothing observed south of these off white cliff. Four mines Kepez Point, four mines in Sarisiglar Bay running NW to SE south of *Messaudieh*, no mines seen running SE from fort 13 but large steamboat in this neighbourhood, picket boat as usual off Suandere River, large steamer similar in appearance to hospital ship painted with two white funnels and four small craft in Dardan Bay. Salvage operations appear to still be in progress on *Saphir*. Minefields north of Narrows not examined.

The location of 'Dardan Bay' may be the northern end of Erenkoi Bay, under the guns of the Dardanos Battery. The references to the 'Messaudieh' and 'Saphir' relate to the Mesudiye, the old ironclad sunk by torpedo in December 1914, and the French submarine Saphir that ran aground off Nagara Point in January 1915. The last sentence of the signal is interesting but maybe misleading as it states that the 'Minefield north of the Narrows not examined'; other than the line from Degirmen Burnu to Canakkale lighthouse, there was no minefield north of the Narrows at this time. From the tone of the signal, one wonders if the VAEMS and his staff understood how formidable the minefield still was. Minesweeping had been carried out in the area the ships were to operate and it was reported as clear of mines. This was as close as 8,000 yards from the Narrows, which was the limit of the known minefield, but picket boats, each armed with a quick-firing 3pr gun, were to accompany each battleship to guard against mines drifting down on the current.

The day of 18 March 1915 was clear and bright, giving perfect conditions for the attack. The First Division, comprising the *Queen Elizabeth* carrying Admiral de Robeck's flag – *Agamemnon, Lord Nelson* and *Inflexible* – was to enter first and take station 14,000 yards from the Narrows to shell the forts there from long range. The Third Division, comprising the French ships *Gaulois, Charlemagne, Bouvet* and *Suffren,* were to hold at 16,000 yards until the forts were dominated, then pass through the First Division up to the limit of the swept area and commence firing at the Narrows forts at closer range. The French ships were to be relieved by ships of the Second Division – *Vengeance, Irresistible, Albion* and *Ocean.* The *Prince George* and *Triumph* would be on the flanks at 15,000 yards taking on Rumeli Mesudiye, Yildiz and Dardanos with their main armament, while suppressing the howitzers and field guns in the hills either side of the Strait with their secondary guns, with *Majestic* and *Swiftsure* supporting them. The *Canopus* and *Cornwallis* were held in reserve.

At 1030 hrs, the First Division entered the Strait and at 1136 hrs, they opened fire on the Narrows forts with the guns in their fore turrets; *Queen Elizabeth* targeted Anadolu Hamidiye; *Agamemnon* fired on Rumeli Mecidiye; *Lord Nelson* on Namazgah; *Inflexible* aimed at Rumeli Hamidiye. The falls of shells appeared to be accurate to observers on the

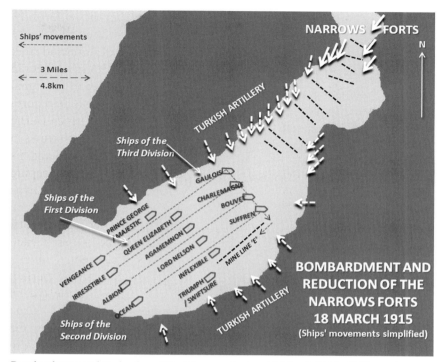

Bombardment and Reduction of the Narrows Forts – 18 March 1915. (© Forrest)

ships, but the reply from the Narrows forts was half-hearted, as if the extreme range of the attackers was too far for their aged guns. Yet as the ships held their position against the current they therefore presented a stationary target for field guns and howitzers, which had began harassing fire. The *Agamemnon* was targeted by a 150mm howitzer battery, which hit her twelve times in half an hour, five times against her armour but seven times above it, causing a great amount of structural damage, so the ship moved to throw off the aim of the Turkish gunners before returning to her original position. As the shells from the ships crashed down around the Narrows, so the distant low-lying targets became obscured by the smoke drifting down the Strait on a southerly breeze. At noon the *Queen Elizabeth's* 15-inch guns began to fire on Cimenlik, which remained a clear target against the sunlit houses of Canakkale, and a double explosion was seen. After nearly an hour the French ships of the Third Division

HMS *Queen Elizabeth* firing her 'X' and 'Y' turret 15-inch guns. (*The Graphic*, 6 March 1915)

steamed through the First Division to add their weight of fire at 10,000 yards, the *Gaulois* and *Charlemagne* along the Gallipoli shore, the *Suffren* and *Bouvet* on the Asian side of the Strait.

The unknown American journalist located in Canakkale, initially frustrated by the time he had spent awaiting an Allied attack, reported what it was like to be on the receiving end of the bombardment:

> On this morning of 18 March my only American colleague (George Schrenier of the Associated Press) and I breakfasted together then walked to the waterfront, to pay my daily visit to the Germans in Fort Cimenlik.... As far as the Germans knew, the *Agamemnon* and its fellow ships that morning would remain at anchor. In their long barracks behind Fort Cimenlik the officers so told us, as we sat with them sipping coffee.
>
> And then a shell burst far down the Strait. We rose. Another shell. An orderly ran up, stiffened to salute, reported the first arrival of enemy warships within the Strait. Commands were shouted. I rushed out to the adjoining wall of the old stone fort and looked toward the sea. The Allied fleet was steaming in single file, firing at objectives far below. Through my binoculars I watched them come, still not believing the awaited attack had begun. The fleet steamed closer, it began manoeuvring in a vast circle, small specks playing follow-your-leader. I could see puffs of smoke as the ships fired, then puffs as the shells exploded on the distant hillsides, and then seconds later hear the booms of explosions.
>
> Here at last was action, even if it did not reach the Narrows. Then a shell burst at Dardanos, a few miles below, another at Fort Hamidieh, still closer. In another moment a shell burst in the water directly in front of me. A geyser fountained up, and shell-fragments screeched over my head. The naval gunners were just getting their range. Next shell fell just in front of Cimenlik, and instead of a geyser of water sent up an upheaval of earth and smoke. Shell followed shell.

I ran to the round stone tower, clambered on its top, and there watched the magnificent spectacle.

The ships were in closer, still in that one-line circle, firing broadside after broadside. On both sides of the Straits the hills blossomed with explosions. The din became terrific. And now the shells fell all about Cimenlik and went beyond into the village. Houses spouted up, filling the air with timbers, tiles and stone. The *Queen Elizabeth* firing 16-inch guns [this is a journalistic error; the *Queen Elizabeth* mounted 15-inch guns] caused the worst havoc. Its shells, distinct from those of *Agamemnon*, *Lord Nelson*, *Inflexible*, *Triumph* and *Prince George* were like a thunderclap that strikes the house.

After an hour's bombardment the forts were completely silent, and observers on the ships began to believe that the Turkish guns had been destroyed. But it was not so; the lull was because the defenders' guns needed to be cleared of sand and earth thrown up by near-misses, and as the French ships steamed closer so the forts took up the fight in earnest. The American journalist continues:

I watched from my round tower only a little while. It was no place for a non-combatant. I decided to make a run for it through the village, so as to gain the hills beyond the town, where the view would be both good and safe. Houses came down in front of me as I loped along the cobblestones. By the time I reached the hills, the forts were returning fire, and for the rest of the afternoon I witnessed the most remarkable for an onlooker of the war.

And all the time, the defending guns were peppering the Dardanelles with shells, causing fountains of water to spout up, some close enough to the ships to deluge them. Other shells found their targets. The howitzers and field guns scattered along both shores kept up a furious fusillade, which, although not fatal for the vessels, were causing casualties. The *Inflexible* was under constant attack; a heavy shell glanced off the ship's port side

An artist's impression of the view from HMS *Triumph* during the assault on the Dardanelles. (*The War Illustrated*, 10 April 1915)

just below the waterline, remarkably only denting the plating; a 150mm howitzer shell destroyed the left gun of 'P' turret, and another shell of the same size hit the foremast close to the flying bridge, killing or wounding everybody within. *Inflexible* was on fire and the fire control communications to the rest of the ship had been destroyed. The ship's picket boat was sunk alongside her. *Inflexible* dropped back from the fray as teams tackled the fires, returning when they were under control, and was hit once more but with little further effect. Later, as the ship manoeuvred in Erenkoi Bay, she hit a mine that blew a large hole in her starboard bow, killing thirty-nine men. Down by the bows *Inflexible* withdrew from the fight, being beached on the island of Tenedos to be patched up before having to steam to Malta on 6 April for dockyard repairs.

Unknown to the Allies, as not having been spotted by aerial reconnaissance, a line of twenty-six mines arranged perpendicular to those that crossed the Strait, and so parallel with the Asian coast, had been laid in Erenkoi Bay at night on 7/8 March 1915 by the minelayer *Nusret*. It is possible that a number of these mines had been swept up prior to 18 March, but as the minesweeper crews could not always identify specific locations, so the remaining mines in Erenkoi Bay remained an unknown threat.

A reconnaissance aircraft flew up the Strait and reported that Dardanos and Cimenlik were abandoned but that the other forts were still occasionally firing. At 1345 hrs, Admiral de Robeck decided that the return fire was sufficiently reduced to call up the minesweepers, and for the ships of the Second Division – *Vengeance*, *Albion*, *Irresistible* and *Ocean* – which had not yet been engaged, to relieve the French ships, which had taken a battering. The *Gaulois* had sustained serious damage, having been hit repeatedly, including a heavy shell impact below the waterline. She took on a list and, with *Dublin* as consort, was forced to run for the Aegean but made it only as far as Rabbit Island, several miles south-west of the entrance to the Strait, where she was beached to prevent her sinking. The departing *Suffren,* steaming ahead of the *Bouvet,* followed a route through Erenkoi Bay that had been taken by the Allied ships before. The *Bouvet* had been firing at Namazgah but she had been hit by two 355mm shells from Anadolu Hamidiye and at least six 6-inch shells from Rumeli Mesudiye, which had accurately targeted the French ship at a range of only 6,000 yards. Two of her guns were out of action, including the forward 305mm, and her bridge and steering compartment were on fire. At 1358 hrs, the ship was seen to blow up; she slowly rolled over while still steaming ahead and sank in just two minutes, taking more than 600 of her crew down with her. A magazine amidships had exploded, so opening up the ship's side to the water.

A French postcard depicting Turkish guns firing at the Allied ships on 18 March 1915. The artist has captured the scene of battle well, showing the three 6-inch guns of Rumeli Mesudiye Battery, although they were not sited so close together. (Author's collection)

Undaunted by the tragic spectacle of the loss of the *Bouvet*, the ships of the Second Division steamed in to 10,600 yds from the Narrows, and began to draw fire from Rumeli Mecidiye and Anadolu Hamidiye. The Second Division's big guns began firing at 1439 hrs, while their secondary armaments were targetting the shore batteries, which were dropping shells around the boats trying to rescue the *Bouvet's* survivors. At 1514 hrs, the *Irresistible* was hit by a shell from a Krupp 355mm L/35. Lance-Corporal Powell, Royal Marine Artillery, aboard *Irresistible* wrote:

> A shell – I think it must have been a 14-inch – hit us somewhere forward. Fair and square it caught us, for the whole ship shook.

The bombardment from the ships continued, but the forts kept up a slow reply; *Irresistible* engaged Namazgah; *Ocean* put five out of seven shells fired into Rumeli Hamidiye; *Vengeance* set the barracks behind Rumeli Mecidiye ablaze. Yet at around 1530 hrs, it was still hot for the Second Division ships, so they were ordered to increase the distance from the big guns that were still effective at Rumeli Mecidiye and Anadolu Hamidiye. Only the Krupp L/35 guns at the Narrows could hope to infict serious damage to the attacking ships, out of range for the Krupp L/22 guns. Had the minefield been cleared so that the warships could proceed toward the Narrows, then the L/22s would have been in action, albeit under increasing heavy fire as the ships closed the distance. An eyewitness account by Midshipman Henry Denham of the *Agamemnon* proves that the long-barrel Krupp guns were effective:

> At 2.30 pm shots fell between us and *Queen Elizabeth*, who was hit twice; we were replying all the time with our 9.2-inch guns singlely.... At 3.30 pm big shots from Fort 19 [Anadolu Hamidiye] were straddling *Irresistible* and soon after, 2nd Division was ordered to extend their distance from the enemy.

HMS *Queen Elizabeth* under fire in the Dardanelles. (Courtesy of the National Museum of the Royal Navy)

The long-range L/35 guns at the Narrows forts eventually fell silent by late-afternoon, again due to the sand and earth and masonry thrown up around them clogging the barrels and mechanisms, but also because many of the demoralized gunners had taken shelter or even fled. Although some of the guns were displaced or damaged, the earth emplacements absorbed much of the energy of the incoming ships' shells, which were not of the correct type for these targets (see Appendix Nine, Shells, Fillings, Fuses and Charges). Many shells simply buried themselves into the soft ground and did not explode. A 15-inch shell from *Queen Elizabeth* is still embedded in the stone wall of Cimenlik Kalesi, having failed to detonate even against a hard target; another shell that may have been from the same salvo ripped off a corner of a magazine but the ammunition contained within did not explode. Yet significant damage was done to the defenders' artillery infrastructure, their command and control and communications, all very necessary to co-ordinate the guns and to bring up ammunition. The screaming arrival of a ship's heavy shell and the resulting earth 'fountain' had a terrible psychological effect on the Turkish soldiers, but for most the impact was survivable unless it was a direct hit. German General Hans Kannengiesser described such an event:

> The shrieking crash of such an armour-piercing shell from a 12 or 14-inch gun, which arrived like a volcanic upheaval, had always a great effect.... The explosive effect of these enormous horrors mostly went through the base into the air, and after several seconds one heard the pieces of shell falling, without a tearing effect, flat to earth. The Turkish soldiers named them 'fountains' as they saw that they mostly escaped with a shock.

Carl Mühlman, a staff officer with Liman von Sanders and the official German historian of the campaign, wrote:

> The craters made by the 38cm shells especially of the *Queen Elizabeth* are gargantuan.... The psychological effect is tremendous.

Turkish artillery officer Major Hansan later wrote:

> We turned our hearts to God and our guns to the enemy and started to bombard *Irresistible*, which was 8,200 metres away.

The potential threat from floating mines was noted by Chief Petty Officer Young aboard *Agamemnon*:

> Some very narrow escapes the '*Aggie*' had during the day's work, 'specially when we managed to get amongst the Turks' floating mines. We got warned once by our piquet [sic] boat there was one 'right ahead' but as ship was going dead slow no difficulty was experienced in dodging it. Was a fine morning, just right for shooting.... It seems the Turk dropped these mines in the water at Chanak when the fleet first appeared in the morning and there always being a 2 to 2.5 knot current here they were now just reaching our ships. Our sweeper got a good many mines however, which we exploded. Our piquet [sic] boats also chased some exploding them by rifle fire.

The same situation was noted by Midshipman Denham of the *Agamemnon*:

> The water must have been thick with mines for we could see a Turkish torpedo boat, a merchantman and two tugs a long way past the Narrows and they must have been heaving mines overboard for all they were worth.

According to General Kannengiesser the Turks did not use floating mines on 18 March. A mine is more deadly when it is submerged and undetected rather than visibly bobbing up and down, therefore offering itself as a target. But the attack on the Narrows was a desperate situation for the Turkish defenders, and so may have led to this frantic action.

Amongst the screech of shells and the crashing columns of water the minesweepers plodded on, incredibly achieving results as they slogged upstream against the current. They passed through the First Division at the 14,000-yard line to reach the Asian side of the lower limit of the minefield, exploding one mine and bringing two others to the surface, which were promptly attacked by picket boats.

The *Irresistible* had a slight list due to battle damage but at 1615 hrs she hit a mine in Erenkoi Bay, causing flooding of the starboard engine room. The bulkhead to the port engine room strained and then buckled under the water pressure, leaving the ship powerless and dead in the water. Down by the stern and static, she was the prime target for the shore batteries, and Captain Dent decided to evacuate her. The destroyer *Wear* hurried alongside to take off the crew, successfully saving twenty-eight officers and 582 men under fire. Aboard the *Wear* was Commodore Roger Keyes, who ordered the captain of the damaged *Ocean*, Captain Hayes-Sadler, to tow *Irresistible* out of danger, but the captain did not do so and, according to historian Sir Robert Rhodes James, '*Ocean* steamed about, blazing away at the forts.'

HMS *Irresistible* strikes a mine on 18 March 1915. (Author's collection)

HMS *Irresistible* abandoned and sinking. (Courtesy of the National Museum of the Royal Navy)

This comment belies the difficulties of towing the 15,800-ton pre-dreadnought that had settled deep in the water, bows on to the Asian shore, out of danger. Captains Dent and Hayes-Sadler conferred, and at 1750 hrs, the tow party previously left aboard were removed and the ship was abandoned. At 1805 hrs, *Ocean,* perhaps only a mile from the sinking *Irresistible*, hit a mine on her starboard side, causing considerable flooding and jamming the helm to port. At almost the same time, a heavy shell struck *Ocean* on the same side, resulting in further flooding so that the ship quickly took on a 15 degree list. Destroyers rushed to her assistance and removed the crew whilst under a crossfire from both shores. Both ships sunk unseen during the night. By 1900 hrs, the battleships, except for those slowly sinking, and all other vessels, had exited the Strait.

The American journalist continues:

> Later I went back to the ruined village with fears for the comrades in Cimenlik and Hamidieh, for their fire had ceased before the fleet had withdrawn. But I found them unscathed, save for minor injuries. In all the twenty forts, 150 casualties were reported. But the Germans were downcast. Only two of the long-range guns remained in action, and ten or eleven of the shorter guns might be remounted before morning. But not enough shells remained for another day's defence ... around twenty per gun.

The actual number of casualties was even less than the journalist believed; only twenty-seven killed, three of whom were German; and sixty-eight wounded, fifteen of whom were German. The majority of the casualties were at Rumeli Mecidiye.

But the Allies were downcast, too, and the blow to British prestige and confidence was shattering. The plan to dominate the forts at the Narrows had almost worked – the Turkish and German gunners had been shell-shocked by the bombardment – but the minesweepers had not had any real chance to do their task: the minefield remained and the defences were still credible. The final result of the day's action was a massive expenditure of shells; the loss of more than 700 sailors; three battleships sunk and three more so seriously damaged (*Inflexible*, *Suffren* and *Gaulois*) that they would require dockyard repairs. The naval assault on the Dardanelles was over: the Allied hammer had been smashed against the Turkish anvil.

When news of the failure to breach the Dardanelles reached the Admiralty in London Winston Churchill was determined to renew the attack, but the pressure for a combined naval and land operation at last prevailed. Yet, even if the Allied warships had broken through to the Sea of Marmara on 18 March, they could not have been supported by transports and colliers that were needed to sustain such an incursion as long as Turkish gunners were still emplaced on shores of the Dardanelles. The *Queen Elizabeth* was powered by oil-fired boilers, so would have required oil tanker support, and it is conjecture to suppose the pride of the Royal Navy would have been risked by progressing into the Sea of Marmara. The ship was withdrawn from the theatre of operations on 12 May 1915, after *Goliath* was torpedoed.

The Turkish guns on both shores had to have been destroyed and the positions captured to ensure freedom of passage through the Dardanelles. Yet, even if the command of the Strait had been in Allied control, there were insufficient numbers of marines and bluejackets with the fleet to have been put ashore to rout the defenders and to garrison the shore batteries. In fact, there were no men in the entire theatre of operations tasked with such a role. Troops were being slowly assembled on the islands of Lemnos and Imbros but as an intended force to occupy Constantinople, based on the assumption that the Royal Navy would successively reach this objective.

CHAPTER 7

'They are Gone'

During the build-up of the Allied naval forces in early 1915, there was a general feeling of inevitability in Constantinople, a certainty that the Allies would sweep past the defences of the Dardanelles and be at the capital in less than twenty-four hours of doing so. Rich merchants moved their families out of the city; foreign embassies sent families home; trains were on standby at Haidar Pasha to evacuate the Sultan, the government and well-placed officials into central Anatolia; important archives from public buildings that were expected to be shelled by the enemy battleships were moved 100 miles to Eskisehir; the banks secreted their cash and gold reserves. There were plans to dynamite some of the ancient buildings of world significance such as the Mosque of Saint Sophia, the former Christian church that became an Islamic mosque after the fall of the city in 1453, and to set fire to hundreds of wooden buildings: the victors would have nothing to show for their efforts except a ruined city. The ordinary Turk with nowhere to go expected to be destroyed by an unmerciful enemy.

Yet on the evening of 18 March 1915, Major General Cevat Pasha, the Turkish commander of the Canakkale Fortified Zone, saw the last Allied warships steam out of the Dardanelles and said:

> They are gone…. They could not break through…. They will not break through.

Unbelievably, the battleships had been repelled but his comments did not disguise the worry that all the defenders shared: what would happen when the Allied fleet returned, probably the next day? German officer Carl Mühlman wrote in his memoirs:

> We could not sleep because of the anxiety of the 19 March.
> With the first light of the day our binoculars began to scan
> the horizon.

Much of Canakkale's centre was in ruins and deserted, with collapsed buildings blocking the streets and quayside, as the town had attracted wayward shells aimed at Anadolu Hamidiye and Cimenlik close by. These two forts, together with those located on the peninsula shore at Rumeli Mecidiye, Rumeli Hamidiye and Namazgah, had drawn ferocious fire from the attackers. The defenders expected another assault and worked feverously through the night to repair the defences by rebuilding the earth ramparts, re-establishing telephone communications and restoring the guns to working condition, where possible. By dawn they had done what they could and were prepared for the next Allied onslaught, which, pessimistically, they expected to be successful. But as 19 March ended, and as each subsequent day did not bring the return of the fleet, Carl Mühlman wrote:

> Neither on 19 March nor on the following days could we see
> any ships except the regular patrol boats. Everyone was
> relieved.

There was a general belief by British planners that the stocks of large calibre ammunition held by the Dardanelles forts had always been low, and that they would run out completely if the naval assault was continued. Evidence now shows that ammunition stocks after the attack were far from low, particularly true of the shorter range Old type shells (see Appendix Nine, Shells, Fillings, Fuses and Charges). The stocks of both Old and New shell types were: 354 of 355mm, of which 40 per cent were the New type; more than 2,900 shells of 210mm to 280mm calibre, of which only 5 per cent were the New type; around 5,000 of 150mm shells for the heavy howitzers and quick-firers, plus a large quantity of those for the smaller calibre field guns. Interesting, too, according to the shell expenditure figures for 18 March, is that Rumeli Hamidiye, armed with two 355mm L/35 guns, did not fire any shells that day, and nor did the single 355mm L/35 gun at Cimenlik. Regarding this latter gun, it is probable that it had been moved to Anadolu Hamidiye, although it may not have been operational on 18 March. This would have been a huge task requiring the efforts of hundreds of men manhandling the 85-ton gun and, separately, the gun mounting and carriage of similar total weight, together with the building of long, easy gradient ramps to the ramparts at each fort for removal and then installation: it does beg the question, why such an effort? Perhaps the L/35 was a replacement for a gun damaged at Anadolu Hamidiye? The advantage of moving the gun was that it was then located approximately 1,000 yards (900m) further south, and therefore closer to the attackers, but such an undertaking may have rendered the gun out of service at a critical time. According to the diary of Major Selahattin Adil, Chief of the Canakkale Fortified Region Headquarters, Cimenlik had ceased to be an operational fort, and the three guns that remained there were being cannibilized for spare parts.

An interesting photograph showing the barrel of a Krupp coastal gun being pulled up to the ramparts at Anadolu Hamidiye. This gun may have been the 355mm that was moved from Cimenlik Kalesi in 1915. (Author's collection)

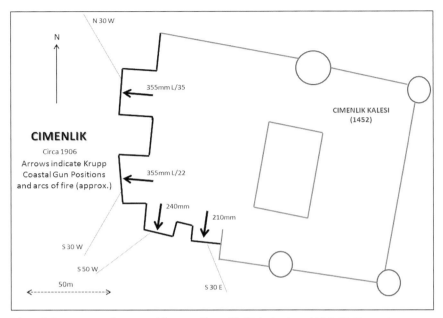

Plan of Krupp coastal gun positions at Cimenlik Kalesi, circa 1906. (© Forrest)

Another reason can be found on a British drawing (reference: National Archives WO301/481) of Cimenlik dated 1908, which shows that both the 355mm guns, the L/35 and the L/22, pointed across the Narrows toward Kilid Bahr, less than a mile away, with the two smaller calibre L/22s facing down the Dardanelles. This was a poor arrangement, as only short-range guns would be facing vessels steaming up from the entrance. However, the angle through which the coastal guns could traverse was 120 degrees, so they could cover the approach to the Narrows from ships steaming *down* the Dardanelles, such as Russian ships that were making for the Aegean. That aside, according to the ammunition expenditure reports, all the heavy calibre defensive fire of 355mm and 240mm shells came from just three forts – Anadolu Hamidiye on the Asian shore, and Namazgah and Rumeli Mecidiye on the opposite shore. Yet, the 355mm shell usage, all of which were high explosive, was just twenty-nine (nineteen New type and ten Old type) fired by the two L/35 guns at Anadolu Hamidiye (or it may have actually been as few as fifteen, depending on research source). This low consumption of these heavy shells and the fact that the two 355mm guns at Rumeli Hamidiye did not fire at all, suggests that the shells may have been husbanded for the expected second battle, but as the total 355mm shell stock after the battle was 354 (136 New/218 Old), it seems odd that more were not fired on 18 March. The 240mm shell expenditure, roughly half of which was high explosive and half armour-piercing, was 186 (107 New/79 Old) fired from a total of sixteen guns at the three combative forts, assuming all guns were operational. On average, this represents fourteen shells per gun, fired in a four to five-hour period, giving an approximate rate of fire of one shell every seventeen to twenty-one minutes. However, it must have been faster than this at the beginning of the battle but slowed as the incoming bombardment intensified, and there were periods of time when the guns could not fire as they had to be cleared of debris. The average is also distorted as guns fell finally silent one-by-one during the action.

In a report dated 8 March 1915 by Captain Fyler of the *Agamemnon,* he recorded the following complimentary comment about the skill of the Turkish gunners during an action that took place the day before:

> The rate of fire of Nos. 13 and 19 Forts was about one salvo per Fort per minute. The salvos fell well together.

There were four 240mm L/35 guns at Fort 13 (Rumeli Mecidiye); at Fort 19 (Anadolu Hamidiye) there were seven 240mm L/35 guns and two 355mm L/35s, so if firing was by salvo – two or more guns firing at the same time – then one salvo per minute was remarkably fast, which may have been true early on in the battle on 18 March.

The process for loading the heavy Krupp coastal guns was labour intensive, each gun requiring a crew of up to twenty, including those bringing the ammunition from the magazines located close to the guns. Each gun would be served from two separate magazines, one providing the shell and the other the propelling charge, because mixed storage would be obvious folly. Rails were laid on the stone base of the gun emplacements for the transportation of the shells, which were clamped to small trucks with four wheels and pushed by hand; non-rail handcarts

A 240mm L/22 Krupp gun of the Madjar Battery protecting the Bosphorus. (Courtesy of the National Museum of the Royal Navy)

The restored Krupp 240mm L/35 at Rumeli Mecidiye showing the wide arc of fire of these guns. Note the figure of Gunner Seyit Ali carrying a shell for loading. (© Forrest)

could be used for lower weight shells and charges. The gun would have to be lowered to the horizontal for loading. On the L/35s a metal mesh platform was located at the rear of each gun on which the loaders would stand, and next to them a davit to lift and swing the shell into the distinctive Krupp cylindrical wedge breech, which would be closed by hand. Access to the platform was by steps, the 355mm L/35 having seven and the 240mm L/35 having five. The older L/22 guns had no such platform, so the gunners stood on the carriage slides. The charge, contained in a brass case much like a rifle cartridge but much larger, would follow the shell, each being rammed into position by the loaders – a strenuous job without the assistance of mechanical aids. The breech was then closed. Elevation was achieved by turning large hand wheels on either side of the gun mounting. The traversing of the gun was also done by muscle power, turning even larger hand wheels at the rear of the carriage to move the gun in an arc about a forward pivot, pulling on gear teeth set into the stone base. Later Krupp coastal guns used electric motors and hydraulic rammers but the Ottoman guns were not fitted with such improvements. Fire control would have been directed by the battery commander located in a position so that he could see the enemy, and by using binoculars, maps and range tables he would determine the bearing and range of the target. As the battery commander could see the enemy, then his position would be exposed and certainly vulnerable, perhaps in a pit on top of an earth-covered magazine or traverse between gun positions. Orders to each gun captain would have been by telephone or by runner. The Krupp guns delivered to the Ottomans during the 1880s had sighting posts set on either side of the barrel, a short post set close to the trunnions and the second, taller post further back on the breech. Here a simple optical sight could be located and adjusted to align with the first sight post, allowing the traverse and elevation of the gun to be adjusted to the prescribed angle and range. The guns were fired by use of a lanyard releasing a firing pin set in the breech block, setting off a small detonator in the base of the charge case. On firing, the gun would recoil up the slide, perhaps as much as 2m, arrested by variable resistance hydraulic-pneumatic brakes.

A remarkable incident occurred at Rumeli Mecidiye during the battle on 18 March, and a Turkish national hero was created – Gunner Seyit Ali Çabuk – recorded as aged twenty-six, one of a crew manning a 240mm L/35 gun. After the shell crane had been disabled by incoming shell

Seyit Ali recreating the lifting of a 240mm shell at Rumeli Mecidiye. Note that the shell is of the 'New' type with a 4crh (calibre radius head), and that a second shell can be seen on a rail truck at ground level. (Author's collection)

splinters Seyit carried the heavy shells up to the platform for loading, not once but three times. The popular mythology that has grown around this incident is that each shell weighed 276kg (607lb), that he fired the gun aided by only one other man, whom history does not recall, as the rest of the crew had been wounded or killed, and that the third shell fired struck the *Ocean*. It was an extraordinary feat of strength if he truly carried each

144

shell unaided up the steps, and it would have been a massive task even for two men to have loaded the breech with shell and charge, elevate the barrel and rotate the carriage to the correct alignment. The memorial statue to Seyit Onbasi (*Onabasi*, Turkish for corporal, as he was promoted after the battle), which stands by the road close to Rumeli Mecidiye, states:

> Corporal Seyit, who is one of thousands of Mehmets, lifted the 140, 190, 215kg shells of those 24cm guns many times.

At the Istanbul Military Museum Seyit Onbasi is shown as a larger-than-life statue mounting the step of the world's sole remaining Krupp 355mm L/35. This representation of him can be found as countless figurines and in heroic images that can be purchased from the trinket stalls at the Turkish memorials in Gallipoli, but in all cases they show a figure with a 355mm shell, not that for the 240mm gun he was serving. What is also interesting is that in the famous photograph of Seyit Onbasi posing with the correct diameter shell carried behind his back, it is a New type steel shell, and therefore lighter in weight compared to the typical cast Old shell. Regardless of construction material, the ability of any man to carry even a 140kg (308lb) shell up five steps to the loading platform and insert it in the breech of the gun, all the time under fire from the attacking ships, is extraordinary!

For all the hundreds of shells fired by the warships at the forts and gun batteries on 18 March, the total number of Germans and Turks killed or seriously wounded was only ninety-five. In return, and in addition to the heavyweight shells fired at the ships, the number of lower calibre shells fired by the defenders that day was 1,833 – 88 per cent of which were from the batteries scattered throughout the Howitzer Zone. Of the 8th Heavy Artillery Regiment in this zone, only three men were killed and eleven wounded, but they scored 139 hits on the attacking ships. The five 150mm guns at Dardanos fired 115 rounds, while the three 6-inch guns at Rumeli Mesudiye fired a credible 114 rounds.

The three forts immediately above the Narrows – Degirmen Burnu (Fort No. 22) on the peninsula side, Anadulo Mecidiye (Fort No. 24) and Nagara Burnu (Fort No. 30) on the Asian shore – did not contribute to the defence of the Dardanelles on 18 March 1915 because of their locations. Forts 22 and 30 did not have line-of-sight to the targets in the Strait, and although Fort 24 did, the three forts were equipped with the short-range L/22 guns. It must have been frustrating for the gunners who were probably itching to fire these old but still powerful weapons.

Could the Royal Navy have succeeded with a second assault?
Technological improvements in ships and gunnery had rendered successive classes of ships redundant; the late-Victorian pre-dreadnoughts were considerably inferior to the super-dreadnoughts that were being built in 1914. Yet the distinction of one ship being superior to another was based on a ship-to-ship fight, such as taking on the German High Sea Fleet, not ship versus fortifications. The first decade of the twentieth century saw the introduction of the big gun battlecruiser as a powerful addition to a battle fleet, but a type of ship that sacrificed armour for speed. Battlecruisers *Indefatigable*, *Indomitable* and *Inflexible*, all of which served in the Dardanelles Campaign, were armed with modern 12-inch guns but they were no better against shore fortifications than any other vessel of the time. Of the combined British and French fleet of all types of pre-dreadnought, battlecruiser and super-dreadnought, two-thirds of them were more than ten years old with reciprocating engines rather than steam turbines; the oldest British pre-dreadnoughts, the *Majestic* and the *Prince George*, dated from 1895. The idea of using older battleships for a purely naval attack on the Dardanelles had been considered by the Committee of Imperial Defence in 1906, and by the beginning of the First World War, many of the ships that were to be sent to the Dardanelles were of an age that they were soon to be scrapped anyway. Winston Churchill wrote:

> In 1905 no one would have risked them in trying to force the Dardanelles. They were our latest vessels and all we had. In 1915 they were surplus and moribund.

Before the disastrous events of 18 March 1915, there had been an attitude of the British War Council that the loss of some ships would have been acceptable to have achieved the goal of reaching Constantinople and so intimidate Turkey. During the Dardanelles Commission enquiry in 1916, Admiral Fisher said that when asked by the Committee of Imperial Defence for his estimate on how many battleships would be lost on a solely naval expedition, he told them, 'Twelve'. This number is close to the estimate of ten predicted by Baron Kolmar von der Goltze, the head of the German Military Mission to Constantinople in the 1880s and 1890s, and aide-de-camp to Ottoman Sultan Mehmet V in November 1914.

In the final analysis, the total battleship losses for the entire Dardanelles and Gallipoli campaigns, including those later sunk by torpedo boat and submarine – *Goliath* by Turkish torpedo boat *Muavenet-i Milliye* on 12 May 1915; *Majestic* and *Triumph* both sunk by the German submarine *U21* on 25 and 27 May 1915 – is less than the quantity that would have been considered justifiable when the decision to force a passage through the Dardanelles was taken in January 1915. Also, if the ships damaged on 18 March 1915 are included, three of them so seriously that they required dockyard repairs and that they were out of action for some time, then the figure is still less than Admiral Fisher's 'Twelve'. When considering lives lost on the ships sunk, only the *Bouvet* and *Goliath* each lost nearly the ship's full complement of crew – 600 of 660, and 570 of 700 respectively – the other ships having mercifully much lower losses.

So, if Admiral Fisher had accepted the idea of losing twelve ships during the build-up of vessels for the assault, why did the British War Cabinet decide not to try again while they were still ahead in the numbers game? There are two reasons: firstly the acceptance of losing twelve ships was made when the idea of a fast assault on the Strait with expendable ships was considered in January 1915. It was in the following month the cautious Admiral Carden had formulated his methodical plan to progressively reduce the forts by weight of shell fire, allowing the minefield to be cleared without significant interference. Therefore, the expectation was that losses would be far fewer than first speculated. Most ships, and especially their precious crews of trained officers and men, were now *not* considered expendable. For a time there were those who still believed that the minefield could be beaten if only a proper job of sweeping could be organized, including Winston Churchill and the Commander in Chief Admiral de Robeck, but that still ignored the second reason. The build-up to the assault had disregarded the real difficulties that defences presented and the strategy applied to the operation had been wrong. So, if the warships had returned on 19 March 1915, or on any day after this date, with another attempt to breach the Narrows and sail on toward Constantinople, they still would not have succeeded as the interlocking defences of forts, gun batteries and the minefield were just too strong. And a breakthrough by the ships would not have secured the passage; ground troops were necessary to take and hold the fortified positions. Yet the realization of total defeat by naval assault took time to accept as more replacement battleships were on their way: *Queen*, *Implacable*, *Prince of Wales*, *London* and the French *Henri IV*.

The Royal Navy did have an opportunity to force the Dardanelles after the pursuit of the *Goeben* and *Breslau* across the Mediterranean during the first few days of the beginning of the war with Germany. British warships entering the Dardanelles uninvited would have undoubtedly

The Narrows, May 2011 – the 216m container ship *Zim Texas* approaching from the south; the length of *Queen Elizabeth* was 196m (indicated by the double-head arrow). Note the location of the forts that defended the Narrows. (© Forrest)

precipitated Turkey immediately aligning with Germany and declaring war on Britain, yet unknown to the British Government, Turkey was already following this path with Germany, although initially hoping to remain as a non-belligerent nation. The powerful British Mediterranean Fleet under the command of Admiral Milne was capable of such a provocative action, consisting of three modern battlecruisers, four armoured cruisers, four light cruisers and fourteen destroyers. The minefield had only two lines until 15 August, when a third was added. The loss of one or two ships would have been certain, but if the ships chosen to break through the minefield had been the oldest ships, perhaps even transports with minimal crews quickly despatched from Malta, the warships could have followed through the gaps made by those that had been sacrificed. It would have been a bold yet horrifying plan, but it would probably have succeeded.

The seeds of the 18 March failure were planted on 3 November 1914 with the attack on the entrance forts, as with every day that passed thereafter, the defences grew even stronger. If the Navy had attempted to steam through the Dardanelles immediately after the bombardment of the entrance forts, at a time when the Turkish gunners were shell-shocked by the explosion of a magazine at Sedd el Bahr and the defences were relatively weak, the probability of successfully reaching Constantinople was still reasonably high. By this time, five lines of mines protected the Narrows, but if old and expendable ships had ploughed up the Strait with more important vessels sailing in the wake of those being forfeited, then Allied warships may well have got through, although how many can only be speculation, and how well they would have been subsequently supported by colliers and transports is another issue. Soon after this the window of opportunity began to close as further lines of mines were added and the Howitzer Zone was created. By March 1915, the Dardanelles were shut and sealed.

In both of the above scenarios the heavy coastal guns, howitzers and field guns would have put up resistance, but how effective and for how long is another unknown. However, it is certain that the loss of life on both sides would have been very small compared to the carnage that was to come on the Gallipoli battlefields.

A postcard of the French pre-dreadnought *Bouvet*. Note the pronounced tumblehome hull and the side-mounted 274mm and 138mm guns. (Author's collection)

The loss of the *Bouvet*

The accepted reason for the loss of the *Bouvet* is that she hit a mine in Erenkoi Bay, and this may well be true. Her rapid sinking in something less than two minutes with smoke pouring from amidships suggests that she sank due to an internal explosion, probably a magazine blowing up, but was this caused by striking a mine or by a shell penetrating the ship? The *Bouvet* was hit by at least eight shells, two of which may have been from a 355mm gun, and her main armament forward gun was put out of action. The four French ships of the Third Division had been as close as 10,000 yards (9,100m) from the Narrows, and many of the Turkish heavy shells fired that day were the armour-piercing New type, which had the range to reach to Erenkoi Bay. Shells from the 6-inch/45s at Rumeli Mesudiye Battery at Suandere Bay also hit the ship, causing serious damage.

150

The *Bouvet's* dated design of a pronounced tumblehome hull, which had been common on wooden-walled warships for centuries but was still peculiar to French battleships built in the 1890s, may have offered an almost flat surface to a plunging shell. The ship was armed with two 305mm/40 guns, one forward and one aft, plus two 274mm/45 guns amidships set on either side of the tumblehome. Also, eight 138mm/45 guns were mounted on the tumblehome, four each side. The magazines were below each gun, which meant that the magazines for the tumblehome guns were close to the hull of the ship: was one of them detonated by an exploding contact mine? The *Bouvet's* sides were armoured, ranging from 400mm thick amidships tapering to 200mm along the ship's length, but this was only a metre or so above and below the waterline. If she did strike a submerged mine then her main armour belt would have offered no protection. Above the main armour was a 100mm belt carried up one deck to protect the ammunition hoists, together with another below this known as a splinter deck, but would these have been able to resist a 725kg armour-piercing shell from a Krupp 355mm L/35 falling at a steep angle at the end of its flight? However, there were parts of the deck devoid of armour: companion ways on the ship's centreline midway between the 274mm turrets. If a shell had plunged into the ship via this access, then it could have readily reached the magazine decks before exploding.

The ship had watertight compartments along her length, and also longitudinal bulkheads, which would have made her likely to capsize with any significant water ingress on one side only. The resulting explosion of a magazine, whatever the cause, would have opened the hull, probably exposing more than one of the ship's watertight compartments, causing her to fill with water and roll over, as she did. Other ships hit mines that day and did not sink quickly, slowly filling with water, enabling the crews to be evacuated or for the ship to be saved. In 1937, French naval historian Paul Chack described the moment of the explosion:

> At that moment a violent jolt shook the hull armour. Lieutenant Quernel said 'We have taken a heavy calibre shell.' A spray of water throws up at the starboard 274mm turret. By the doorway thick yellow smoke makes people

believe that the explosion is from a projectile inside the ship. 'I rather believe that it is a mine,' responds Captain Rageot de la Touche.

Captain Rageot de la Touche did not survive the sinking but five officers did, including Lieutenant Quernel, who described a huge gap in the deck caused by a shell that struck near to the rear turret. The ship was on fire below deck, but men remained at their stations in the awful conditions that asphyxiated many of them. The second in command, Commander Autric, believed that the ship had been torpedoed, and went to investigate. He did not survive.

Sir Julian Corbett wrote a significant description of the sinking:

> The French flagship (*Suffren*) had just passed through the British line, and the *Bouvet* was about to do so, when a huge column of reddish black smoke shot up from under her. Whether it was from a shell or a mine could not be seen. It was followed almost immediately by another, higher and more dense, which seemed to tell a magazine had gone. As the smoke cleared she was seen to have taken on a heavy list, and then in two minutes she turned turtle and went down.

The acclaimed Turkish diver Tosun Sezen dived on the *Bouvet* in 1968, when working for the Ministry of Finance to remove metal from the wreck. The ship had taken four days to locate using photographs of the sinking to spot for landmarks and a magnetometer to detect the mass of steel. He reported that the ship is lying by the stern and at an angle with the starboard propeller shaft visible, so revealing that side of the hull where a massive rent is located amidships which has almost ripped the ship apart. He also dived on the wreck of the *Irresistible,* recovering more than 100 tons of bronze, and the hole caused by the mine that sank this ship is only about a metre in diameter.

It is beyond reasonable doubt that a devastating internal explosion sank the *Bouvet*, but we may never know if this was as a result of striking a mine, from a shell or shells penetrating her hull to cause a terrible fire that detonated a magazine, or from a cruel combination of both.

CHAPTER 8

Submarines, Destroyers and More Guns

Submarine actions in the Dardanelles

British submarines operating in the Sea of Marmara were an important weapon during the battle for Gallipoli by seriously disrupting Turkish shipping that was supporting the army on the peninsula, and so forcing much of the supplies and reinforcements to a long and arduous overland route. Although submarines provided some successes in what otherwise was a generally disastrous campaign, it was not without cost: eight were lost in 1915 and another in 1918. Winston Churchill recognized the contribution of submarines and wrote:

> The Naval History of Britain contains no page more wonderful than that which records the prowess of her submarines at the Dardanelles.

The first to arrive were three B class submarines despatched from Malta in September 1914, with the mission to patrol the entrance to the Dardanelles and prevent the exit of the *Goeben* and *Breslau*. Built by Vickers at Barrow-in-Furness from October 1904 to February 1906, the B class were small and underpowered compared to the latest E class boats being built for the Royal Navy. Displacing just 313 tons submerged and powered by a single 600hp petrol engine, plus an 180hp electric motor for when underwater, the B class were capable of only 8 knots submerged, but were at their limits to tackle the difficult currents of the Dardanelles. Yet on 13 December 1914, the *B11* did penetrate the Strait to sink with a single torpedo the *Mesudiye* in Sarisiglar Bay, a few kilometres south of Canakkale. It was an incredible exploit by the crew and the submarine, considering that they had to negotiate five lines of mines submerged at a depth of 80 feet. The return journey was made at periscope depth through the minefield because the compass had fogged and it was impossible to navigate at depth. The *B11*'s commander, Lieutenant Norman Holbrook, was awarded the first Victoria Cross for the Submarine Service, and every other crew member was recognized with a gallantry award. A total of six B class boats operated in or off the Dardanelles, but were replaced with the bigger and more powerful E class submarines from April 1915.

The E class displaced 810 tons submerged and were powered by two 800hp Vickers diesel engines, plus two electric motors (either 600hp giving 9.5 knots underwater, or 840hp giving 10.25 knots underwater). The first E class boat to arrive was the Australian *AE2*, but she was damaged in a grounding incident off Mudros harbour on 10 March 1915, and was towed to Malta for repairs, returning the following month when British submarines of the same class were arriving. On 25 April – the day of the Allied invasion of Gallipoli – the *AE2* was the first Allied submarine to successfully transit the Dardanelles to access the Sea of Marmara. The passage through the Strait was not without incident as, after successfully clearing the minefield and torpedoing a Turkish gunboat, she ran aground close to one of the Canakkale forts but was able to free herself within a few minutes. Commanded by Lieutenant Commander Henry Stoker, the boat settled on the bottom of the Dardanelles to await nightfall, later surfacing to recharge her batteries. The old Turkish battleships *Turgut Reis* and the *Hayreddin Barbarossa* were anchored off Maidos, firing over the Gallipoli peninsula at the Ari Burnu landings, but quickly raised anchor and steamed off toward the Sea of Marmara as soon as the *AE2* was reported. Yet only five days later, the *AE2* was lost in the Sea of Marmara in an exchange against the Turkish torpedo boat *Sultanhisar*, although the crew of the submarine were rescued and became prisoners of war.

In 1915, two British E class submarines were lost in the Dardanelles and another in the Sea of Marmara, but others successfully reached as far as Constantinople to cause havoc with Turkish shipping. On 17 April, the *E15* was the first loss when she ran aground on a shoal near Kepez Point, having been swept uncontrollably along by the vicious current. Unfortunately, the boat was in sight of the Dardanos Battery, which opened fire on the stranded vessel, killing the commander, Lieutenant Commander Theodore Brodie; six more crewmen were killed by the release of chlorine gas caused by sea water coming in contact with the batteries. The remainder of the crew abandoned the submarine and were taken prisoner. Yet that was not the end of the affair because the stranded submarine was regarded as a prize for the Turks but an embarrassment for the British: the *E15* had to be destroyed. The first attempt was made by the *B6* but the torpedo missed. Then the destroyers *Grampus* and *Scorpion* attempted but failed to find her in the dark, and the following morning, the *B11* also tried but failed due to fog. An attempt to bomb the submarine from an aircraft was unsuccessful. The *Triumph* and *Majestic* tried firing from long range but missed. It took a courageous night expedition in the best traditions of the Royal Navy to achieve where others had failed, as two little picket boats, one each from the *Triumph* and *Majestic,* were able to get close enough to torpedo the *E15* on the night of 18 April. Each boat carried two 18-inch torpedoes mounted in a

A restored Royal Navy 50-foot steam picket boat photographed in Portsmouth Harbour (*Pinnace* No. 199). This type of robust little vessel mounted a 3pr Hotchkiss gun forward and was used extensively during the Dardanelles Campaign for ship-to-ship traffic, as rescue craft and even for minesweeping. (© Ryan)

simple arrangement to drop them from the boat's side when ready. The boats were more than 7 miles inside the Dardanelles before being picked up by a searchlight, which invited a whole barrage to be fired at them as more searchlights lit up their progress. The boats chugged on unscathed as fast as their little engines could carry them against the current, then a stray searchlight beam illuminated the stranded *E15*. This enabled the *Majestic*'s picket boat, commanded by Lieutenant Goodwin, to fire its first torpedo, which missed. The picket boat then took a shell in its stern but fired the second torpedo. The *Triumph's* picket boat also fired both of her torpedoes, and one of the three hit the submarine below the waterline just forward of the conning tower. *Majestic*'s boat was abandoned and the crew taken off by the *Triumph's* boat commanded by Lieutenant Commander Robinson, hero and Victoria Cross winner of the landing at the Orhaniye Battery on 26 February. One sailor was mortally wounded but those on the *Triumph's* crowded boat made good their escape out of the Dardanelles as the Turkish gunners fired on the drifting wreck of the abandoned picket boat.

The first British E class submarine to enter the Sea of Marmara was the *E14* on 27 April 1915, just two days after the *AE2*. The *E14* has the distinction that two of her captains were awarded the Victoria Cross – Lieutenant Commander Edward Boyle and Lieutenant Commander Geoffrey White – albeit the latter's was posthumous. Boyle took the *E14* through the Dardanelles on three successful patrols, including sinking the 5,000-ton ex-White Star Line *Guj Djemel* crowded with 6,000 troops and a battery of field guns en route to Gallipoli, but it was under the command of White in 1918 that she was lost. On 28 January 1918, the *E14* was sent into the Dardanelles because the *Yavuz Sultan Selim* (*Goeben*) was reported to be aground near Nagara Point, having being damaged during a raid into the Aegean. It took some time for the *E14* to negotiate the minefield and pass through the Narrows, but once close to where the wounded ship had been last reported White discovered that she was gone, having been refloated and was being towed to Constantinople for repairs. White attempted to torpedo another enemy ship in the area. Unfortunately, the torpedo exploded prematurely, damaging the submarine, forcing it close to the surface and so attracting gunfire from the shore batteries. White took the boat deep but it was leaking and uncontrollable, and with the air supply almost exhausted he decided to surface. The submarine began to run for the entrance of the Strait, but was too badly damaged to escape, so the captain took her close to shore to give the crew a chance of survival. Lieutenant Commander White stayed aboard but was killed by shellfire, although nine men out of a complement of thirty did survive and were taken prisoner.

Perhaps the most successful of the E class submarines was the *E11*, with three unbeaten sorties into the Sea of Marmara, in which she accounted for more than eighty vessels of various types, from battleship to sailing barge. Under the command of Lieutenant Commander Martin Nasmith, the *E11* entered the Sea of Marmara for the first time on 18 May 1915, and was the first enemy warship to arrive off Constantinople since Admiral Duckworth's ships in 1807. Nasmith torpedoed the transport *Stamboul* moored alongside the Tophane Arsenal, causing panic in the city. On 8 August 1915, the *E11* sunk the battleship *Hayreddin Barbarossa* off Bulair. During her return through the Dardanelles the submarine snagged a moored mine off Kilid Bahr, which was dragged all the way out of the Strait before it could be removed, the mine having been finely balanced just above the foredeck by the weight of its sinker. It was removed by going full astern and blowing the aft tanks to keep the bows submerged, and the rush of water swept the mine off the forward

British submarine *E11* returning from a successful patrol in the Sea of Marmara. (Courtesy of the National Museum of the Royal Navy)

hydroplane. After her third patrol the tired *E11* was replaced by the *E2* commanded by Lieutenant Commander David de Stocks, which went on to survive the war.

The *E7* was lost on 4 September 1915 en route into the Sea of Marmara when she became entangled in the submarine net stretched across the Strait off Nagara Point. In a bizarre incident the *E7* was sunk with the assistance of the German commander of the *UB14*, Oberleutnant Heino von Heimburg, when his submarine was laid up in Canakkale for repairs. The *E7* was stuck fast by the stern for around twelve hours, all efforts to free her by blowing tanks having proved fruitless, but this action had alerted the Turks to her predicament. A busy gaggle of patrol boats circled around on the surface and dropped charges, but they failed to destroy the submarine or even bring her to the surface. During these events von Heimburg rowed out in a skiff with two members of his crew and, at considerable personal risk, lowered and detonated a succession of small mines. After several damaging explosions close to the immovable submarine, her captain, Lieutenant Commander Archibald Cochrane, decided the *E7* could not escape, so he brought her to the surface to save the crew but promptly scuttled the boat, which now lies at a depth of 96m.

The same Nagara Point anti-submarine net nearly claimed the *E12* in November 1915 as it was returning from a record-breaking patrol that had lasted forty days, during which she had accounted for thirty-four vessels, and had taken her as far as Constantinople. Commanded by Lieutenant Commander Bruce, the boat was caught in the anti-submarine net by the forward hydroplanes but broke free. Released but dragging a part of the net, the submarine was pulled down to 75m before she could be controlled. Leaking badly, the *E12* met another unknown obstruction further south, which removed the dragging net, and the boat made good its escape.

The final E class that operated in the Dardanelles was the *E20*, sadly sunk by von Heimburg's *UB14* on 6 November 1915. The French submarine *Torquoise* ran aground near Nagara Point on 30 October 1915, and was captured intact, together with her orders, which the captain, Lieutenant Ravenel, had not destroyed. She had been due to rendezvous with the *E20* in the Sea of Marmara but the *UB14* kept the appointment instead, surprising the British submarine and sinking her with a single torpedo. The *Torquoise* was refloated by the Turks after a few days and renamed the *Mustadieh Ombashi,* eventually being returned to France after the cessation of hostilities.

French submarines were larger than the British B class but smaller than the E class, typically between 425 tons to 550 tons submerged. In addition to the *Torquoise*, three others were lost in the Dardanelles. The first French submarine to attempt to break through the Dardanelles was the *Saphir* on 15 January 1915. Commanded by Captain Fournier, the boat ran aground off Nagara Point, probably battered by the tricky currents, and was shelled by the shore batteries, resulting in half of her crew being killed, including the captain, the remainder being captured. The *Joule* was lost on 1 May 1915, when she hit a mine off Kepez Point, disappearing with all hands, and now lies on the bottom at a depth of 44m. On 27 July 1915, the *Mariotte* successfully cleared the minefield but was caught in a new anti-submarine net north of the Narrows. Forced to the surface the boat was shelled by the shore batteries and scuttled by her crew, sinking in shallow water. One other French submarine – the *Bernouilli* – operated and survived the Dardanelles but was lost in the Aegean in 1918.

According to Robert Rhodes James, more than forty German submarines were active in the Mediterranean in 1915, but as they were concentrated at the western end, they did not seriously threaten Allied transports during the Gallipoli Campaign. However, two notable attacks were made on Gallipoli transport vessels in 1915: the 11,000-ton *Royal Edward* was en route to Mudros from Alexandria but was sunk in the Aegean on 13 August with considerable loss of life; on 2 September, the 12,000-ton *Southland* was torpedoed but did not sink, eventually being beached on Lemnos. Both ships were torpedoed by von Heimburg in the *UB14,* and in addition to these two attacks the submarine had previously sunk the 10,000-ton Italian armoured cruiser *Amalfi.* These were impressive achievements for a submarine designed for coastal operations, and one even smaller and less powerful than the British B class. The UB boats that operated in the Aegean and Black Sea were shipped in sections by rail to Pola (now Pula, Croatia) for assembly and then sea trials with the Pola Flotilla based there and at Cattaro (now Kotor, Montenegro). Four of these submarines were transferred in this way – *UB3*, *UB7*, *UB8* and *UB14* – and all of them were then selected for service with the Constantinople Flotilla to operate in the Black Sea. The *UB3* did not reach the Dardanelles, disappearing without explanation close to her last believed position near Smyrna (now Izmir). According to the German Official History, the *UB8* transited the Dardanelles on 2 June and the *UB7* on 19 June.

Another successful German submarine of the Gallipoli campaign was the *U21* under the command of Captain Otto Hersing, sinking the pre-dreadnoughts *Triumph* on 25 May 1915 and the *Majestic* two days later, and then the 5,600-ton steamer *Carthage* off Cape Helles on 4 July. Similar in size to the British E class, the *U21* was the first of these ocean-going U-boats to make the long journey from Wilhelmshaven, Germany, via the North Sea and the Atlantic, entering the Mediterranean via the Straits of Gibraltar. The *U21's* audacious success against the *Triumph* was responsible for the recall of the major warships and transports to the safer anchorages of Imbros and Lemnos, but the *Majestic* returned the following day to anchor off Morto Bay. Although she was surrounded by patrol craft and with a torpedo net screen, Hersing struck again at 0645 hrs on the 27 May to send the *Majestic* to the bottom. This marked the end of the reign of the vulnerable battleships spending too much time in the Dardanelles and the waters off Gallipoli, as cruisers and destroyers took up an even more active role.

The Dardanelles has a strong surface current that runs out toward the Aegean but also has a reverse undercurrent, which, once understood, enabled submarines to successfully use this natural feature. Allied submarines passed through the Dardanelles twenty-seven times, and on every occasion ran the gauntlet of mines, anti-submarine nets, patrol craft, searchlights, shore forts and gun batteries. German submarines had it easier. The German Official History provides the following method employed to accept friendly submarines:

> Special preparations were necessary to receive them and a navigable channel had to be made, the route marked as unobtrusively as possible. Small barrel buoys were laid at the end of the rows of mines and at points where navigation was difficult. The channel was cleared of mines by small boats.

The use of depth was critical as between 25m to 30m there was no current.

German submarines became more aggressive at the eastern end of the Mediterranean after 1915, with those of the Pola Flotilla achieving a maximum strength of thirty-three boats. The Constantinople Flotilla had a maximum strength of eleven boats but these were the coastal type, and were not particularly successful in the Black Sea as there were few opportunities to attack Russian ships. A total of fourteen boats served in the Constantinople Flotilla but six were lost in operations.

Destroyer actions in the Dardanelles
Although the larger Allied warships had generally retreated from the Dardanelles after the loss of the *Triumph* and *Majestic,* it was not the case for smaller, faster vessels such as destroyers. As the battles for the peninsula continued throughout 1915, destroyers would frequently rush up and down the Strait firing on Turkish positions, including those in reserve areas. Particular attention was given to the gun batteries that were emplaced to shell French ground troops dug in around Morto Bay, so enticing them to divert their attention to the ships and waste ammunition. Harold Tumman of the destroyer *Harpy* described the reasons why:

> The object of this is to induce the wily Turk to chuck away some valuable ammunition, and incidentally, to enable our guns to obtain some valuable information with regard to the Turkish guns, batteries and searchlights, etc.

But he also wrote of the difficulty in spotting enemy guns:

> The Turks certainly know how to effectively conceal their guns, and as most of the batteries are mobile, it requires the greatest vigilance on our part to locate them, and, although we know within a little how many guns there are on the Asiatic side of the Straits, it is impossible to obtain the exact number on account of their mobility, as they are constantly shifting them.

Harold Tumman also wrote of a night-time 'leg-pulling' expedition to harass the Turkish gunners, as a dummy picket boat was created out of wood and canvas with an oil drum for a funnel half-filled with oil and cotton waste. The dummy boat, complete with a figurine of a coxswain, was quietly put in the water just off the Suandere Bay, the oil ignited to represent the boat under steam, and then set adrift. The destroyer then:

> Rushed a good distance above the dummy, before turning preparatory to greasing for the entrance [of the Strait]. The searchlights almost immediately flashed out and got it in the beams, but before the guns could open we flashed passed it on our return journey.... All the guns in creation appeared to be concentrating on that inoffensive bit of canvas and a few planks of wood, shots being furiously rained on it from Suandere Battery, Domuz, Kepez Point and Erenkoi Bay. On observing the flashes of these various guns, Tott's Battery and several field batteries on the French flank opened fire on them. To add to the general racket, as we went hustling past Domuz, we opened up a rapid fire on the Turkish Reserve lines, to such a good purpose, that we got off sixty rounds of shrapnel before losing the range.

The Turkish gunners soon realized that the dummy picket boat was not 'what it appeared to be ...' and their searchlights began to search for a real target:

> We had just got below de Tott's Battery, when suddenly, an additional searchlight, well down toward Kum Kale, switched dead on to us, entirely illuminating us at the first attempt. Naturally we were prepared for a devilish hot time, but our luck was in, for the light did not burn for more than thirty seconds. It appears that the *Foxhound*, anticipating some such move at that particular spot, had crept right inshore, under where the beam of light would play, and almost simultaneously with the switching on of the light, 'bang' went her 4-inch gun with a round of Lyditte, which had the immediate and much desired effect of switching off the gas.... Only one round fell anywhere near us.

The destroyers were able to steam up and down the Dardanelles with relative ease in the course of their patrols, sometimes as many as five times in a day, although all the time attracting Turkish gunfire:

> We ambled gracefully up the Strait. As it is now broad daylight.... The various hostile guns and batteries ... opened fire with every available gun. However, a little skilful manipulation of the helm, and a judicious manipulation increase or decrease of speed as the circumstances warranted, nullified the frenzied efforts of the Turkish gun-layers.

On 22 June, the *Harpy*, *Scourge*, *Foxhound*, *Savage* and *Grampus* swept up the Strait at 0500 hrs chasing a Turkish transport that had been spotted trying to cross from one shore to the other in darkness of the previous night. The destroyers exchanged fire with the shore guns while also firing

A Beagle class destroyer, believed to be HMS *Grampus,* en-route to Suvla Bay with soldiers of the Manchester Regiment aboard. Note what appears to be the starboard minesweeping kite at the ship's stern. (Courtesy of the National Museum of the Royal Navy)

on the hapless transport until she stopped. The wounded were evacuated and the prize taken in tow:

> Of course, we were not having things entirely our own way, for the Turks at Domuz Headland, as well as the batteries at Kepez Point and Erenkoi Bay, commenced pouring in shells by the dozen, as well as the occasional 'Whistler' from the big guns at Chanak itself.

The destroyers were under fire for more than an hour, including a short time when three of the vessels were stationary, taking the transport in tow, and received only three hits between them, with one seaman being slightly wounded. The *Harpy* was hit in the Wireless Room, which caught fire, but the flames were extinguished by hosing it down. However, as the burning room was above the galley, a freshly-cooked breakfast was ruined:

> Twenty-four eggs and twelve juicy rashers.... I wish the gunlayer that had sent that shot from Asia, could have heard his pedigree as expressed by our messdeck. He would have certainly thought that 'Allah' had forsaken him entirely.

The prize ship was towed to Kephalos Bay at Imbros and moored close to the armoured cruiser *Blenheim*, but before the transport could be searched:

> She suddenly turned turtle and sank like a stone, to the intense disgust of everyone concerned.

The 'human shield' defence

The Allied shelling of the towns on the shores of the Dardanelles such as Canakkale and Maidos had caused localized devastation. In response to this, a form of defence used by the Turks was a 'human shield' of civilians within a battle area to stop the shelling by the ships. Fortunately, this barbaric use of non-combatants did not end in tragedy but it is a reflection of the desperation felt by Enver Pasha, to retaliate against the inaccurate reports of Turkish civilian deaths in the shelling zones. In May 1915, the town of Gallipoli was targeted by indirect fire from British warships in the Aegean because it was being used as a headquarters location for the Turkish military, the civilians having already been evacuated. A series of misinformed reports of civilian casualties, either deliberately explosive or simply wrong, reached Enver, who proposed to round up some 3,000 British and French residents of Constantinople, ship them to the peninsula and imprison them in Gallipoli town. It was only after the energetic intervention of the American Ambassador to Constantinople, Henry Morgenthau, that the number was reduced to a total of fifty men, young and healthy so that they could survive the expected deprivations. Their ordeal lasted only a week because the British did stop shelling the town, but this was because the Turkish Army scattered their troop concentrations and headquarters staff.

Another unacceptable extension to the use of civilians was the proposal to place British and French nationals on troop transports in the hope of discouraging Allied submarines from sinking them. Fortunately, no such placements occurred. The irony is that the majority of the British and French residents of Constantinople at that time considered themselves Turkish, having lived within the Ottoman Empire most, if not all, their lives.

The redeployment of the coastal guns
The British landings of 25 April 1915 at Cape Helles, the French at Kum Kale (albeit for only two days) and the Anzacs at Ari Burnu led to a massive entrenchment of both armies and to stalemate. After two months of fighting at Helles and Ari Burnu, General Liman von Sanders was convinced that the land assault was now the main thrust of the Allies, and so a redeployment of heavy guns to bombard the invaders on the beaches and their supply ships when anchored off shore was necessary. This was also the case later in the year when a further landing at Suvla Bay took place, and a battery of 240mm L/22s was set up at Anafarta. Initially one battery of 105mm and three batteries of 150mm howitzers were released to the Helles front, but the use of the heavy coastal guns that for decades had silently protected the Strait needed to be re-evaluated. Moving artillery, particularly heavyweight guns, across the hills surrounding the

Dardanelles without mechanical transport, and therefore reliant on teams of oxen and hundreds of men, was an immense and strenuous task. It is impossible to date when each gun was moved but German maps (reference: *Der Krieg in Den Turkischen Gewassern* by Herman Loren) showing the disposition of gun batteries in 1915, 1916 and 1917 illustrate the changing nature of the threat. In May 1915, two 150mm QF guns from the *Yavuz Sultan Selim* were removed and shipped to Gallipoli with 1,000 rounds of ammunition, although one gun and half the shells were lost on a transport that was torpedoed off Marmara Island on 24 May. More secondary ships' guns and ammunition were transferred; four 88mm from the *Yavuz Sultan Selim,* two of the same from the *Hayreddin Barbarossa* before she was sunk, and two 105mm from the *Turgut Reis*. After the final Allied evacuation in early 1916, more long-range guns, including those from ships, were sited on both sides of the entrance to the Dardanelles. Although the Allied troops had left Gallipoli, they were still on the offshore islands of Lemnos, Imbros and Tenedos. The Royal Navy continued to use the anchorages of Mudros (Lemnos) and Kephalos Bay (Imbros), patrolling and mining the waters off the Dardanelles.

As the fighting settled to a war of attrition on the soil of Gallipoli, the Turkish artillery on the Asian shore was supplemented with heavier weight guns including one known as 'Asiatic Annie'. This endearing name given by British troops at Helles to a gun that was trying to kill them is misleading because it was not a single gun but a new battery at Intepe, arranged as a pair of 210mm L/22s and later a pair of 240mm L/22s, concentrating their fire on the beaches at Helles and Morto Bay, which were full of men, stores and equipment. On maximum range with the Old type shell, the fire from these guns was intermittent rather than a bombardment. A lookout was posted on a tower of the ruined Sedd el Bahr fort watching for the flash of an Intepe gun and, once seen, then a bugler would blow a long low G note to warn all who could hear it. Men would scramble for whatever cover was available, and according to Ordinary Seaman Joe Murray, Hood Battalion, 2nd Naval Brigade, Royal Naval Division:

> We had 28 seconds; I think that was the time it took the shell to come over.... Eight times out of ten they never exploded; dud shells. But it was frightening for all that.

The guns at Intepe were installed during the mid-1915 upgrading of the defences and probably came from Degirmen Burnu and Anadulo Mecidiye. The only land-based gun that could seriously challenge them was the British 5-inch breech-loading 60pr, but there were precious few of these, and they were constantly demanded for shelling Turkish positions on the peninsula. There is an interesting account from one of Asiatic Annie's gunners:

> I have my field glasses in front of me. In Seddülbahir, between their Headquarters and their trenches, are units marching to the front. 'Go ahead, Intepe, fire !', I say to myself. I can see the enemy, can't you? Less than a minute later a few salvos are fired from Intepe. One, fired with great accuracy falls on the group and blows it to pieces ! Enemy soldiers fly and fall everywhere. The battleship in front of us gets angry, becoming furious again. Intepe fires again. The ship replies with hundreds of shells again. The battleship's guns begin to fire. Intepe is silenced. The guns continue firing for hours. Intepe keeps silent for hours. Enemy planes appear over Intepe. The plane flies to find the Intepe batteries and locate them for the enemy ships so that the ships may shoot at them. The planes keep circling the skies over Intepe. But the enemy doesn't know and is not aware there are two battery positions at Intepe: A real one, is seriously hidden. Another, is fake, and in the open. The gun barrels in the open consist of boiler pipes, you see ? Every day hundreds of shells and bombs are fired by those ignorant of what our 'boiler-pipes' really are.... What an amusing sight this is.

The original Intepe Battery comprised four mobile 120mm L/30 howitzers, having been heavily engaged against the warships as they moved in and out of the Dardanelles earlier in the campaign. When the French Senegalese troops landed close to the ruin of Kum Kale on 25 April as a diversion to the British landing at Helles, Turkish troops backed by the Intepe howitzers ensured that the invaders were not allowed to penetrate any more than one kilometre. The French troops evacuated to plan on 27 April. The Intepe Battery was heavily shelled from the sea and sustained many casualties.

As 1915 turned to summer and then autumn, British aerial observation of the fall of shells had improved enough to assist ships' gunnery. Old cruisers such as *Endymion*, *Theseus* and *Grafton* based at Kephalos Bay, patrolled in turn off Cape Helles and would be instructed to fire at concealed Turkish batteries on the peninsula and the Asian coast. The time chosen for the shelling was often late in the afternoon when the sun was behind the ship but the land well illuminated. As soon as the spotter aircraft was in position, the ship would hold location and fire a ranging shot. The naval artist Norman Wilkinson, while serving with the Royal Naval Volunteer Reserve, witnessed such events:

> The range, usually about 8,000 yards, was arrived at by the navigator, who knowing our own distance from the coast to the yard, would then use a squared map on which every known Turkish battery was marked.

The aircraft would contact the ship by radio soon after the first shot to issue corrections, and the gun would fire again.

> Then just over our point of aim a dirty yellowish cloud would rise…. After four or five shots the aeroplane would make the signal 'O K,' and rapid fire was opened from all guns which bear on the side engaged.

The Turkish howitzers would return fire, often at extreme range so that the angle of descent of the shell was very steep:

> Should we be hit, the shell was likely to fall on our unarmoured decks…. Comparatively small shells had caused damage out of all proportion to the size of the projectiles.

German maps showing the disposition of Turkish guns in 1917 indicates that Intepe finally had six L/22 guns, and that there were a further three batteries within a few kilometres: Masirlik with six 240mm L/22s; Cakaltepe with three 150mm SK L/40s; Topcamlar with three 240mm

L/35s. Ultimately these batteries had even more heavy guns, as the Narrows forts were stripped of the old Krupp coastal artillery, dug into deep pits that afforded them almost complete protection from anything other than a direct hit.

By January 1916, all of the British and Allied troops had been removed from Gallipoli in a remarkable series of evacuations that duped the Turkish defenders and resulted in no loss of life, but the islands close to the Gallipoli peninsula were still manned by British troops. As 1916 became 1917, the British ships that continued to use Kephalos Bay at Imbros were subjected to shelling from a long-range German gun, a 210mm SK L/40 located at Cape Helles. This gun was removed from the SMS *Roon*, an armoured cruiser launched in 1903 at Kiel and fitted with

A Turkish officer and troops inspect an abandoned French 240mm gun at Cape Helles after the Allied evacuation. This gun is still there today. (Author's collection)

The Krupp 210mm SK L/40 from the SMS *Roon*, sited near to Cape Helles to shell British ships in Kephalos Bay, Imbros. (Author's collection)

German gunners loading the Krupp 210mm SK L/40 from the SMS *Roon*. (Author's collection)

four 210mm guns arranged in twin turrets. The ship was disarmed in November 1916, and one gun was sent to Gallipoli, where it was built into a circular pit, approximately 20m in diameter, with a central pivot giving 360-degree freedom of rotation. At a maximum elevation of 30 degrees, the gun had a range of 16,300m (17,830 yards) firing a 108kg (238lb) shell. The barrel of the gun is still there today.

The Battle of Imbros

Before the end of the war the Ottoman Navy ventured out of the Dardanelles for one last battle, taking the initiative to attack British ships at Kephalos Bay. A squadron of British warships, including the pre-dreadnoughts *Agamemnon* and *Lord Nelson*, were tasked to prevent such a breakout but the *Lord Nelson* was steaming toward Salonika, ferrying the squadron's admiral to a conference, and the *Agamemnon* was anchored at Mudros. Without battleships to confront the enemy, the destroyers and monitors at Kephalos were no match for the *Yavuz Sultan Selim* and the *Midilli*, formerly the *Goeben* and *Breslau*; the destroyers were fast but had only 4-inch guns; the monitors were armed with heavy coastal bombardment guns but were incredibly slow.

On 20 January 1918, the attacking ships carefully exited the Dardanelles and headed north along the Gallipoli coast. Although the Turks were aware that British minelayers had seeded these waters, their information on the extent of the minefields proved to be woefully inadequate. The *Yavuz Sultan Selim* soon hit a mine, which did not cause significant damage, so she was able to continue. After bombarding the signal station at Kephalos Point the Ottoman ships were sighted by the destroyer *Lizard*, which attempted to engage them, but she could not close to torpedo range due to the heavy fire directed at her. Two monitors were in the Kephalos Bay, the *Raglan* and the *M28*, and the *Yavuz Sultan Selim* aimed her fire at them, while the *Midilli* continued to fire at *Lizard*. A second destroyer, the *Tigress,* joined her companion in an attempt to lay a smokescreen to cloak the monitors but this did not work as they were too slow to get away. The well-aimed shells from the *Yavuz Sultan Selim* hit the *Raglan* several times as she attempted return fire with her two American-manufactured 14-inch Mk II/45 guns, but it was ineffective as the gunnery control team had been killed. The *Raglan* took more hits and her guns fell silent, then she was hit in the magazine, causing her to explode and sink with the loss of 127 lives. The *Yavuz Sultan Selim* continued to fire on the *M28*, striking her amidships, which caused a fire. She also sank when her magazine exploded, although most of her crew were rescued by other British vessels.

With the *Lizard* and *Tigress* taking station to shadow the two raiders as they headed south, British aircraft from Mudros were spotted, which caused the *Midilli* to take the lead because of her superior anti-aircraft armament, but she struck a mine. Soon after this the *Yavuz Sultan Selim* also hit a mine, and then the *Midilli* struck more mines, perhaps as many as four, and sank quickly with the loss of 330 of her crew. The *Yavuz Sultan Selim* hit another mine and had to abandon the doomed *Midilli* to head for the sanctuary of the Dardanelles. A screen of Ottoman destroyers prevented *Lizard* or *Tigress* from closing on the wounded ship, escorting her through the entrance as the shore batteries fired on the British destroyers and aircraft.

The *Yavuz Sultan Selim* was beached near Nagara Point to prevent her sinking, and after five days of temporary repairs was pulled off by the *Turget Reis* and towed to Constantinople for further repairs. During the time the ship was beached she was attacked by Royal Naval Air Service aircraft and was hit twice, but the bombs were too small to cause any damage. On 24 January 1918, she was shelled by the 9.2-inch Mk X/46.7 gun of the monitor *M17*, which fired ten rounds indirectly over the peninsula, but the monitor was chased off by Turkish artillery before any hits could be scored. The *Goeben* had escaped from the Royal Navy for the second time in her life.

CHAPTER 9

The Chanak Crisis and After

The Dardanelles remained tightly shut throughout the rest of the First World War. The Turkish defenders and their German commanders had not stopped expecting a second invasion, yet, ironically, when it did come there was no opposition to it at all. Journalist Harry Collinson Owen reported on the arrival of British troops at Cape Helles on 10 November 1918:

> By the time we returned to Cape Helles a big transport and an old type cruiser, both loaded with British troops, were lying there. The unwieldy craft nosed slowly ashore and put her nose to the pier just alongside the bow of the *River Clyde.* Our men – troops who have seen much hard service in Macedonia – stepped ashore with their kits, and that was all the incident there was to the second landing in Gallipoli.

Of course, by this date the war with Turkey was over.

Armistice talks between Britain and Turkey began on 26 October 1918 and were concluded four days later aboard the *Agamemnon,* veteran of the assault on the Dardanelles in 1915, anchored at Mudros harbour, Lemnos. The Mudros Armistice took effect from noon on 31 October 1918 and was signed by Admiral Gough-Calthorpe, senior British officer present, and by Reuf Bey, Turkish Minister of Marine Affairs. The terms were far-reaching: the Allies were to occupy the Dardanelles and Bosphorus forts; the Turks had to ensure that all minefields therein were cleared to achieve safe access to the Black Sea; all Turkish vessels of war were to be surrendered; the Turkish Army was to be demobilized wherever it was, except where needed for internal order; all weapons, ammunition and military stores were to be surrendered. In addition, all Allied prisoners had to be assembled in Constantinople to await repatriation, and all German troops and civilians were to be ejected from Turkish soil. According to author, military historian and Member of Parliament David Walder:

> Nearly 9,500 German and 1,000 Austrian soldiers under Liman von Sanders obeyed their orders and quietly took themselves off to Haider Pasha, a suburb on the Asiatic shore, to await repatriation.

Other, heavier conditions that were imposed under the Treaty of Sevres in 1920 effectively broke up the Ottoman Empire for good. On 12 November 1918, Admiral Gough-Calthorpe aboard the dreadnought battleship *Superb,* flagship of the British Eastern Mediterranean Squadron, led a combined fleet of British and French ships through the Dardanelles to Constantinople. After four years and three months since the light cruiser *Weymouth* had sought permission to enter the Dardanelles and had been refused, and three years and eight months since three Allied battleships had been sent to the bottom of the Strait, British and French warships at last transited the Dardanelles under the now silent guns of the forts and batteries. Admiral Gough-Calthorpe was soon to become the British High Commissioner to Constantinople. In August 1919 he was replaced by Admiral de Robeck, former Commander-in-Chief of the Allied naval assault on the Dardanelles in 1915.

The fortifications and gun batteries had been abandoned. As British troops began their occupation of the Gallipoli peninsula and the Asian side of the Dardanelles, the Turkish troops were ordered to assembly areas. Harry Collinson Owen noted, first at Cape Helles and then later in Canakkale:

> The Turkish troops occupying the peninsula had been removed some days before, and for the time being not a

British soldiers examining one of the two Krupp 240mm L/35 guns at Ertugrul above V Beach, circa 1919. The barrel of this gun and parts of its mounting are still there today. Note the ruined barrack behind the gun emplacement, which was destroyed by Allied shell fire in 1915. (Courtesy of the National Museum of the Royal Navy)

Rumeli Mecidiye fort under British occupation, circa 1919, with Krupp 240mm L/35 guns still emplaced. (Courtesy of the National Museum of the Royal Navy)

single Turk was to be seen.... Everywhere, too, were elaborate telephone connections. Here, on the ground which we had won and given up again, the Turks were expecting to fight us once more. The two heavy guns we had captured and blew up were still lying there, not far from a modern heavy battery with deep ammunition dugouts cut in rocky soil and a plentiful supply of 6-inch shells neatly arranged in galleries.... At Chanak were Turks in plenty, both soldiers and otherwise, and everybody appeared quite well fed. The population appeared pleased to see a group of British officers walking about, glad that the war for them was over.... Hamidieh fort was quite deserted.... A small party of Turkish soldiers will be temporarily left to put the guns clean and in order, and we shall hold the forts until such time as the Allies shall have decided what is exactly to happen to the Dardanelles in the future.

French troops were added to those from Britain on Gallipoli. A French brigade marched into Constantinople as a fleet of British, French, Italian and Greek ships arrived carrying more troops into Turkey. As the troops were deployed, so Constantinople became under foreign rule for the first time since Sultan Mehmed II had taken the city in 1453. On 8 February 1919, French General Louis Franchet d'Espèrey entered the city on a white horse, reproducing Mehmed II's grand entrance. The General was instantly hated by the local population when he rode his horse over a Turkish flag to signify that Ottoman sovereignty over the imperial city was over. The army of occupation steadily took control of Constantinople, much of Eastern Thrace and the Turkish Straits, ensuring Allied warships had full access at all times. British Prime Minister David Lloyd George was aggressively anti-Turk and was in no doubt that the Straits were not to be given up:

Can we leave those gates which were slammed in our face under the same gate-keeper? They were shut treacherously in our face. We cannot trust the same porter.... The Turk must be deprived of the power to veto development of rich lands under his rule.

At the Paris Peace Conference in January 1919, where the victorious nations met to determine the terms to be applied to the defeated Central Powers, a special commission discussed the mandates to be applied to the Ottoman Empire. This was intended to be a qualification to the secret deals that had been struck at the beginning of the war to carve up the empire, with Britain, France, Italy and Greece all laying their claims. Lloyd George was actively pro-Greek and in May 1919, supported the landing of a Greek army at Smyrna (now Izmir) in Anatolia.

The reaction of the disorganized and dispirited Turks to the loss of Smyrna and to the way their country was being dismembered was smouldering anger, and a new nationalism began to grow centred around the leadership of Mustafa Kemal who, for a while, was supposedly working with the Allies to oversee the disbandment of the Ottoman Army. This was not the case; men and war materials were being removed from the areas of Allied control and moved to Central Anatolia. The rise of the Turkish National Movement put Mustafa Kemal and the new nationalist government on a collision course with both the old Ottoman State and the Allies, particularly the Greeks, who brutally pushed into Anatolia with the objective of taking the city of Angora (Angora became Ankara in 1930). They were violently repulsed and eventually abandoned their claim to the region, evacuating their troops via Smyrna in September 1922. The destruction of Smyrna was a vicious and cataclysmic episode wrought on the city's population, but with the rout and ejection of the Greek Army, Mustafa Kemal said:

> There is nothing to fight about any more. The frontiers we claim for Turkey exclude Syria and Mesopotamia but compose all the areas principally populated by the Turkish race.... We are prepared to give every security for the free passage of the Dardanelles, which we will undertake not to fortify. It is only right that the Powers should agree to our creating such defensive works on the Sea of Marmara as will protect Constantinople against a surprise attack.

But during the Greek retreat Winston Churchill had said of the Dardanelles:

To ensure the safety of the Greek Army ... the line of deep water separating Asia from Europe was a line of great significance and we must make that secure by every means within our power.

And of the demands made by Mustafa Kemal's government to rid Turkey of any army of occupation, Churchill said:

If assented to, involve nothing less than the loss of the whole results of the victory over Turkey in the last war.... The British Government regard the effective and permanent freedom of the Straits as a vital necessity for the sake of which they are prepared to make exertions.

The British defence of Canakkale
In 1921 a Neutral Zone was created along the Asian side of the Dardanelles, the Sea of Marmara and the Bosphorus with the objective

A photograph that probably dates from 1922 of Canakkale quayside with Cimenlik Kalesi to the right. (Author's collection)

of preventing the Turkish Army in Anatolia having access to a shoreline, so preventing them from crossing to Europe. It was an arbitrary line of demarcation, without any tactical thought of how to defend it. As the Turks swept towards Constantinople in the north and toward the Dardanelles from central Anatolia, pushing back the Greeks as they advanced, the Allies found themselves in a precarious position.

Lloyd George agreed with Churchill's views regarding the significance of the Dardanelles and, initially referring back to the First World War, said:

> In no circumstance could we allow the Gallipoli peninsula to be held by the Turks. It was the most important strategic position in the world and the closing of the Straits had prolonged the war by two years.

And of the current crisis he said:

> It was inconceivable that we should allow the Turks to gain possession of the Gallipoli peninsula and we should fight to prevent their doing so. The peninsular was easily defended against a great sea power like ourselves and if it were to be in the occupation of a great sea power, it would be impregnable.

British ships off Constantinople and in the Sea of Marmara had only one exit to Home Waters – the Dardanelles – and the lessons of the Gallipoli Campaign were still fresh in everyone's mind: whoever held the coast dominated the Strait. Even if British troops held on to the Gallipoli shore, to have lost the Asian side would have been disastrous as Turkish artillery would threaten the passage of every vessel. Britain's decision to deny the Turkish nationalists the Dardanelles became known as the Chanak Crisis.

The defence of Canakkale began in the middle of September 1922. The commanding officer, Colonel Shuttleworth, was pessimistically told that the defence of the town was unlikely to be prolonged and that he should plan to ultimately evacuate under fire to the Gallipoli peninsula. Initially, the forces at his disposition were few, just one infantry battalion,

A view of Anadolu Mecidiye, circa 1922. (Author's collection)

92nd Battery Royal Field Artillery armed with 18prs, a section of Royal Engineers and a squadron of the 3rd Hussars. Later reinforcements did bolster numbers, including a number of Italian and French troops, but the potential size of the Turkish Nationalist Army was huge. Colonel Shuttleworth considered that the perimeter was too long, so contracted the defence to a ring of about 4 miles around Canakkale connected by the coast road, which went past Anadolu Mecidiye to a defensive position at Nagara Point. This ensured control of the Narrows, the most important part of the Strait. Like the troops on Gallipoli in 1915, the British troops at Canakkale dug in to form a trench and wire boundary up to 2 miles from the town. Those that were not digging were patrolling, and the mounted 3rd Hussars became the Colonel's 'eyes and ears'. Aircraft, supplied by the carrier *Pegasus*, were later used for reconnaissance.

HMS *Ajax*, a King George V class battleship, anchored in the Narrows to add her substantial firepower of ten 13.5-inch guns to the defence. Yet as powerful as these guns were, being able to fire a 1250lb high explosive shell over 13 miles, they would have been largely ineffective against the Turkish infantry, which were to take up positions close to the town. The ship's secondary armament of sixteen 4-inch guns was more useful, if needed. HMS *Marlborough*, an Iron Duke class battleship with heavier secondary armaments compared to *Ajax*, arrived and landed naval machine gun teams to increase the defences. Yet they were still not enough troops, and the battleships might have to act as evacuation ships rather than guardians.

French troops had largely taken over the occupation of the Gallipoli peninsula since 1919, but, concerned about the British Cabinet's inept handling of the affair and after a political settlement with the new Turkish government, France began to remove her combatants from Turkish soil. By late September 1922, all French and Italian troops had gone, so British soldiers and sailors stood alone to defend the Dardanelles against an expected Turkish onslaught. Turkish cavalry crossed into the Neutral Zone on 23 September 1923, and were intercepted by a patrol from the 3rd Hussars, but as the Turks did not recognize the concept of such a zone they politely refused to withdraw. Sensibly, the British patrol, which was seriously outnumbered, departed to report the incursion.

As the British strengthened their defences, so the Turkish guns that

An aerial photograph of the Narrows, 1922 – looking south with Cimenlik Kalesi to the left and Kilid Bahr to the right, showing transports, a destroyer and in the centre distance an Iron Duke class battleship, either HMS *Benbow* or HMS *Marlborough*. (Author's collection)

The 355mm L/22 at Cimenlik Kalesi with its barrel blown off overlooking the Narrows. The photograph was probably taken during the British occupation. (Author's collection)

were still emplaced from the previous decade, such as at Dardanos, were systematically destroyed by Royal Navy and British Army teams. Some of these were now forty-five years old but they were still considered a threat to the British positions and ships, so their breeches were removed and thrown into the sea, and their barrels blown off using shells from the stocks of ammunition still within the magazines and bunkers. These, too, were blown up to ensure that the Turkish nationalists had no ready supply of war material.

British diplomatic messages from the highest levels were directed to the new government, but to no avail as Mustafa Kemal obstinately chose not to respond. Turkish troops moved closer to Canakkale and to Constantinople, as British reinforcements arrived to take up positions both at the tiny enclave and also in the capital. The artillery available at

Canakkale and on Gallipoli now amounted to fourteen 18prs, twenty-six howitzers from 3.7-inch to 6-inch, fifteen naval 12prs, plus 6-inch guns unshipped from the Iron Duke class battleship *Benbow*. Four battleships, four light cruisers and eight destroyers lay at anchor in or close to the Narrows, and it became so crowded that incoming troopships and transports had difficulty in finding suitable anchorages. The Royal Air Force was also in strength with a squadron of Sopwith Snipes and another of Bristol Fighters, with two more squadrons on their way from Egypt.

Turkish troops were soon emplaced very close to the perimeter wire and would approach right up to it talking a little English, possibly picked up as prisoners of war, and exchanging small gifts for cigarettes. General Charles Harington Harington, Commander-in-Chief of all British forces in Turkey, described them as: 'Grinning through the wire.'

On other occasions they would taunt the British defenders, who were under very strict rules not to react or to be provocative in any way. However, no one wanted war, not even Mustafa Kemal, who had instructed his troops not to enflame the delicate situation.

Yet as each day of frustrating political manoeuvring passed so war drew closer. General Harington was instructed by the British Cabinet to issue an uncompromising ultimatum to the Turkish commander of the soldiers surrounding Canakkale to withdraw from the Neutral Zone: if they did not do so, then a state of war would exist between Britain and Turkey. The reality that all this effort was being employed to defend a little Turkish coastal town of no real significance to Britain from a nationalist army who, by rights, was entitled to it was not lost on the British public. London newspapers began to ask 'Why?' The *Daily Mail* was fiercely against the possibility of another war over such an unimportant place, and on 20 September 1922 described Canakkale as:

Chanak ... a little lonely shabby town.

Lloyd George called for the backing from the Dominions but Canada, Australia and South Africa were tired, having sacrificed enough of their young men during the previous war, and only New Zealand reluctantly agreed to send troops.

However, war was averted, largely due to the tireless endeavour of

General Harington and the diplomatic efforts of the French government. A conference between Britain, France, Italy and the Turkish Nationalists was held in early October 1922 at a place called Mudunia, a small town on the shores of the Sea of Marmara, with an agreement being concluded on 11 October 1922. The Armistice of Mudunia between the Allies and the Grand National Assembly of Turkey at last recognized Turkish sovereignty over Constantinople and the Dardanelles, together ensuring that Turkey regained much of Eastern Thrace. The Chanak Crisis had passed but in England Lloyd George had become isolated, resigning as Prime Minister on 22 October 1922. This was the beginning of the end of occupation in Turkey, and in the following year British troops left Constantinople and the shores of the Dardanelles forever.

The Republic of Turkey
The Turkish Grand National Assembly abolished the Sultanate, and on 17 November 1922, Sultan Mehmet VI left Constantinople aboard the British battleship *Malaya* heading into exile in Malta and later Italy. His last sight of the remains of the Ottoman Empire would have been the shores either side of the entrance to the Dardanelles. Now that the defunct empire was to be replaced by the Republic of Turkey, a new treaty with the Allies was required to supersede the Treaty of Sevres. On 24 July 1923, the Treaty of Lausanne was signed, which laid down the process for transition from foreign occupation, the defining of new boundaries and international recognition of the new state. Allied troops finally left Constantinople during September 1923, and on 29 October, the Republic of Turkey was proclaimed, with its capital as Angora. There were restrictions to the size of the Turkish armed forces, also the necessity to demilitarize certain areas such as the Dardanelles to a distance of up to 20km from the shore, therefore including the Gallipoli peninsula, but the new Republic was more focused on internal issues and had no external ambitions anyway.

The Straits Commission was formed under the auspices of the League of Nations to supervise the demilitarization, ensuring the Dardanelles and Bosphorus remained open to all international traffic. In 1936, this arrangement was updated by the Montreux Convention Regarding the Regime of the Turkish Straits. With this new agreement Turkey had at last control of its own waterways, restricting non-Turkish military vessels and prohibiting some types of warships such as aircraft carriers, but still had to guarantee the free passage of all commercial traffic. Turkish troops entered former demilitarized areas, which were then off-limits to everyone else, remaining so for the rest of the twentieth century. On the peninsula, which had been deserted at the end of the First World War, the sparse civilian communities that had returned were moved close to Eceabat (formally Maidos). A new fortifications building programme commenced on the Gallipoli peninsula, many in locations that defended the original 1915 invasion beaches, and along the Asian shore of the Dardanelles. The shoreline was laced with barbed wire, machine gun pits were dug, reinforced concrete block houses constructed, telephone lines were strung, and gun batteries were emplaced. Turkey had virtually no remaining big coastal defence Krupp *Ringkanones* from the previous century, and although a few of these outdated weapons still remained intact but derelict on the Bosphorus there were none operational in the Dardanelles. Turkey had no money to purchase more modern guns to defend against another possible incursion into the Strait, so an odd assortment of quick-firers and heavyweight guns were installed as batteries at various locations, having been removed from what had remained of the ancient Ottoman Navy many years earlier. Many of these batteries still exist and will be described in Chapter Ten.

Turkey remained neutral through most of the Second World War, joining on the side of the Allies in February 1945 as a gesture to ensure membership of the United Nations. Yet Turkey's neutrality and then co-operation did not mean an end to tragedy in the Dardanelles.

The loss of submarines *Atilay* and *Dumlupinar*

The Dardanelles were to take two more submarines to join the wrecks of the *E7*, *E14*, *E15*, *Joule*, *Mariotte* and *Saphir*, but these submarines were Turkish, not British or French. The first was the *Atilay,* one of a class of four constructed at the Haliç Shipyard and launched on 19 May 1939, being the first Turkish-built submarine of the twentieth century. The boat was lost with all hands at the entrance to the Dardanelles on 14 July 1942, during a routine operation, checking a newly constructed underwater detection cable. The *Atilay* set off from Canakkale on the surface, dived

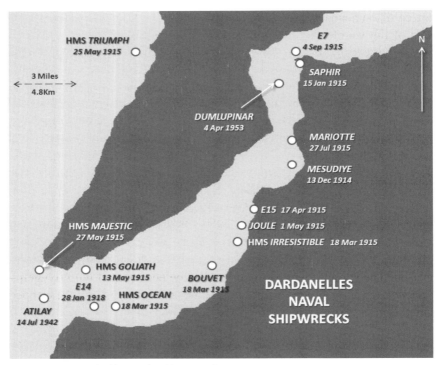

Dardanelles Naval Shipwrecks. (© Forrest)

off Morto Bay but did not surface as scheduled. It was surmised that she hit a mine, probably a relic of the First World War, as during the search operation two unexpected mines were discovered and destroyed. The boat's emergency buoy was found but not the wreck or any sign of her thirty-man crew. In 1992, divers discovered the wreck at a depth of 68m with a hole in her side that had been caused by an explosion.

The *Dumlupinar* was formally the USS *Blower*; at 2,400 tons (submerged) the largest submarine that the Turkish Navy has operated. Commissioned in 1944 for the US Navy, she was transferred to the Turkish Navy under the Mutual Defence Assistance Programme in 1950, being recommissioned as the TCG *Dumlupinar*. While returning from NATO exercise Blue Sea on 4 April 1953, at 0210 hrs the *Dumlupinar* was struck by the Swedish cargo ship *Naboland* in fog off Canakkale. The watch did not see the approaching ship until it was on top of the boat, the collision being on the starboard side level with the torpedo room. Only two of the watch survived, others being thrown into the water, two of whom were killed by the propellers of the *Naboland* as it ploughed over the submarine, which immediately started to sink by the bow; moments later there was an explosion. The *Naboland* stopped and lowered her boats, alerting the authorities so that a search for survivors could be rapidly implemented. The submarine's emergency communications buoy had been released, and it was discovered that twenty-two survivors were trapped in the stern torpedo compartment. Led by Lieutenant Selami, the men patiently awaited rescue at a depth of 90m, enduring terrible conditions of cold, darkness and increasingly poisoned air. The submarine rescue vessel *Kurtaran* – American-built and originally the USS *Bluebird*, which was purchased by the Turkish Navy in 1950 – arrived and divers were sent down. Sadly, the turbulent waters of the Dardanelles defeated all attempts to extract the men, and after three days, the rescue efforts ceased. The submariners had been told to be economical with oxygen – no smoking, movement or talking – but the last message from the trapped submariners was the sound of praying.

CHAPTER 10

The Fortifications Today

How to get to the Dardanelles

As the Dardanelles is an international waterway the obvious way to see it is by ship, but few enthusiasts of fortifications will be satisfied with just trying to photograph the numerous forts and gun batteries from a distance without an opportunity to land and explore. With the exception of the ancient stone castles of Sedd el Bahr, Kilid Bahr and Cimenlik Kalesi, there is actually little to see from a ship, as the nineteenth-century forts of earth-covered traverses and magazines present a very low profile. The gun batteries that were scattered in the hills on either shore are impossible to locate from the sea. However, cruising slowly up or down the Strait does provide a chance to understand what sailors in 1915 saw of the land on either side, and to try to imagine the fall of shells and the columns of spouting water that greeted the warships.

Other than fortifications, there are a number of impressive sights that are worth photographing from the deck of a ship. On the Gallipoli shore at the tip of the peninsula is the Helles Memorial commemorating many of the Commonwealth dead who have no known grave. The 33m tall obelisk was built in 1924 of rough stone and stands brilliant white in the sunshine. Moving through the entrance of the Dardanelles is the huge and impressive Turkish Martyrs' Memorial at Eski Hisarlik Point that was completed in 1960. Close to the Narrows is the less obvious statue of Seyit Ali in front of Rumeli Mecidiye fort, but it is easy to spot by looking for the trinket stalls and the tour buses that call at this location. Passing through the Narrows is an exciting opportunity to appreciate just how narrow the passage is, and to wonder what damage the big Krupp guns at Namazgah would have inflicted upon the warships had they cleared the minefield. Next are the walls and towers of Kilid Bahr that have commanded the Narrows for five and a half centuries. On the opposite shore is the low profile of Cimenlik Kalesi, as old but not as impressive as its neighbour. Between the castle and the town of Canakkale can be seen the open park of the naval museum and, if you are lucky, a seagoing replica of the minelayer *Nusret* moored at the pier. Above Canakkale is the huge 18 MART 1915 sign, white letters and numbers on a red field, constantly reminding the local population of that epic day. Returning to view the Gallipoli shore the Dur Yolcu memorial can be seen, a white figure of a Turkish Soldier and words of poetry carved into the hillside. Below is Degirmen Burnu, an out-of-bounds fort as it is still an active military base. Further on above Eceabat is a huge Turkish flag on the side of another hill. The excitement is over once past Nagara Point, but the attractive shores of the Dardanelles run for another 22 miles until the town of Gelibolu, where the Strait opens into the Sea of Marmara. Although some of the smaller cruise ships may anchor off Canakkale for a few hours, Istanbul is the destination for all cruises and for visitors by air, so

Degirmen Burnu today taken from the Dardanelles, easy to locate because it is below the Dur Yolcu poem. The arrows indicate the approximate positions of the former Krupp gun emplacements. (© Forrest)

it is here where one must start the journey of exploration of the Dardanelles.

British, Australian, New Zealander and other visitors to the region are generally not there to discover the fortifications but to see the Gallipoli landing beaches, the battlefields and numerous sad but beautiful Allied cemeteries. Turkish visitors, arriving by the coachload from Istanbul on a long day of travelling and zipping around the Turkish memorials, do now include a twenty-minute stop at Rumeli Mecidiye to learn of Corporal Seyit's heroic actions. Yet few visitors of any nationality investigate the history of the fortifications, therefore missing a fundamental part of the story of the defence of the Dardanelles and why the Allies decided to invade the Gallipoli peninsula in 1915. A tour of the fortifications must obviously include the more accepted locations, such as the beaches and selected cemeteries and memorials, so one should allow four to five days, although six to seven would be better to thoroughly investigate all that remains. There are a number of UK-based historic tours companies providing well organized package trips to Gallipoli. For the more independent traveller there are several local tour guides who know the battlefields well, although those that know of the hidden gun batteries are very few. For the intrepid 'fort hunter' transport is essential; four-wheel drive preferable but not crucial except for some of the remote locations.

Arriving in Istanbul by air, one can fly to either of Istanbul's international airports – Atatürk Havalimani, 10 miles west of the city, or Sabiha Gökçen, which is 30 miles to the east. Car hire is available at both airports. The driving time from Atatürk Havalimani Airport to the peninsula is around five hours – six hours from Sabiha Gökçen – and the main roads are good if one chooses the E80/O-3 motorway where electronic tolls are collected (you will need to buy a pass when arranging car hire). Do not be tempted to save driving distance by selecting shorter routes because these will either plunge you into terrible city traffic or take you on poorly maintained gravel roads. Around 50 miles west of Istanbul take the E84/D110 to Tekirdağ, bypassing the town on a new ring road, then on to Keşan, where one turns south on the E87/D550 to Gelibolu, Eceabat and the Canakkale ferry. There are restaurants and comfort stops en route.

There are a number of good hotels in Canakkale and a couple on the Gallipoli peninsula. A visitor may decide to split the visit by staying on both sides of the Dardanelles, although this is not essential. The ferries from Eceabat and Kilitbahir are easy, regular and inexpensive, particularly as a foot passenger, so it is possible to stay on the peninsula and cross daily to the Asian side. However, to do justice to the fortifications by exploring as many as possible, and to enjoy the cheerful town of Canakkale for at least one evening, a split stay is recommended.

But before even arriving in this area, a fortifications aficionado has an opportunity to visit a fort on the Bulair Lines, which cross the narrowest part of the Gallipoli peninsula, constructed to resist an army approaching from the north. Built at the time of the Crimean War by a combined Anglo-French effort, and upgraded twenty years later, the Lines were a continuous earthwork with redoubts and forts, but only the centrally located fort remains for exploration, known variously as Cimpe Kalesi, Merkez Tabya or Fort Sultan. At 170 metres elevation the fort is in a high commanding position and provided interlocking fire with two other forts – Fort Victoria 800 metres to the east overlooking the Sea of Marmara,

Cimpe Kalesi or Fort Sultan, centrally located on the Bulair Lines. (© Forrest)

and Fort Napoleon 1,600 metres to the west. The perceived Russian threat of invasion in the 1850s was a reality in 1877, when Russia declared war on Turkey once again, and Cimpe Kalesi was armed with 150mm L/26 and 90mm L/22 Krupp guns. Today the fort is derelict, with empty gun positions, caponiers and magazines to explore. It is easy to find by diverting off the E87/D550 at Bolayir and driving through the village on its only road. A line of concrete pill boxes dating from the remilitarization period can be seen either side of the road, and the fort is on the crest of the approaching hill, with vehicle access from the rear.

Fortifications that cannot be visited

Restrictions apply at several of the old fortifications that still serve as bases for the Turkish military. Warning signs prohibiting entry and taking photographs abound on all fences, some of which are run as a pair with a 3m gap between them to create a 'dead zone'. Armed sentries patrol the fences and perimeter watchtowers are strategically positioned; barriers,

This is how close an intrepid fort hunter can get to Anadulo Mecidiye. Ignore these signs at your peril! (© Forrest)

guard houses and checkpoints are obvious at the entrances. Even slowing down in one's car to peer beyond the entrance to these military areas (in the vain hope of seeing something of historic interest) invites immediate interest from the gate sentries with their automatic weapons. This actually happened to the author at Degirmen Burnu, below the *Dur Yolcu* poem blazoned on the hillside above the European shore, so acts of such bravado are not recommended. On the opposite shore at the entrance to Anadulo Mecidiye, just north of Canakkale and along the busy and fashionable promenade, similar controls are in place. On the hillside above this fort is the 18 MART 1915 sign, which is also behind wire and inaccessible. The plateau area above Anadulo Mecidiye is being developed as high-rise accommodation with a large community park and entertainment area. Not far from here is the access to Nagara Burnu, but this is similarly protected, although the guard post is several hundred metres along the access road, which has a chicane of large diameter yellow painted balls, perhaps which were once ammunition for an ancient bombard?

To the south of Canakkale is the deserted fort of Anadolu Hamidiye, which was manned by German artillerymen firing the long-range Krupp *Ringkanones*, and was a prime target for many of the Allied naval guns. Although abandoned and with the parade area and ramparts overgrown

Anadolu Hamidiye was already derelict when this photograph was taken in 2005, but it shows the magazines and casemates located in and under the traverses between each gun emplacement. The blast walls date from the re-militarization period. (© Goossens)

by tall grass, the fort is still restricted and surrounded by a 2m high stone wall topped with wire of a similar height. The main access gates were chained and locked during the author's visit but the magazines still appear intact (from a distance), having concrete blast walls in front of them, which are definitely post-First World War. Although metal 'Forbidden Zone' and '*No Fotograf*' signs are attached to the rusting wire, modern five-story apartments overlook the fort, which must give the residents a splendid view, if they were so interested. Perhaps, one day, this area will be open to public access.

The final fortification that is out-of-bounds to fort hunters is the remote Kum Kale on the Asian side of the entrance to the Dardanelles, an hour's drive from Canakkale. Although historically significant, with the ruins of the castle dating back to 1657, all the same restrictions as to the other named forts apply. It is possible to bypass this military area and move on to Orhaniye, which is well worth visiting.

Fortifications and gun batteries that can be easily found on the Gallipoli peninsula

As any battlefield historian or fortifications enthusiast knows, one must respect the historical content of where one visits. And as many former places of conflict are shrouded in sorrow for those who fell, so one must step softly and observe the words on the *Dur Yolcu* hillside written by the Turkish poet Necmettin Halil Onan:

> Traveller, Halt
> The soil you tread once witnessed the end of an era.
> Listen, in this quiet mound
> There once beat the heart of a nation.

Deference is required to the land on which a visitor may explore because all of it is owned by someone – the military, private landowners or the Turkish nation. So, observe the basic rules: do not trespass; do not cause damage; do not remove artefacts; revere the fallen of all nationalities; be polite to all people. Some of the gun batteries and forts are in remote areas where it is the natural habitat for snakes, so care must be taken and a walking cane recommended. Watch out, too, for feral dogs!

The first fortification that is easy to find on the Gallipoli peninsula is in the town of Gelibolu, formerly Gallipoli, although it is only a part of the castle that was built by the Ottomans when they were developing the harbour in the fifteenth century. It is not easy to park in the town and there is little to see, but it may make a useful break in the journey from Istanbul. The drive along the eastern shore of the Dardanelles on the E87/D550 from Gelibolu to Eceabat gives an opportunity to admire that part of the Strait that was not fortified, being north of Nagara Point.

Boghali Kalesi – At about 4km from Eceabat, just before a right turn to Bigali, the ruin of Boghali Kalesi is found on the shore opposite Nagara Point. Built in 1807 as a response to Admiral Duckworth's enterprise and armed with smooth-bore muzzle-loaders, the castle walls and the gateways still stand, as do what remains of some of the buildings within. The wall overlooking the straight is 2m thick, pierced with twenty-nine embrasures, although the number of guns installed was probably only ever half this number. Nature is slowly reclaiming this fortification but it

Boghali Kalesi in 2010. (© Forrest)

The remains of an anti-submarine net stanchion in Kilye Koyu Bay. (© Forrest)

is worth the stop to admire the commanding view it has of the ancient Hellespont. This part of the shore was the European end of Xerxes' bridge of boats. Boghali Kalesi became redundant with the introduction of the Krupp coastal artillery further to the south, although it was used as a barracks and store beyond this time. Just 2km further on in Kilye Koyu Bay are the remains of an anti-submarine net stanchion, which lies rusting in the water, although the current position does not necessarily indicate where it was located when in use. There were at least two nets stretched across the Strait off Nagara Point, and both stanchions and moored ships were used to secure them. On the shore of the bay is the ruin of an ancient stone watchtower. Set back on the west side of the road is the Gallipoli National Park Visitors' Centre, where a large-scale relief map of the peninsula is well worth viewing.

The town of Eceabat (originally Maidos) was devastated by Allied shelling in 1915, but today it exists because of the ferries that depart every half an hour to Canakkale. Just a few metres from the entrance to the ferry terminal is a statue of Kemal Ataturk, which is flanked by the breech ends of four Krupp 150mm guns, the barrels having been blown off and the sliding breech blocks removed. As the date on one of them is 1876, they were probably the L/26 model that was used at the Yildiz Battery, some 7km from Eceabat. Interestingly, too, on display is an inert 355mm shell of the Old type, i.e. 2crh.

The blown barrels of four Krupp 150mm L/26 guns now on display close to the ferry terminal in Eceabat. Between the front two barrels is an inert 355mm shell. (© Forrest)

Camburnu Tabyasi – 2 kilometres further along the coast road is the ruin of Camburnu Fort, which can be found on the shore at a sharp right-hand bend when exiting Eceabat. It is easy to locate as it is next to a building that houses the administration offices for the Gallipoli National Park. Built at the same time as Boghali Kalesi, the fort was equipped with up to twenty smooth-bore muzzle-loaders arranged in an arc. Other than the gun wall facing across the Strait, little of the other walls and nothing of

The ruin of Camburnu in 2010. (© Forrest)

the fort's buildings remain. A Turkish military hospital was located here in 1915, and Allied troops encamped here during the period of occupation from 1918 to 1922.

Kilid Bahr – Continue south along the coast road, passing the entrance to the military complex at Degirmen Burnu and then the ferry terminal, and into the little village where the striking castle Kilid Bahr rises above buildings. The road passes through a narrow gateway in the castle's curtain wall and easy parking is available at the main entrance. This is a fascinating building (described in Chapter Three) that is accessed after paying a small entrance fee. It is possible to enter the central keep to look up at the evidence of six floors within the massive structure. The climb to the top of the walls is not for the faint-hearted as the steps are uneven and there are no handrails, but the view across the Narrows to Cimenlik Kalesi is worth the effort. And by looking south from the outer wall, the V-shaped Namazgah can be seen just a few hundred metres away.

THE FORTIFICATIONS TODAY

Namazgah – The fort developed from Kilid Bahr during the French-inspired improvements in the first half of the nineteenth century, but was fully modernized by 1893, with the final installation of sixteen Krupp coastal guns set on raised emplacements. Today, the coast road that passes Kilid Bahr and Namazgah is actually within what used to be the fortified area, as is the car and coach parking at this fort. A visitor has full access to wander around, and of particular interest are the magazines, one of which is now a visitors' centre and museum, while the other is set under the raised terreplein at the point of the fort. Each of the masonry gun positions are supported by earth-covered ready-use magazines set in the traverses, some of which may be open for inspection. The two southernmost positions were for the long-range 240mm L/35 guns, which were in action on 18 March 1915. Namazgah has been subject to recent renovations and is popular with coach tour parties because of its size, ease of access and its museum. After visiting Namazgah do not return to your car because it is easy to miss the next fort, which is just a short distance away.

A photograph of Namazgah taken from the hill behind the fort. The right-hand gun emplacements, which face south, are clearly visible. (© Forrest)

Rumeli Hamidiye – It is a two-minute walk to this fort, so it is not necessary to move a parked vehicle. Leave Namazgah from the 240mm gun positions and walk along the road for 50m, and on the opposite side is the metal-gated access to Rumeli Hamidiye. The gate is decrepit and was unlocked at the time of the author's visit, and the fort can be found a further 50m through the pine trees. Built in 1896, two 355mm L/35s were set in masonry revetments with earth-covered magazines in the traverses. There is still evidence of damage to the stonework caused by incoming shell fragments. The whole site is overgrown and although entry to the magazines is possible, a visitor needs to be careful of the piles of unwholesome rubbish and numerous buzzing insects!

Rumeli Hamidiye is still very original, although overgrown today. (© Forrest)

Evidence of battle damage can still be seen on one of Rumeli Hamidiye's magazines. (© Forrest)

Rumeli Mecidiye – Just 1km further along the road is Rumeli Mecidiye, where Seyit Ali became a Turkish hero. The gun positions are in a line and of similar design to the neighbouring forts, but they are elevated from the road and accessed up a steep ramp. At the time of the author's last visit, admission to the fort was uncontrolled but the area was being fenced to manage entry. There is a small cemetery at the entrance containing the remains of those who were killed on 18 March 1915, and beside the road below is the previously mentioned statue of Seyit Ali, trinket stalls and parking. The Turkish Ministry of Culture and Tourism has recently funded a 1.7m TL renovation of Rumeli Mecidiye, repairing the gun emplacements and magazines but also laying paving where none originally existed. The effect is clinical rather than authentic but the most important addition is a Krupp 240mm L/35 on a complete traversing carriage. This gun was transferred from Izmir and is complemented by

Rumeli Mecidiye during the renovation work in 2010. In the distance is the town of Canakkale. Compare this photograph to that taken in 1919 on page 175. (© Forrest)

A closer view of Krupp 240mm L/35 at Rumeli Mecidiye in a restored gun emplacement and Gunner Seyit Ali mistakenly labouring under the weight of 355mm shell! Note the rails leading to the shell store. (© Forrest)

three bronze figures, one of whom is Seyit Ali preparing to mount the steps to the loading platform (although the lifting davit is in place). Unfortunately, the sculptor has fallen into the trap of providing the plucky gunner with a 355mm shell to load into the 240mm breech – just as well he is not under fire anymore! The rails for the shell carts leading from the adjacent magazine are still present in most of the gun positions, as are many of the carriage traverse pivots. To the rear of the fort there are ground-level ruins of the accommodation and store buildings.

Moving south to Cape Helles, through the village of Alcitepe (formerly Krithia), where there is a small private museum full of artefacts recovered from the battlefields in the area, there are a lot more fortifications that are easy to find.

Sedd el Bahr – The best approach to Sedd el Bahr is to drive into Seddülbahir village toward the Camber, but do not drive down to it. Park instead at the top of the slope by the memorial to those killed in the 3 November 1914 attack. You are now by the main gate to the fort, which is locked. Walk down to the Camber, passing a small cemetery, and turn right along the shore, where easy access to the ruined castle can be made.

The east wall of Sedd el Bahr. In the grass is a destroyed Krupp 280mm L/22. In the far distance is the Turkish Martyrs Memorial at Eski Hisarlik Burnu. (© Forrest)

During the re-militarization of the defences this fort was an important location, being opposite Kum Kale on the Asian shore, but it is now abandoned by the military and surrounded by rusting wire. Various twentieth-century buildings stand decaying, and the parade area is a wide expanse where signs of temporary buildings remain. The most interesting features are found at other areas of the fort such as the shore-level arches in the east wall, where ancient bombards would have been placed; the ruin of the tower destroyed by Allied gunfire; the north tower with its vast vaulted ceiling; the sunken magazines that were constructed in the 1880s to serve the Krupp guns set above them; the brick rings where more modern quick-firers were placed; the breech-less barrels of two Krupp L/22s seemingly just cast aside. Great care should be taken as the stone steps and some structures within the fort are in poor condition. From here it is a short drive to Cape Helles, where there is ample parking next to the British and Commonwealth memorial.

Ertugrul Battery – this battery of two Krupp 240mm L/35s is similar in layout to Rumeli Hamidiye but has been subject to a similar makeover as at Namazgah and Rumeli Mecidiye, and like those it is a popular stop for Turkish tourist coaches. There is a small entrance fee to the battery and the first stop is a museum in the east magazine. More interesting is the bent barrel of one of the 240mm L/35s that defended this position, so arranged to point across the entrance to the Dardanelles (see page 101).

The restored Ertugrul battery today. The left magazine is now a small museum. Compare this photograph to that taken in 1915 on page 97. (© Forrest)

A British-made Armstrong 4.7-inch/50 gun from the cruiser *Hamidiye*, in a low barbette emplacement on V Beach. (© Forrest)

V Beach Battery – V Beach lies between the ruin of Sedd el Bahr and the Ertugrul Battery, and was where the converted collier *River Clyde* disgorged men from the Hampshire Regiment and fusiliers from the Royal Munster and Royal Dublins into a devastating wall of rifle and machine gun fire on 25 April 1915. The V beach cemetery is close to two concrete emplacements built in the late 1930s, where pedestal mounted British 4.7-inch/50 quick-firing guns were installed *en barbette*, so that they each fired over the crest of a low parapet. One still remains, but in poor condition and with the breech removed. These guns were from Turkish cruiser *Hamidiye*, built in 1903 at the Elswick works of Armstrong-Whitworth in Northumberland. The *Hamidiye* was the ship that had tried to lure the powerful Greek *Averof* away from the entrance to the Dardanelles in January 1914, during the First Balkan War. The gun emplacements are connected by a concrete slab-topped tunnel, which is in poor condition, so should not be entered.

The barrel of a Krupp 150mm SK L/40 near to the Helles Memorial. (© Forrest)

Staying in the Cape Helles area, there are several other guns worth trying to find, the easiest of which is the barrel of a Krupp 150mm SK L/40 just 30m north of the Helles Memorial. Dated 1898, this gun was one of three of this type mounted between V Beach and W Beach, also known as Lancashire Landing, after the Allied evacuations. A second gun of this type is located 50m south of the memorial but is easy to miss if the crops are high.

Harder to find fortifications and gun batteries on Gallipoli peninsula
The Gallipoli peninsula became a national park in 1973 and has been heavily planted with pine. Of the peninsula's 33,000 hectares of land, more than half is now covered by forest, so in some areas the density of vegetation can make finding the forts and gun batteries more difficult.

Helles French Battery – Leaving the Helles car park on foot walk back along the road to the junction, turn left for 50m then head north along an overgrown track. After a few minutes walking the track turns left and then right. Off to the right is a pair of Desbois de Boussechausse 240mm guns, with another pair straight ahead, and all are in overgrown, water-filled pits. The guns were manufactured in Nantes in 1884 and formed a French battery that shelled the Turkish positions north of Morto Bay, some 3km away, and all still face in that direction. They were abandoned when the French evacuated the peninsula but it seems these guns were considered too ancient even for the Turks and did not become a part of their arsenal. None of the guns have breeches, and only one does not have its barrel blown off.

One of four French 240mm guns that remain at Cape Helles. Compare this photograph to that on page 169. (© Forrest)

The barrel of the Krupp 210mm SK L/40 from the SMS *Roon* may still be found at its emplacement. (© Forrest)

Helles German Gun – the 210mm SK L/40 from the SMS *Roon* (described in Chapter Eight) can still be found 300m north of the French battery, although it is not obvious as the location is overgrown. Only the barrel is still there, pointing over the water-filled gun emplacement, the carriage and mounting having been removed years before, probably for their scrap value. Not surprisingly, the sliding breech is missing but there is a large crack across the breech casing as if an explosive charge had been laid in it. Behind the gun but in a thicket is evidence of the gunners' camp with the outline of dug trenches. Facing west from here and across agricultural land there are four water-filled gun pits between 400m to 1,000m away, where 88mm SK L/45 quick-firers were emplaced, used in both anti-ship and anti-aircraft roles.

de Tott's Battery and more French guns – At Eski Hisarlik Burnu (Old Fortress Point), where the Turkish Martyrs' Memorial now stands, remnants of the stone walls of de Tott's Battery can still be discovered at the south-western point. The walls of the battery have been incorporated within the gardens and park surrounding the memorial and are easily missed. From here can be seen the village of Seddülbahir on the other side of Morto Bay. To the right is S Beach, where the South Wales Borderers successfully landed on 25 April 1915, and set back from the beach is the dramatic French National Cemetery. On the west side of the Martyrs' Memorial are a selection of guns from various periods of history, including nineteenth-century iron smooth-bore muzzle-loaders, probably 24prs or equivalent, cast in Liege, France and, therefore, almost certainly original to de Tott's Battery. Coach and car parking for the memorial and its gardens is a few hundred metres away, but close to the parking area are two French 138mm L/45 guns, one visible from the road but the other hidden in the trees.

The **Eski Hisarlik French Battery** is interesting because the guns are secondary armament from certain types of French pre-dreadnought battleships, dating from the 1890s. They cannot be from the lost *Bouvet*, so these guns were probably removed from either the *Charlemagne* or

One of two 138mm L/45 naval guns from a French pre-dreadnought that may still be found at Eski Hisarlik. (© Forrest)

Gaulois, each of which were fitted with ten of them. This was done to boost the French firepower after the Allied landings but then they were abandoned during the evacuation of the area. They are still with their 360-degree pedestal mountings, so they could have shelled Turkish positions to the north of the position, to the south toward Kum Kale, and also directed their fire at the Intepe Battery.

Returning north from Morto Bay and Cape Helles, via Alcitepe, the road back to Kilitbahir follows a valley to the shores of the Dardanelles at Suandere Bay. It is worth stopping here to look across the Dardanelles as this was the southern limit of the minefield and the turning point for the destroyers in their dashes up and down the Strait. In fact, this position is roughly central within the Howitzer Zone, so the whole area would have been dotted with the mobile batteries that caused so much havoc to the minesweeping efforts. South amongst the dense pine of the hillsides was the semi-permanent **Domuz Dere Battery** of 150mm L/26 howitzers, which, so far, has eluded the author even with a guide and a four-wheel drive! But driving a short distance north of Suandere Bay is what remains of the **Rumeli Mesudiye Battery** set above the road, the concrete barbette emplacements for three 6-inch/45s still remaining. These guns were from the sunken *Mesudiye,* and were in action by 18 March 1915, repeatedly striking the French battleship *Bouvet,* perhaps even fatally.

Yildiz Battery – The last 'hard to find' battery in this area is Yildiz, set up high on a hillside above Rumeli Mecidiye, and the enthusiastic fort hunter must drive a climbing route through the rear of Kilitbahir village into the pine forest. Approximately a kilometre after entering the pines a small stone water cistern can be found on the edge of a clearing, and a short distance from here in amongst the trees is the ground-level ruin of an accommodation building. The gun positions are another 100m through the trees and are not readily visible until one is close, the stone-built earth-covered magazines being most obvious. Of these there are four, two arranged as a pair and the other two singularly. On top of the most southerly magazine is a fire control position sunk into the earth, but today there is no view from here to the Dardanelles because of the trees. This battery was equipped with six 150mm L/26 howitzers, but nothing remains of the emplacements except some steps and low stone barbette

Two of the magazines at the Yildiz Battery. (© Forrest)

walls disappearing under the vegetation. Another magazine can be found 200m to the north set deep into the ground with an earth mound above it, having been constructed to supply four 87mm L/24 mortars.

Aegean coastal gun batteries

There are only a few fortifications and gun positions of interest on the Aegean coast of the Gallipoli peninsula around what was the Anzac beachhead. Of course, there are numerous other places of significance in this savagely contested area, but they are beyond the remit of this book.

The destroyed 6-inch/45 gun from the *Mesudiye* located on the Sari Bair Ridge. (© Forrest)

Starting at the Gaba Tepe Information Centre it is necessary to drive a one-way circular route to tour the Sari Bair Ridge, on which are dotted many cemeteries and memorials. Passing Lone Pine Cemetery, Quinn's Post Cemetery and then the Turkish 57th Regiment Memorial, look for the sign to the Baby 700 Cemetery, and just after this is a short track to the right to another 6-inch gun from the *Mesudiye*, its barrel blown off and breech missing.

The circular route around the ridge affords many beautiful views of the area but returning to the start point, drive north toward Anzac Cove along what became known to the invaders as Brighton Beach. It was here that the Anzac landing was intended to take place rather than where it actually did, being more suitable for an amphibious landing as it is 2km long with a gently rising hinterland, although it was well defended by the Turks. There are still concrete machine gun pillboxes located at either end of the beach, dating from the period of remilitarization in the 1930s, and another further on at Anzac. All are derelict with two gently falling into the sea due to coastal erosion.

A machine gun 'pill box' close to Gaba Tepe dating from the re-militarisation period, now derelict and falling into the sea. In the far distance is Ari Burnu, where the Anzacs landed in 1915, but the beach behind the pill box is where they should have come ashore. (© Forrest)

Kucukanafarta Battery – The final gun battery to visit is approximately 8km north of here at Kucukanafarta, where two Krupp 240mm L/22 guns stand, one complete on its mounting but without its breech or carriage, the other as just a stunted barrel. The later is dated 1875 and identified as No. 6, possibly making it the oldest remaining Krupp coastal gun that defended the Dardanelles. These two guns were emplaced here to shell

One of two Krupp 240mm L/22 guns of the Kucukanafarta Battery. These guns targeted the ships supporting the Suvla Bay landings. (© Forrest)

Suvla Bay after the landings in August 1915, and were probably from Degirmen Burnu fort.

Fortifications and guns batteries that can be easily found on the Asian coast

The best place to start a tour on the Asian side is at Republic Square (Cumhuriyet Meydani) in Canakkale, just 200m from the ferry terminal. There are two guns here, a Krupp 240mm L/35 gun with the breech in place and mounted on its carriage, and the barrel only of a British 6-inch/45. It is said that the Krupp was one of those located at Anadolu Hamidiye, which is a reasonable conclusion as the fort is just a kilometre away, although other sources suggest that it could have come from Rumeli Mecidiye. What is intriguing is the damage on the mounting below the left-hand trunnion, suggesting that a ship's small calibre shell struck just below the barrel but failed to explode: if so, it was lucky for the gun crew

Republic Square in Canakkale: a Krupp 240mm L/35 and the barrel only of a British 6-inch L/45 from the Rumeli Mesudiye Battery. Note the damage to the gun's mounting (below the trunnion), probably caused by a shell that failed to explode. (© Forrest)

The blown-up barrel of a Krupp 240mm L/35 from the Orhaniye Battery, now at the Canakkale Naval Museum. In the background is the keep of Cimenlik Kalesi. (© Forrest)

that it was not a 12-inch shell that struck the gun! Speculatively, could this damage have been caused by the detonation of a charge laid by one of the landing parties? The other barrel is a Vickers 6-inch/45 Mk VII naval gun from the *Mesudiye,* apparently from the Rumeli Mesudiye Battery on the peninsula, one of ten installed during the ship's 1903 refit. All of these guns were later recovered from the wreck and used at various locations, including those previously described and others that will follow.

The Canakkale Naval Museum is a short walk south from Republic Square, being located in the original headquarters building of the Canakkale Strait Forces and Fortification Command. Access to the museum is through a park that displays dozens of guns, some of which date back to the eighteenth century, and of different countries of origin – Britain, France, Russia, Germany, Austria and Turkey. A few are complete on their carriages but many are just gun barrels, two of which have had demolition charges exploded in them, one of them being a 240mm L/35 from Orhaniye. Other exhibits include mines, torpedoes and the remains of the German submarine *UB46*, which was sunk by a Russian mine off the entrance to the Bosphorus in December 1916. Until 2011, a full-scale reproduction of the minelayer *Nusret* was prominently displayed outside the museum on a raised area of concrete, but this has been removed and replaced by a splendid full-scale seagoing replica of the ship, which is moored at the front of the museum (see page 68). Built at the Gölcük Shipyard Command, the 30m long, 180-ton ship is capable of 12 knots and is complete with dummy mines correct to its time of action. This vessel will recreate its exploits on the Dardanelles for important visitors but, hopefully, without actually laying any mines!

A small charge is paid to enter Cimenlik Kalesi. There is an additional fee for a photograph licence, which is worthwhile because two dozen more guns of various types can be found there including field guns, howitzers, mortars and three Krupp 150mm L/26s. The museum inside the castle keep is good but the light level is kept low, presumably for the preservation of artefacts. Externally, the 1880s' ramparts are not accessible to the public, although there is an opportunity to view the hole in the castle's wall where a 15-inch shell from the *Queen Elizabeth* struck but did not explode: it is still embeded there.

The north wall of Cimenlik Kalesi today, showing the penetration damage of a 15-inch shell from the *Queen Elizabeth* that failed to explode. The shell is still inside the hole in the wall. (© Forrest)

The stunted remains of one of five Krupp 150mm SK L/40 guns of the Dardanos Battery. The distant headland in the centre of the picture is Eski Hisarlik Burnu. The open sea to the left of the headland is the entrance to the Dardanelles. (© Forrest)

Dardanos Battery – This battery can be found driving south from Canakkale on the E87/D550 for about 10km and looking for the signpost on the right-hand side of the road. The battery is 1km from the E87 but before arriving one passes the small Hasan Mevsuf cemetery dedicated to those killed by Allied shelling in this area. Although five guns of this Krupp 150mm SK L/40 quick-firer battery remain, the site is disappointing as the guns are not in their original barbette emplacements but are now displayed in an unnatural fenced area next to a huge radar navigation tower. The barrels of three guns were blown off during the British occupation but it is odd that the other two have their barrels intact, a possible reason being that these particular guns may have been re-located here post-First World War, during the period of re-militarization. The armoured turrets that once protected the guns and their crew are missing. The only impressive thing about Dardanos is the commanding views both up and down the Strait.

One of two 6-inch/45 MkVII EOC guns of the Mesudiye Battery. (© Forrest)

Mesudiye Battery – Two more 6-inch/45 Mk VII EOC guns from the *Mesudiye* can still be found at the Mesudiye Battery, roughly equidistant between Kum Kale and Canakkale, just north of Güzelyali and signposted from the E87/D550 main road. The two guns are in open concrete barbette emplacements built in 1938 and linked by a magazine tunnel within a now popular wooded picnic and camping park, but the trees are dense so that the Dardanelles are barely visible from this position. However, these guns and others from the *Mesudiye* positioned elsewhere would have been a strong defensive asset, as this mark of gun had a range of 14,000m with a 45kg high explosive shell.

Turgut Reis Battery – This battery is near to the Mesudiye Battery but on the opposite side of the E87/D550 and approached along a track that climbs upwards for about a kilometre. The *Turgut Reis* was originally the German SMS *Weissenburg*, a Brandenburg class pre-dreadnought commissioned in 1893 but sold to Turkey in 1910. The ship was fitted with four Krupp 280mm SK L/40 and two 280mm SK L/35 guns arranged

One of two turrets from the pre-dreadnought *Turgut Reis* equipped with Krupp 280mm L/35 guns, now located 2 kilometres inland. (© Forrest)

as pairs in low profile armoured turrets. Two of these turrets were emplaced on the hillside during the 1930s remilitarization programme, and are approximately 200m apart. Although 2km inland, the 18,000m range of these guns enabled them to cover the entire length of the Dardanelles from the entrance to the Narrows. It is possible to enter the turrets but the sliding breeches of all four guns have been removed.

Orhaniye – The road to Orhaniye is found by turning right off the E87/D550 toward Yenişehir and Kum Kale, passing through a new village of that name (which has a curious short length of dual carriageway) and on toward the old fort at the entrance to the Dardanelles. The road is narrow but reasonably straight, passing through a flat agricultural area of

The Orhaniye Battery is still very original, although the emplacements for the two Krupp 240mm L/35s have evidence of structures having been built in them after the guns were removed. (© Forrest)

the Menderes River. Orhaniye is reasonably easy to find as it sits on tree-covered high ground to the right of the road 2km to the south-west of Kum Kale fort. The trees have grown up during the passage of time, as originally this was a barren location, but the position has excellent views of the southern approach to the entrance of the Strait. Built in late 1880s and fitted with two Krupp 240mm L/35 guns in masonry gun positions, their huge cast steel traverse pivots are still in place. Flanking these are three well-preserved magazines and gun crew casemates built into the traverses, the centre one having an anchor motif above its entrance. In one of the gun emplacements there is evidence of a temporary building having been constructed later in the life of the battery, and this is also apparent to the rear, where the original barracks once stood but were destroyed by shelling. After intensive bombardment of the Orhaniye Battery in February 1915, the two Krupp guns were finally put out of action by the landing parties and played no further part in the war. At the southernmost magazine, steps lead to what remains of a target and rangefinder's position, although this may not be from the First World War, as during the late 1930s several additional guns were emplaced behind low brick and concrete barbette walls in front of the old battery. One pedestal mounted gun still remains but without a breech. This is a 6-inch/ 45 Mk VII EOC from the *Mesudiye,* one of four from a battery set up close to Kum Kale later during the First World War. It appears that at least one gun from this battery was moved to Orhaniye at a much later time; two others are to be found at Cakaltepe.

The ruin of Kum Kale at the entrance to the Dardanelles is within a restricted military area. Note: two twentieth-century pill boxes on the shore; the Turkish Martyrs Memorial at Eski Hisarlik Burnu; the 6-inch/45 gun in the foreground. (© Forrest)

Harder to find fortifications and gun batteries on the Asian coast
By 1917, at least twelve additional batteries had been sited around Kepez, Dardanos, Erenkoi, Halileli and Yenisehir, equipped with guns ranging from 87mm howitzers in an anti-aircraft role to 240mm L/35s moved from the Narrows forts. Evidence of most of these positions has been lost although a few do remain, but they can be hard to find. The use of a local guide with specialist knowledge and a four-wheel drive vehicle is recommended.

Intepe Battery – Starting from the new Kum Kale village, take a narrow turning to the north soon after entering the village, and after 2km along an unmade road a small Turkish cemetery will be seen on the left. This is the last resting place of fourteen artillerymen of the Intepe Battery, which was originally equipped with four 120mm L/30s. These guns were effective against the French landings at Kum Kale but were targeted

The position of the second Intepe Battery, better known to the troops at Cape Helles as 'Asiatic Annie'. The arrow indicates the location of a part-buried Krupp gun barrel amongst the crops. (© Forrest)

themselves by Allied ships soon after, and nothing now remains of the battery. The position of the cemetery is misleading because a second battery was established 1km further along the road (known to British troops as 'Asiatic Annie' – see Chapter Eight) consisting of pair of 210mm L/22s and a pair of 240mm L/22s. There is evidence of one of these guns as part of a buried barrel is visible in a field, but it is easily missed if the planted crops are tall.

Kum Kale/Cakaltepe Battery – Following the unmade road, which has now become a track down to the sea, a small harbour is discovered with two more pedestal mounted 6-inch/45 Mk VII British-made guns from the *Mesudiye*. Each gun is in a concrete emplacement from the late 1930s, with a 2m thick concrete heavy protective 'eyebrow', reminiscent of the Second World War Atlantic Wall defences on the French and Belgium coasts. The guns have an excellent view to the north over Erenkoi Bay, but as with all others of this type, the breeches have been removed and the condition of them is so poor due to surface corrosion it is impossible to identify the manufacturer's markings.

The 1930s' Cakaltepe Battery overlooking Erenkoi Bay. Each of the two gun positions utilized a 6-inch/45 from the *Mesudiye*. (© Forrest)

223

Cakaltepe/Halileli Battery – What remains of this battery, which dates from 1916, is difficult to find but can be approached from two ways, either from the south before entering new Kum Kale or following the track from the Kum Kale/Cakaltepe Battery and turning inland. The only indicator to the proximity of the battery is a small cemetery with two graves, and a small Turkish flag on a rudimentary pole. Here one must park a vehicle as the battery is 400m to the east across agricultural fields and set behind a natural rise in the land, so as to fire indirectly without revealing the battery's position. Three Krupp 150mm SK L/40 guns were emplaced and it is still possible to identify at least one of the flattened earth areas of the gun emplacement. Only one barrel remains, its breech blown off and nearly totally buried in the soil. The remains of the gun's pedestal mounting can be found in a field a few hundred metres away.

Eric Goossens, local historian and owner of the Gallipoli Houses Hotel, stands in one of the three (now hard to find) emplacements for a Krupp 150mm SK L/40 at the Cakaltepe Halileli Battery. (© Forrest)

Topcamlar Battery – Following the track further to the east the use of a four-wheel drive is now essential, particularly in wet weather, as the Topcamlar Battery is set on the reverse side of a hill that is approached up a climbing track. Three Krupp 240mm L/35 guns were emplaced and all barrels still remain with their mountings but have been thrown onto their sides as the traversing carriages have been removed, probably for scrap. It is still possible to identify two of the tumbledown magazines next to the guns, and behind the emplacements are a series of cuttings leading to a flat area where, presumably, the artillerymen's tented camp was located. The most likely origin of these guns was that they were moved from Anadolu Hamidiye in 1916.

The Topcamlar Battery. The arrow indicates one of the three Krupp 240mm L/35 guns that remain. (© Forrest)

The barrel and mounting of a Krupp 240mm L/22 at the Erenkoi Battery. (© Forrest)

Erenkoi Battery – Moving further east along the coast, the Erenkoi Battery is set in deep pits along the crest of a hill. It was here that seven Krupp 240mm L/22 guns were positioned in 1916, taken from the Narrows forts. All of the guns and most of their mountings and carriages are still there but pushed on their sides, and are very difficult to get to because of the undergrowth that fills the pits. Confusingly, the Erenkoi Battery is near the village of Intepe, as Erenkoi was renamed in the 1930s, and is located close to the E87/D550.

Istanbul

There are two other important places to visit that relate to the defence of the Dardanelles, but they are not on the shores of the Strait. Returning to Istanbul, the Naval Museum at Beşiktaş and the Military Museum at Harbiye will provide further interest and information. Both are easy to

226

find using public transport, or even easier by taxi. The Naval Museum is close to the Beşiktaş pier terminal, so a ferry from the Golden Horn is a stimulating way of getting there. This museum is small and contains mainly scale models of past Turkish warships, numerous paintings, examples of naval uniforms, and also some artefacts from the *Yavuz Sultan Selim* (*Goeben*). Sadly, this ship of great historical importance was broken up in 1973.

The Military Museum is more exciting, with many examples of field pieces from different periods of history. In front of the main entrance is the world's last surviving Krupp 355mm L/35, complete on its mounting and traversing carriage. The giant gun with its 12.4m long barrel is displayed with a larger than life Seyit Ali, who is cast in dull green resin to represent bronze, standing 2.3m tall and carrying a correspondingly even larger shell than he actually did. According to an information panel close by, this gun was one of two recovered from the Dardanelles (although the panel does not give a date) and was assigned to the 65th Division in Balikesir. Both guns were later transported to Izmir but one of them was dropped in the sea and was not recovered.

The last surviving Krupp 355mm L/35 outside the Istanbul Military Museum. (© Forrest)

APPENDIX 1

Krupp Coastal Defence Guns Purchased by Ottoman Turkey

Bore sizes 210mm-355 mm

Year	Size & Type	Quantity
1873	210mm L/22	28
	240mm L/22	50
	260mm L/22	10
	280mm L/22	12
1875	355mm L/22	1
1885	240mm L/35	22
	355mm L/35	7
1886	240mm L/35	4
	Total	134

Source: forum.axishistory.com

APPENDIX 2

Krupp Coastal Defence Gun Locations on the Dardanelles

Bore sizes 210mm-355 mm

British Fort No.	Fort Name	Size & Type	Quantity
1	Ertugrul Battery	240mm L/35	2
3	Sedd el Bahr	240mm L/22	2
		260mm L/22	2
		280mm L/22	2
4	Orhaniye Battery	240mm L/35	2
6	Kum Kale	210mm L/22	1
		240mm L/22	2
		260mm L/22	2
		280mm L/22	2
13	Rumeli Mecidiye	240mm L/35	4
		280mm L/22	2
16	Rumeli Hamidiye (Hamidieh II)	355mm L/35	2
17	Namazgah	210mm L/22	7
		240mm L/22	5
		260mm L/22	2
		240mm L/35	2
19	Anadolu Hamidiye (Hamidieh I)	240mm L/35	7
		355mm L/35	2
20	Cimenlik (Hamidieh III)	210mm L/22	1
		240mm L/22	1
		355mm L/22	1
		355mm L/35	1
22	Degirmen Burnu	210mm L/22	1
		240mm L/22	6
24	Anadulo Mecidiye	210mm L/22	1
		240mm L/22	3
		260mm L/22	3
		280mm L/22	3
30	Nagara Burnu	240mm L/22	6
		260mm L/22	1
	Total		78

Sources: *Der Krieg in Den Turkischen Gewassern* by Hermann Loren; *Gallipoli – The Ottoman Campaign* by Edward J. Erickson; *A Military Atlas of World War One* by Arthur Banks; *History of the Great War: Naval Operations Vol. II* by Sir Julian S. Corbett.

APPENDIX 3

Dardanelles Gun Batteries –
18 March 1915

Excludes coastal guns identified in Appendix 2 but includes mobile batteries.

European Shore (North-East to South-West)

Battery Name / British Fort No.	Size & Type	Quantity
Yildiz / 9	150mm L/26	6
	87mm L/24	4
Havuzlar	120mm L/24	4
	87mm L/24	10
Kum Burnu	120mm L/24	4
	47mm L/40	6
Rumeli Mesudiye / 7	6-inch/45	3
Suandere North	120mm L/24	4
	87mm L/24	4
	75mm L/40 QF	4
	47mm L/40	6
Suandere South	210mm L/6.4 Mortar	10
	120mm L/24	4
	88mm SK L/30 QF	4
Tenkir Dere	150mm L/10.8	4
Domuz Dere	150mm L/10.8	4
Kereves Dere	120mm L/11.6	6
Eski Hisarlik	150mm L/10.8	4
	Total	91

Asian Shore (North-East to South-West)

Battery Name / British Fort No.	Size & Type	Quantity
Nagara Burnu	150mm L/26	5
Anadulo Mecidiye	210mm L/6.4 Mortar	6
Cimenlik Kalesi	150mm L/14	4
Kepez	87mm L/24	6
	75mm L/40 QF	3
	57mm L/40 QF	3
	Nordenfelt	6
Dardanos / 8	150mm SK L/40	5
Ak Tepe	150mm L/26	4
	87mm L/24 QF	4
	75mm L/30	4
	57mm L/40 QF	6
Karantina	150mm L/10.8	8
	120mm L/11.4	2
Erenkoi/Eski Kale	150mm L/10.8	12
	120mm L/30	4
Intepe	120mm L/30	4
	Total	86

Sources: *Der Krieg in Den Turkischen Gewassern* by Hermann Loren; *Gallipoli – The Ottoman Campaign* by Edward J. Erickson; *A Military Atlas of World War One* by Arthur Banks; *History of the Great War: Naval Operations Vol. II* by Sir Julian S. Corbett.

APPENDIX 4a

Dardanelles Minefield up to 18 March 1915

Original Lines of Mines						Additional Mines to Reduce then Close the Strait			
No.*	Date	Location	Details	Vessel	Qty	Date	Details	Qty	Total
II	4 August 1914	Havuzlar – Kepez	Depth 4.5m Interval 80-100m	*Selanik*	22	19 August 1914 / 1 October 1914	Closure of passages on both shores	8 / 9	39
III	6 August 1914	North of Havuzlar – Dergirmen	Depth 4m Interval 75m 2 mines exploded	*Selanik*	26	17 August 1914 / 19 August 1914 / 1 October 1914	Narrowing passage on on Asian shore then full closure	4 / 8 / 9	47
I	15 August 1914	North of Soganli Valley – Kepez lighthouse	Depth 4.5m Interval 50m 1 mine exploded	*Intibah*	40	24 August 1914 / 27 September 1914	Narrowing passage on Gallipoli shore then full closure	3 / 4	47
Ia	24 September 1914	South of Soganli Valley		*Intibah*	29				29
IV	1 October 1914	South of Namazgah – Anadolu Hamidiye	Depth 2.5m 1 mine exploded	*Intibah*	29				29
Ib	9 November 1914	North of Line I	1 mine exploded	*Samsun*	16				16
IIa	17 December 1914	South of Havuzlar – Kepez line	1 mine exploded	*Nusret*	50				50
IVa	17 December 1914	South of Line IV		*Nusret*	28				28
IVb	30 December 1914	South of IV a		*Nusret*	39				39
V	26 February 1915	Cape Degirmen – Canakkale lighthouse	Depth 4m	*Intibah*	53				53
E	8 March 1915	Erenkoi Bay	Interval 100m	*Nusret*	26				26
					358			45	**403**

This table is reproduced in part, courtesy of *Expedition to the Golden Horn: Military Operations in the Dardanelles and on the Aegean Sea* by Piotr Nykiel.
Number* – Line Number refers to German drawing No. 7 from *Der Krieg in Den Turkischen Gewassern* by Hermann Loren.

APPENDIX 4b

Dardanelles Minefield and Anti-Submarine Nets from 28 March to December 1915

Number	Date	Location	Qty
T2	28 March 1915	Centred between Domus Dere and Erenkoi Bay	9
T1	31 March 1915	South of T2 close to Domus Dere	10
U	22 May 1915	The Narrows - Cimenlik to Namazgah	20
U1	20 June 1915	The Narrows - Cimenlik to Kilid Bahr	21
U2	29 August 1915	Centre of channel off Nagara Point	15
U3	September 1915	Extension to East of U2	3
VI	30 September 1915	Angled South of Ia	47
VII	11 December 1915	South of VI	48
			173

A-S Net	Date	Location
1	26 July 1915	Centre of channel off Nagara Point
2	24 December 1915	Centre of channel off Nagara Point

Source: *Der Krieg in Den Turkischen Gewassern* by Hermann Loren

APPENDIX 5

Extracts from the Foreign Committee Paper (No. 93) March 1886

Source: The National Archives: ADM231/8 No. 93, March 1886

SCHEMES FOR ATTACKING FORTS
Admiral Sir Geoffrey Hornby, K.C.B., 1880

In 1880, as in 1878, it was the opinion of Admiral Sir Geoffrey Hornby, also of the senior officers serving under him in the latter year, that with a squadron of seven ironclads and a corvette, it would be better to pass Forts Namazieh [Namazgah] and Sultanieh [Cimenlik], so as to envelope and silence Fort Medjidieh [Anadolu Mecidiye], and then to drop down and silence the two former, than to tell off a weak squadron to attack each fort simultaneously.

He was of the opinion that, if the heavily armed forts of the Dardanelles were to be attacked by ironclads, the ships should be anchored, which would necessitate their being very near the shore. In that position, and inasmuch as the guns in the forts are mounted in wide embrasures, their fire would be best subdued by shrapnel shell and case shot. Machine guns mounted in the tops would also be specially effective.

Admiral Hornby added, however, that when the new forts are built (they were completed in 1883) the propriety of attacking the whole position by fleet alone, will be placed in a very different light.

Lieutenant Bourke, R.N., 1883

In 1883, Lieutenant Bourke, R.N., considered that the best method of forcing the Dardanelles would be to push up at high speed above Fort Nagara Kalesi [Nagara Burnu], and then concentrate the whole force on each individual from the northward.

Captain Rawson, R.N., 1883

Captain Rawson, R.N., in forwarding the above report by Lieutenant Bourke, R.N., remarked that from his own observations of the forts in the Narrows, he also was of opinion that an attacking fleet should force its way to the east of Fort Nagara Kalesi, and then, concentrating on each fort in succession, work its way down again. By this means the four strongest forts, viz: Nagara Kalesi, Medjidieh, Namazieh and Sultanieh, could all be taken in reverse or in flank, and the only modern fort which would be able to bring its guns to bear directly would be that of Derma Burnu [Degirmen Burnu]. Should the enemy have ships and torpedo boats to assist in the defence, these should be specifically engaged by torpedo boats of the squadron.

Abstract from the Foreign Committee Paper (No. 65), 1885
The new works above referred to by Admiral Sir Geoffrey Hornby, are ten in number, eight being on the European and two on the Asian side. [These included redoubts, where both 150mm howitzers and 200mm mortars were located in open barbette positions. One of the positions was Boghali Kalesi, where fourteen smooth-bore guns and two 150mm mortars were located.] They are situated on high ground commanding the channel and waterside forts, but those on the European side are in turn commanded by heights in their immediate rear.

The forts in the rear of the two principal waterside forts on the European side, i.e. Namazieh and Derma Burnu, command, moreover, the two principal waterside forts on the Asiatic side, i.e. Sultanieh and Medjidieh.

The Key of the position is a plateau 653 feet high, on the European side in the rear of Fort Derma Burnu, from which are completely commanded the whole of the waterside forts on both sides of the channel as well as four southernmost hill forts on the European side, the latter being taken in reverse.

A force occupying this hill with field and machine guns would render untenable the whole of the above mentioned works on the European side, and would greatly assist ships in attacking the forts on the Asiatic side.

The seizure of this hill would therefore be the first objective of a land force.

In a paper prepared in the Intelligence Department of the War Office in 1880, it is stated that if a Brigade of Infantry 2,500 strong could land secretly on each shore of the Dardanelles, they could possess themselves of the forts, and thus secure the command of the Straits.

The new hill forts were not built when this was written, but since they are commanded in reverse by the height which was then and still is the objective, this statement equally applies to the existing conditions.

In the War Office paper it was suggested that the force for the European side should be landed on the west side of the Gallipoli peninsula, in the bay to the south of Gaba Tepe, which is some 7 or 8 miles from the height in question.

Kepez Bay, 5 miles south of Chanak, is the landing place proposed for the force operating on the Asiatic side. Its objective would be the ridge extending from the village of Karaivren to Nagara, which completely commands Forts Sultanieh, Medjidieh and Nagara Kalesi, the two latter being within musketry range.

The two Brigades could be landed simultaneously at daybreak, the Fleet with the Asiatic Brigade passing Forts Seddul Bahr [Sedd el Bahr] and Koum Kaleh-si [Kum Kale] at the entrance, just before light dawned.

The presence of the Fleet would ensure the garrisons of the forts at the Narrows remained at their guns, thus preventing their moving out to attack either of the brigades.

The heights on both sides having been seized by the troops, a simultaneous attack could be made on Forts Namazieh, Derma Burnu, Sultanieh and Medjidieh by the Fleet and the troops, the former passing the batteries and enfilading them from upstream, anchoring for the purpose.

The waterside batteries being low, not having more than 30 feet command (with the exception of Fort Namazieh which has 60 feet), and their embrasures being very wide, the fire of machine guns and rifles from the tops of the ships would search out the whole of the works, since they are deficient in cover.

Having silenced these forts, and rendered their guns temporarily unserviceable, the Fleet could then move up to the attack of Fort Nagara Kalesi.

This work could be attacked on three sides by the Fleet and on the fourth by the troops, who would also take the two detached batteries on the ridge to the rear.

There would then remain only the four northernmost hill forts [directly opposite Nagara Burnu] on the European side, which, from their height, would be difficult to silence from the ships, but being all commanded by heights a short distance to their rear, they could be rendered untenable by the land force on the European side.

It is considered necessary that the landing of the Brigades should be of the nature of a surprise, in order that time may not be given for reinforcing the Dardanelles garrisons from Constantinople, which could be effected in 24 hours. Any strengthening of these garrisons would necessitate a corresponding increase in the strength of the landing force.

APPENDIX 6

British and French Battleships used in the Dardanelles Campaign up to 18 March 1915

Type	Ship	Class	Launched	Displacement (tons)	Main Armament	Quantity
Super-Dreadnought	HMS *Queen Elizabeth*	Queen Elizabeth	1913	33,000	BL 15-inch Mk I /42	8
Battlecruiser	HMS *Indefatigable*	Indefatigable	1909	22,000	BL 12-inch Mk X /45	8
Battlecruiser	HMS *Indomitable*	Invincible	1907	20,700	BL 12-inch Mk X /45	8
Battlecruiser	HMS *Inflexible*	Invincible	1907	20,700	BL 12-inch Mk X /45	8
Pre-Dreadnought	HMS *Agamemnon*	Lord Nelson	1906	16,500	BL 12-inch Mk X /45	4
Pre-Dreadnought	HMS *Lord Nelson*	Lord Nelson	1906	16,500	BL 12-inch Mk X /45	4
Pre-Dreadnought	HMS *Cornwallis*	Duncan	1901	14,000	BL 12-inch Mk IX /40	4
Pre-Dreadnought	HMS *Irresistible*	Formidable	1898	15,800	BL 12-inch Mk IX /40	4
Pre-Dreadnought	HMS *Vengeance*	Canopus	1899	12,950	BL 12-inch Mk VIII /35	4
Pre-Dreadnought	HMS *Albion*	Canopus	1898	12,950	BL 12-inch Mk VIII /35	4
Pre-Dreadnought	HMS *Ocean*	Canopus	1898	12,950	BL 12-inch Mk VIII /35	4
Pre-Dreadnought	HMS *Goliath*	Canopus	1898	12,950	BL 12-inch Mk VIII /35	4
Pre-Dreadnought	HMS *Canopus*	Canopus	1897	12,950	BL 12-inch Mk VIII /35	4
Pre-Dreadnought	HMS *Majestic*	Majestic	1895	14,900	BL 12-inch Mk VIII /35	4
Pre-Dreadnought	HMS *Prince George*	Majestic	1895	14,900	BL 12-inch Mk VIII /35	4
Pre-Dreadnought	HMS *Swiftsure*	Swiftsure	1903	11,800	BL 10-inch Mk VI /45	4
Pre-Dreadnought	HMS *Triumph*	Swiftsure	1903	11,800	BL 10-inch Mk VII /45	4
Pre-Dreadnought	*Verite*	Liberte	1907	14,900	305mm /40 Model 1893/96	4
Pre-Dreadnought	*Bouvet*	Bouvet	1896	12,200	305mm /40 Model 1893/96 274mm /45 Model 1893	2 2
Pre-Dreadnought	*Charlemagne*	Charlemagne	1895	11,300	305mm /40 Model 1893/96	4
Pre-Dreadnought	*Gaulois*	Charlemagne	1896	11,300	305mm /40 Model 1893/96	4
Pre-Dreadnought	*Suffren*	Suffren	1899	12,750	305mm /40 Model 1893/96	4

APPENDIX 7

The Power of the Guns

The range of any gun is directly related to its barrel length: the longer the barrel the greater the range of the projectile fired. The nomenclature applied to the description of a gun includes a suffix, i.e. /40, /42 or L/22, L/35, where the number signifies a multiplication of the bore to achieve the barrel length.

The 15-inch Mk I/42 – the barrel length being 52 feet, 6 inches long; 42 times the calibre – guns of the *Queen Elizabeth* had a range of 23,734 yards (21,702m) at the maximum elevation of 20 degrees. The *Queen Elizabeth's* gun mountings were modified in the mid-1930s to elevate to 30 degrees, extending their range to 32,500 yards (29,720m) using a 6crh (calibre radius head) projectile.

The best range that the heaviest of the Krupp guns, the 355mm L/35 – the barrel length being 12.425m long; 35 times the calibre – could offer was 18,500 yards (16,900m) and so could not outshoot this ship. But comparing 10-inch guns: the British EOC BL10-inch Mk VI/45 guns fitted to *Swiftsure* and the Vickers BL10-inch Mk VII/45 on *Triumph* ranged to 14,860 yards (13,600m), less than the Krupp 240mm L/35, which had a range of up to 16,190 yards (14,800m).

The 12-inch guns fitted to the British ships were Armstrong/EOC or Vickers of three types. Firstly, the Mk VIII/35 fitted to the nineteenth-century pre-dreadnoughts *Vengeance*, *Albion*, *Ocean*, *Canopus*, *Goliath*, *Majestic* and *Prince George* had a maximum range of around 14,860 yards (13,600m), and so could be outranged by any of the Krupp L/35 guns at the Narrows. Secondly, the Mk IX/40s on *Cornwallis* and *Irresistible*, with a range of 15,600 yd (14,260m), were also inferior to the long-barrel Krupp guns. Finally, the Mk X/45 on *Agamemnon*, *Lord Nelson*, *Indefatigable*, *Indomitable* and *Inflexible* with a range of 16,450 to 18,850 yards (15,040m to 17,230m) depending on the shell profile, just exceeded the range of the 240mm L/35 coastal guns and matched the 355mm L/35. The Krupp L/22 guns of all bore sizes defending the Dardanelles had considerably less range than the naval guns employed against them, typically around 8,750 yards (8,000m), and were of little use unless the ships came very close.

Table of comparison: British, French and Turkish main armaments
The range all types of guns, both naval and coastal, are influenced by many

	Shell Type	Main Armament	Range	@ elevation	Shell Weight
British	4crh	BL 15-inch Mk I /42	23,730 yards / 21,700m	20 deg	1920lb / 871kg
British	2crh	BL 12-inch Mk X /45	16,450 yards / 15,040m	13.5 deg	850lb / 386kg
British	4crh	BL 12-inch Mk X /45	18,850 yards / 17,230m	13.5 deg	850lb / 386kg
British	2crh	BL 12-inch Mk IX /40	15,600 yards / 14,260m	13.5 deg	850lb / 386kg
British	2crh	BL 12-inch Mk VIII /35	14,860 yards / 13,600m	13.5 deg	850lb / 386kg
British	2crh	BL 10-inch Mk VI /45	14,800 yards / 13,600m	13.5 deg	500lb / 227kg
British	2crh	BL 10-inch Mk VII /45	14,800 yards / 13,600m	13.5 deg	500lb / 227kg

	Shell Type	Main Armament	Range	@ elevation	Shell Weight	
French	2crh	305mm / 40 Model 1893/96	13,120 yards / 12,000m	15 deg	770lb / 349kg	
Turkish	New	355mm L/35	18,500 yards / 16,900m		1597lb / 725kg AP	1366lb / 620kg HE
Turkish	New	240mm L/35	16,190 yards / 14,800m			474lb / 215kg Frag
Turkish	New	280mm L/22	8,700 yards / 8,000m			
Turkish	Old	355mm L/35	11,800 yards / 10,800m			
Turkish	Old	240mm L/35	12,030 yards / 11,000m			
Turkish	Old	280mm L/22	8,300 yards / 7,600m			

Notes

The range figures quoted are based on those established by each manufacturer when a gun was new.
Range assumes using Full Service Charge.
crh – calibre radius head.
For the definitions of 'New' and 'Old' Turkish shells, refer to Appendix 9.
Sources: www.navweaps.com; www.navyingallipoli.com

variables, such as charge strength, shell type and weight, and the condition of a gun's bore. These elements are also related to each other in that, for example, guns would fire reduced charges whenever possible to lessen the effect of barrel wear. And different shells will have different driving band interference qualities, which will also influence barrel wear, the driving band of a shell being a band of soft metal on the external diameter. When the shell is fired the pressure of the propellant swages the metal of the band into the rifling of the gun barrel, both providing a seal to prevent the gases from blowing past the shell and to engage with the rifling to spin-stabilize the shell.

The life expectancy of big naval guns was calculable and based on the number of rounds fired; for example, the 12-inch Mk X/45 had a barrel life of around 220 rounds. In January 1915, *Indefatigable*, which had fired on the forts at the entrance to the Dardanelles the previous November, was directed to Malta for a refit, including the replacement of a number of worn gun barrels.

The range progressively reduced with every firing as the barrel wore and the clearance around the shell minutely increased, so allowing a leakage of propelling gases. In trials of large calibre naval guns conducted by Krupp before the First World War, they concluded that the range reduced by 10m (11 yards) with each firing.

APPENDIX 8

The Director Fire Control System

A t the beginning of the First World War the Royal Navy had made considerable efforts to improve the techniques for computing the range of sea targets and tracking them as they moved, largely thanks to efforts by officers such as Percy Scott and Frederic Dreyer. Admiral Scott had commanded HMS *Excellent*, the Royal Navy's gunnery school, and Admiral Dreyer was involved with numerous gunnery trials and committees throughout his naval career, including developing the Dreyer Table of gun corrections. Improvements in optical range finding equipment produced by Glasgow-based Barr and Stroud, and refinements of the Director Fire Control System, meant that by 1914, some British capital ships were reasonably equipped in this aspect of gunnery to go to war. Yet it was not until 1916 that the Royal Navy was properly prepared. The Director Fire Control System meant that all a ship's main armament could bear on a target, each gun setting a slightly different shell trajectory to allow for its position on the ship, so as to land all the shells at the same position and the same time when fired as a salvo. The effect could be devastating but, if the salvo missed, then a correction could be made by the Director Controller to all guns at the same time. This system was to be used to good effect at the Battle of Jutland in 1916, albeit with some reservations outside of the scope of this book. However, good as this system was for its day it still relied on the human eye to determine correction, and it would not be until the advent of radar that a much better system was established. In the event of the Director Fire Control System being disabled, each gun turret could maintain local control to lay and fire its guns. The German company Zeiss was producing excellent quality optical equipment at the beginning of the First World War, and Turkey did receive German stereoscopic rangefinders, which were employed in the Dardanelles defences.

APPENDIX 9

Shells, Fillings, Fuses and Charges

Shells

The Krupp coastal guns in the forts of the Dardanelles were supplied with an assortment of shells dependant on diameter and purpose: 210mm, 240mm, 260mm, 280mm, 355mm; Shrapnel/Fragmentation, High Explosive, Armour-Piercing, some of which were tipped with a soft iron cap for improved armour penetration, and all with a variety of impact, timed or delayed fuses. There was a mixture of what has become known as New and Old shell types, which relates to the materials of manufacture and to the streamlining of the shell profile for improved range. Old shells were made from chilled cast iron, which was very thick and consequently contained a small amount of explosive for a given diameter. They were relatively cheap to manufacture and entirely suitable against ironclad ships, the perceived threat the Ottomans expected when they purchased their first Krupp coastal guns in the 1870s. However, as technology moved on this material was not shockproof enough for the explosive fillings developed at the end of the nineteenth century, and inadequate for piercing the armour of modern battleships, even if capped. New shells were manufactured from forged and machined steel to contain the massive forces, and these thin-walled shells carried more explosive to greater range thanks to streamlining. The nose profile of an Old shell measured 2crh (calibre radius head), which is the relationship between the contour of the nose and the calibre of the shell; that of the New shell was 4crh. British main armament shells were also of either 2crh or 4crh depending on the type of gun employed, the more modern using the streamlined 4crh (see Appendix Seven, Table of Comparison: British, French and Turkish Main Armaments).

Guns of longer range than the opposition have an obvious advantage but to capitalize on this the delivery of the heaviest projectile is also important. The Krupp 355mm L/35 gun could deliver a 725kg (1595lb) armour-piercing shell or a 620kg (1365lb) high explosive shell, both of which were heavier compared to the shells fired by the majority of the British ships and all of the French ships. Only the *Queen Elizabeth* fired a heavier shell than the largest Krupp guns – 1,920lb (871kg). The Krupp L/22 guns of all bore sizes fired lower weight shells than most of the Allied guns.

APPENDIX 9

Fillings

An essential part of any shell is the explosive filling, generally known as the 'bursting charge'. Until the early twentieth century, British bursting charges were predominantly black powder, which is hygroscopic and has to be stored in a damp-free environment. The powder would be either poured into the shell cavity or held in a loosely restrained bag at the base of the shell, but by 1910, the Royal Navy had adopted lyddite as a bursting charge. Lyddite – British picric acid, a chemical compound called trinitrophenol – was first tested at Lydd in Kent (hence lyddite). When used as a bursting charge lyddite had two to three times the explosive power of black powder for the same weight, but was found to be more sensitive and could explode immediately on contact with a target, rather than be able to penetrate any thickness of armour. By 1914, TNT – trinitrotoluene – was considered a safer explosive for filling shells and more reliable as a bursting charge, and would therefore replace lyddite. However, at the outbreak of the First World War, the trials of this new bursting compound had not been concluded so British naval shells were still powder- or lyddite-filled.

When the decision to send the *Queen Elizabeth* to the Dardanelles was taken, the ship carried no high explosive shells, and more than 50 per cent of all her shells were powder-filled. Winston Churchill wrote to the Director of Naval Ordnance:

> We cannot rest content with 15-inch shells being powder filled....
> Has any attempt been made to use TNT in shells of the larger guns?

Incredibly, black powder shell fillings continued for naval use well into the 1930s, and even during the Second World War.

German shell production had incorporated TNT since around 1902, so it is likely that the New shells provided to the Turkish guns used TNT as a bursting charge, although the Old shells were still black powder-filled.

Fuses

The obvious benefit of the New shells used by the defenders of the Dardanelles was increased range and the penetration of the armour-piercing types against ships. The Turkish and German gunners had another advantage over their British naval opposition, that of the appropriate type of shell and fuse combination – specifically armour-piercing with graze fuses located at the base of the shell. A base fuse is not initiated at the moment of impact, allowing an armour-piercing shell to continue into the target before exploding.

With the exception of masonry targets such as the old towers at Sedd el Bahr, the British ships were firing at guns located low in earthworks that were difficult to see precisely, and magazines protected with several metres of earth above them. The type of shell required to destroy such a target would be a delayed action high explosive type, allowing the shell to penetrate the earth to reach the magazine before exploding. The best type of gun to deliver such a shell would be a howitzer with its high angle plunging shot, not a flat trajectory ship's gun. Few ships carried high explosive shells with lyddite as a bursting charge, and where they did they were fused with direct action fuses designed to explode on contact with a reasonably solid surface, not delayed action as was required for this type of shore target. The amount of smoke and earth thrown into the air during the later bombardments did suggested success to the naval gunnery observers, while in reality the explosions did little more than remodel the landscape.

Charges

The Royal Navy had used cordite – a compound of nitrocellulose, nitroglycerine and mineral jelly (essentially, 'Vaseline') extruded in the form of thin sticks or 'cords' – as a shell propellant since the 1890s, being vastly superior to black powder. This smokeless propellant allowed higher velocities to be achieved with a more controlled burn rate whilst maintaining moderate pressures, as well as reducing smoke and barrel fouling. For any shell diameter the use of cordite reduced the charge weight by around 70 per cent compared to black powder to achieve the same muzzle velocity, so this meant that ships' guns could be designed with smaller chambers and longer bores, with a corresponding increase in range. The naval charges for the main armament were silk-bagged as cylinders, nominally 1.5 times the bore, four of which would be required as a 'full charge'. Quick-firing guns up to 6-inch bore would generally use brass cartridge cases, although bagged charges were also common on this size of gun.

Conclusion

So, because of the poor combination of shell types, bursting charges and fuses, the British ships were inadequately prepared to beat the coastal guns into submission. It was little better with the French ships as they still continued to use powder filling, although some of their shells may have used melinite, similar to lyddite, as a bursting charge that had been adopted by them at the beginning of the twentieth century. Add to this to the fact that flat trajectory ships' guns were of the wrong type to attack the shore fortifications of the Dardanelles, the chance of overall success by naval bombardment was always very low.

Bibliography

Books

Encyclopaedia Iranica: (New York: Columbia University, 1996)

Jane's Fighting Ships of World War 1 (London: Studio Editions, 1990)

Agoston, Gabor: *Guns for the Sultan: Military Power and the Weapons Industry in the Ottoman Empire* (Cambridge University Press, 2005)

Askin, Mustafa: *Gallipoli – A Turning Point* (Canakkale: Keskin Color Kartpostalcilik Ltd. Post-2002)

Banks, Arthur: *A Military Atlas of World War One* (Barnsley: Pen & Sword Books, 1997)

Beehler, Commodore W.H.: *The History of the Italian-Turkish War, September 29, 1911-October 18, 1912* (Annapolis: Advertiser Republican, 1913)

Calwell, Major-General Sir C.E.: *Experiences of a Dugout* (London: Constable & Company, 1920)

Chack, Paul: *Marins à la bataille: Des Dardanelles aux brumes du nord* (Paris: 1937)

Churchill, Winston: *The World Crisis 1911-1918* (London: Thornton Butterworth, 1931)

Corbett, Sir Julian S.: *History of the Great War: Naval Operations Vol. II* (London: Longmans, Green & Co., 1921)

Denham, H.M.: *Dardanelles – A Midshipman's Diary 1915-16* (London: John Murray, 1981)

Ellis, John: *The Social History of the Machine Gun* (New York: Pantheon Books, 1975)

Erickson, Edward J.: *Gallipoli – The Ottoman Campaign* (Barnsley: Pen & Sword Military, 2010)

Feron, Luc: *Cuirasse D'Escadre Bouvet* (Falmes, Belgium: Editions Edimo, 1996)

Fisher, Admiral of the Fleet Lord John: *Fisher - Memories and Records* (London: Hodder & Stoughton, 1919)

Goodwin, Jason: *Lords of the Horizons* (London: Vintage Books, 1999)

Grant, Jonathan A.: *Rulers, Guns and Money* (Cambridge: Harvard University Press, 2007)

Grey, Edwyn: *Nineteenth-Century Torpedoes and their Inventors* (Annapolis: Naval Institute Press, 2004)

Heinl, Robert Debs: *Dictionary of Military and Naval Quotations* (Annapolis: Naval Institute Press, 1966)

Hickey, Michael: *Gallipoli* (London: John Murray, 1995)

Holt, Tonie and Valmi: *Major & Mrs Holt's Battlefield Guide to Gallipoli* (Barnsley: Leo Cooper, 2000)

Horne, Charles F.: *The Source Records of the Great War, Volume VI* (National Alumini, 1923)

Jager, Herbert: *German Artillery of World War One* (Marlborough: The Crowood Press, 2001)

James, Sir Robert Rhodes: *Gallipoli* (London: Pimlico, 1999)

Kannengiesser, Hans: *The Campaign in Gallipoli* (London: Hutchinson & Co. Ltd., 1928)

Loren, Hermann: *Der Krieg in Den Turkischen Gewassern* (Berlin: 1926)

Manchester, William: *The Arms of Krupp* (London: Little, Brown & Co., 2003)

Masefield, John: *Gallipoli* (London: William Heinemann, 1926)

McGregor, Andrew: *A Military History of Modern Egypt: from the Ottoman Conquest to the Ramadan War* (Westport: Praeger Publishers, 2006)

McMeekin, Sean: *The Berlin-Baghdad Express: The Ottoman Empire and Germany: Bid for World Power, 1898-1919* (London: Allen Lane, 2010)

Melegari, Vezio: *The Great Military Sieges* (London: New English Library, 1972)

Moore, David: *A Handbook of Military Terms* (Fareham: Palmerston Forts Society, 1996)

Morgenthau, Henry: *Ambassador Morgenthau's Story* (New York: Doubleday, Page & Company, 1918)

Murray, J.: *Gallipoli – As I Saw It* (London: William Kimber, 1965)

Nicolle, David: *Ottoman Fortifications 1300-1710* (Botley: Osprey Publishing, 2010)

Nykiel, Piotr: *Expedition to the Golden Horn. Military Operations in the Dardanelles and on the Aegean Sea (August 1914-March 1915)* (Krakow: Wydawnictwo Arkadiusz Wingert, 2008)

Shankland, Peter and Hunter, Anthony: *Dardanelles Patrol* (St Albans: Granada Publishing, 1983)

Snelling, Steven: *VCs of the First World War: Gallipoli* (Gloucestershire: Sutton Publishing, 1995)

Stoker, Donald J: *Grant Girding For Battle – The arms trade in a global perspective, 1815-1940* (Westport: Praeger Publishers, 2003)

Talbot, Frederick A.: *Submarines – Their Mechanism and Operation* (London: William Heineman, 1915)

Terraine, John: *White Heat, The New Warfare 1914-18* (Chatham: Mackays of Chatham Ltd, 1982)

Van der Vat, Dan: *The Ship that Changed the World* (London: Grafton Books, 1986)

Van der Vat, Dan: *The Dardanelles Disaster* (London: Duckworth Overlook, 2009)

Walder, David: *The Chanak Affair* (London: Hutchinson & Co., 1969)

Wilkinson, Norman: *A Brush With Life* (London: Seeley Service & Co. Ltd., 1969)

Wilson, H.N.: *Battleships in Action, Volume II* (London: Sampson Low, Marston & Co., 1926)

Wilson, H.N.: *The Great War, Volume III* (London: Amalgamated Press, 1916)

Magazines, newspapers, conference papers, personal papers and other sources

Anonymous: *Yesterday's Wrong Turning* (1938)

French, David: *The Origins of the Dardanelles Campaign Reconsidered* (Wiley Online Library, 2007)

Gallipoli Association: *Ordinary Seaman Joe Murray*, Hood Battalion, 2nd Naval Brigade, RND: *Gallipoli – As I Saw It*

Heunis, M.C.: *The Boer Krupp Guns* (Winchester: The Redan, *Journal of the Palmerston Forts Society*, No. 66, February 2006)

BIBLIOGRAPHY

McCallum, Iain: *Ships versus Forts: Crimea to the Dardanelles – The Naval Projectiles at the Dardanelles* (Royal Naval Museum Paper, 1999)

Mehmet Hilmi Bey memoirs: *Canakkale was not passed* (*Scientific American*, 1915)

National Museum of the Royal Navy (NMRN) Manuscript 2005.79, Diary kept by Harold Tumman, HMS *Harpy*

NMRN, Manuscript 1992.431/1 and 1992.431/2, Diary kept by Chief Petty Officer A.W. Young, HMS *Agamemnon*

NMRN, Manuscript 1981/608.1, diary kept by Chief Bandsman Herbert Reely, HMS *Inflexible*.

NMRN, German Official History, *The Naval War 1914-1918, Mediterranean Part 1* (Berlin: date not specified)

Sleeman, C. Lieutenant R.N.: *The Lay and other Locomotive Torpedoes considered for the purpose of Coast Defence, and also as the armament of Ships, Torpedo and Submarine Boats* (London, date not specified)

Şükrü Fuad Gücüyener: *The Gunners of Intepe, Çanakkale Recollections/Volume III* (Istanbul, 2005)

The *Daily Mail* (London, 1922)

The Daily News (London, 1877)

The Gallipolian No. 85

The Graphic (London, 1894)

The London Gazette (London, 1915)

The National Archives (London)

The Penny Illustrated Paper (London, 1878, 1891)

Yorulmaz, Naci: *Trade Activities of German Armaments Industry in the Ottoman Market* (Berlin Free University, 2007)

Specialist websites

forum.axishistory.com
uboat.net
www.canakkalesavalar.net
www.galipolli.co.tr/silent_witness
www.galipolli-association.org
www.iranicaonline.org
www.mfa.gov.tr
www.navweaps.com
www.navyingallipoli.com
www.oldmagazinearticles.com
www.savaskarakas.com
www.thebookoftravels.org
www.turkeyswar.com
www.turkiye-wrecks.com

Index

INDEX

INDEX